JESUS MATTERS

JESUS MATTERS

good
news
for
the
21st
century

edited by James R. Krabill and David W. Shenk
foreword by Shane Claiborne

Herald Press

Scottdale, Pennsylvania
Waterloo, Ontario

Library of Congress Cataloging-in-Publication Data

Jesus matters : good news for the 21st century / edited by James R.
Krabill and David W. Shenk.
    p. cm.
Includes bibliographical references.
ISBN 978-0-8361-9448-7 (pbk. : alk. paper)
1. Jesus Christ. I. Krabill, James R., 1951- II. Shenk, David W., 1937-
BT205.J46 2009
232–dc22

                                                                    2009002225

JESUS MATTERS
Copyright © 2009 by Herald Press, Scottdale, Pa. 15683
  Published simultaneously in Canada by Herald Press,
  Waterloo, Ont. N2L 6H7. All rights reserved
International Standard Book Number: 978-0-8361-9448-7
Library of Congress Catalog Card Number: 2009002225
Printed in the United States of America
Book design by Joshua Byler
Cover by Reuben Graham

14 13 12 11 10 09   10 9 8 7 6 5 4 3 2 1

To order or request information please call 1-800-245-7894
or visit www.heraldpress.com.

Contents

Foreword

Several years ago a friend of mine was being interviewed by a secular-Jewish-country-radio talk show host (that's quite a combination). The DJ was talking with my friend about the contemporary movement in the church where there is a reshaping of evangelicalism, a renewal of radical discipleship, signs of a church that is closer to the poor and further from the drums of war.

The talk show host confessed to my friend that there were many things he wrestled with as he read the Bible—things he found confusing, troubling, hard to reconcile. But then his face lit up and he said with a smile, "But I love the stuff in red," referring to the words of Jesus in the Gospels which are often set apart in red letters. He went on, "And you all seem to take that stuff in red seriously, you should call yourselves 'Red Letter Christians.'" So we did.

> Gandhi was once asked if he was a Christian and he responded: "I love Jesus, I just wish the Christians took him more seriously."

Gandhi was once asked if he was a Christian and he responded: "I love Jesus, I just wish the Christians took him more seriously." How beautiful it is to see a new movement of Christians who are taking Jesus seriously.

As evidenced in the pages of this book, there is a movement of these "red-letter Christians" who are reading the words of Jesus and asking, "What if he really meant the things he said?" As we dare to follow the words of Jesus, we find ourselves at odds with many of the patterns of this world, and even at odds with many things that have come to characterize much of the church, including evangelical Christianity.

This book is one more sign of a generation that has not given up on Jesus, despite the embarrassing and scandalous things Christians have done in his name. It is evidence of a generation that has not even given up on the church but is tirelessly proclaiming—"We will stop complaining about the church we have experienced and work on becoming the change we dream of!"

One of the things I love about *Jesus Matters* is that it bridges the generations and busts through the walls of homogeneity. The writers are young and old, male and female, a diverse spectrum of background and experience that reflects the diversity of God's kingdom. We need this kind of revolutionary chorus of voices in the church—of new Anabaptists, new monastics, a new reformation, another great awakening—that can lead us into this century.

We certainly need older folks who are willing to come alongside a new generation of Christians and allow them to re-imagine church and make their own mistakes. And we also need younger folks who know they don't have to make all the same mistakes as their parents and who want to come alongside elders who have treasures of wisdom and scars to prove it. Each of these essays is a harmony, a dazzling fulfillment of the hope echoed in Scripture: "Your sons and daughters will prophesy, your young men will see visions, your old men will dream dreams."[1]

These authors invite us to set aside our political agendas, our committee meetings, our ideologies and stale arguments— and to dream about the One who is the Way, the Truth, and the Life, amid this world of shortcuts, deception, and death. I think you will find, as I have, that the words of Jesus are as relevant to the world that we live in as they were two thousand years ago.

I was on a plane once and the guy sitting next to me said, "So what is it that you do?" I decided to have a little fun. "I'm a preacher," I said with a smirk.

The man returned the smirk and said, "I never would have

known." And then he said something interesting, "Well, you shouldn't be short of preaching material these days. After all, this is the apocalypse!"

Granted, the guy may have read too many Tim LaHaye books (that old "Left Behind" series), but I think he was onto something. These are incredible times to be alive. *Apocalypse*, like *revelation*, literally means an "unveiling" or "disclosure," a "ripping away the veil"—sort of like in the Wizard of Oz when they pull open the curtain and see a little man behind all the hoorah. Now we are seeing what lies behind Wall Street—and it's brittle. In wars around the globe, we are seeing the sour fruits of the myth of redemptive violence. And the words of Jesus could not be more fresh and magical. The lilies and the sparrows still shame Wall Street's splendor. Jesus' warning that if we pick up the sword we will die by it has proved true over and over. Help us, Lord Jesus.

These authors invite us to set aside our political agendas, our committee meetings, our ideologies and stale arguments—and to dream about the One who is the Way, the Truth, and the Life.

How desperate people are for hope, for freedom from fear, for a sense of security as markets flail. And yet we so quickly lose our lives as we try to find them and gain the whole world but lose our soul. Many are tempted to give up and resign themselves to a cynical nihilism. Others are tempted to misplace their hope in politicians, armies, 401ks, celebrities, or Caesars. But the authors of this book cry out with a childlike innocence of that old hymn: "My hope is built on nothing less than Jesus' blood and righteousness . . . On Christ, the solid Rock, I stand; all other ground is sinking sand." What a refreshing place to find all hope, wisdom, and love. All other ground is sinking sand.

Shane Claiborne
February 2009

Introduction
The North American Context

The story is told of a university student who, running to catch a two-hour final exam in chemistry, encountered the campus chaplain in the hallway. Breezing by without missing a beat, the student blurted out, "Will you pray for me at four p.m.?"

"Of course," replied the chaplain, calling after her. "But why do you want me to wait until then?"

"My exam begins at three p.m.," she shouted back, "and I'd like an hour to see if I can do it on my own."

Does Jesus or the God he proclaimed have any relevance to our modern situation or to the pending exam of the college coed described here? We are writing this introduction at a time when the United States and the global economic system are under incredible strain. People are afraid. They fear that the world is on the edge of economic collapse precipitated by greed. The September 11, 2001, attacks against key symbols of U.S. political, economic, and military power have imprinted the North American and global psychic with deep underlying paranoia. The United States has responded by engaging in several wars and military incursions that are draining life and wealth with no satisfactory resolution on the horizon.

> Do times such as these offer North Americans an opportunity to look beyond themselves to God and those things that make for meaning and hope in a world otherwise falling apart?

Many have hoped that the historic watershed represented by the Barack Obama presidency would usher in the genuine change that is needed. Yet there is a nagging feeling that the challenges largely exceed our capabilities or the wisdom of anyone in leadership. Do times such as these offer North Americans an opportunity to look beyond themselves to God and those things that make for meaning and hope in a world otherwise falling apart?

In the book *Habits of the Heart*, Robert Bellah and his research team observe that within the North American context the God who speaks is seldom listened to and rarely obeyed.[2] The individual has replaced God as the center of worship and authority. In a society that creates and venerates self-reliant heroes, rugged pioneers, crusty cowboys, and hard-boiled entrepreneurs, it should not surprise us that our capacity for commitment to God and to each other is seriously diminished and underdeveloped. What people want and feel they need in a context shaped predominately by self-centered individualism is a personalized, custom-built religious experience—a natural outgrowth of the mix 'em, match 'em cafeteria-style consumer culture in which we live.

We now encounter, not just one, or even several, but *many* stories about "truth"—as many stories in fact as there are people to develop them—and all are considered of equal veracity, weight, and value.

Charles Strohmer, writer and lecturer on contemporary religious trends, calls this "The New Spirituality"—a swirl of practices and beliefs inspired by elements of Eastern religions, New Ageism, self-help and pop psychologies, the occult, and "a dash of Western optimism" reinforced by "whatever current scientific theories can be assumed." No two persons put these elements together in exactly the same way since each is striving to design a spiritual "product" that suits their individual needs.[3]

The result, of course, is that we now encounter, not just one, or even several, but *many* stories about "truth"—as many stories in fact as there are people to develop them—and all are considered of equal veracity, weight, and value.

What a Trend We Have in Jesus

Into this mix comes the Jesus story, elements of which appear in today's culture to be more popular than ever. Dozens of films have featured Jesus in recent years, ranging from *The Da Vinci Code* and Mel Gibson's blockbuster, *The Passion of the Christ*, to lesser-known comedies like *Jesus Christ Vampire Hunter* and *Talladega Nights: The Ballad of Ricky Bobby*. In this latter production—which has engendered a following of almost cultic proportions—Jesus is presented as a baby adorned in golden, fleece diapers and becomes the object of prayer for actor Will Ferrell.

Jesus also makes frequent television appearances on *South Park*, *The Simpsons*, Carlos Mencia's comedy hit *The Mind of Mencia*, and in the passionate prayers of Dog the Bounty Hunter when he gathers his posse to prepare for a manhunt. Neil Saavedra elevates Jesus to talk-show status on his popular Sunday morning radio program *The Jesus Christ Show*, which helps listeners to imagine what it might be like if Jesus were a resident of southern California taking questions from callers on his own talk show.

There is virtually no area of pop culture that remains untouched by the Jesus factor, from the music scene and the sports world to tattoo art and the fashion industry with its popular line of T-shirts (one website—cafepress.com—offers 129,000 designs) and bling-bling jewelry. Singer-actress Madonna has long dangled a crucifix around her neck as part of her personal fashion statement. The reason for this is quite simple and unapologetically irreverent. "I have always been attracted to naked men," she says.[4]

The September 11 attacks against U.S. symbols of power have driven many to a search for national identity and spiritual roots. That quest could lead to an encounter with the Jesus of the Bible and indeed for some Jesus *has* provided welcome spiritual

There is virtually no area of pop culture that remains untouched by the Jesus factor.

resource. In many other instances, however, the Jesus embraced is little more than a tribal or nationalistic patriotic concoction— a Jesus clothed in the American flag, a cross wrapped in red, white, and blue.

Will the *Real* Jesus Please Stand Up?

Where and when Jesus lived and what he actually said and did are virtually absent from most of these popular depictions. If one takes the time to dig a bit deeper and explore what twenty-first-century North Americans truly know or think about Jesus, one will encounter quite a spectrum of responses, including some of the following:

> Where and when Jesus lived and what he actually said and did are virtually absent from most of these popular depictions.

- **LEGEND: Jesus never lived.** A recent survey in Britain and some parallel research being conducted among U.S. youth reveals that a high percentage of those interviewed believe Jesus to be a fictitious figure who never actually lived. On the other hand, why does this even matter? Most people don't spend much time obsessing over the origins of Santa Claus, but that doesn't keep them in the slightest from making the plump and jolly, white-bearded grand-pappy an integral part of their annual holiday festivities.

- **LOST: Jesus is unknowable to us.** Jesus *did* actually exist as a living person, but there is, unfortunately, no way to peel off the multiple encrusted layers of what others have said and thought about him. Even the New Testament documents tell us far more about the Gospel writers them-selves and about the early church than they do about Jesus. What we actually know of him is minimal, if anything at all. One famous group of scholars known as the Jesus Seminar has since 1985 taken upon themselves the task of determining which of the words and deeds attributed to Jesus in the Gospels are, in fact, authentic. By means of a rather complex voting system using colored beads, they have concluded that 82 percent of Jesus' words were not actually spoken by him. Only one of Jesus' statements survived from the Gospel of Mark; in John's Gospel, the scholars were unable to find a single saying that, in their opinion, was traceable to the historical Jesus.

• **LUDICROUS: Jesus is incomprehensible to modern people.** It is possible, perhaps even likely, that Jesus was a wonderful first-century teacher, but much of his ministry and message is unintelligible in our modern scientific age. Once you clean up some of the supernatural gibberish by eliminating the miracles, angels, and evil spirits, then you start to have something folks today can relate to. Already in the early nineteenth century, Thomas Jefferson, a son of the Enlightenment and America's third president, was greatly annoyed by the supernatural worldview presented in the Bible. With scalpel in hand, Jefferson surgically removed from the New Testament gospels everything that seemed to him incompatible with contemporary scientific discoveries. Only one in ten verses made the cut. All miracles, including the resurrection, were struck from the text, and Jefferson was left with a forty-six-page primer of morality that he entitled *The Philosophy of Jesus of Nazareth*.

> Already in the early nineteenth century, Thomas Jefferson, a son of the Enlightenment and America's third president, was greatly annoyed by the supernatural worldview presented in the Bible.

• **LIKEABLE: Jesus is a nice guy.** There are parts of Jesus' message that are indeed appealing—his emphasis, for example, on peace, kindness, dignity, justice, and freedom. He is certainly one of the greatest moral teachers that ever lived. It's the "Son of God," "forgiveness of sins," "I am the way," and "final judgment" stuff that creates distance between us and people of other religious traditions and seems unnecessary and irrelevant to Jesus' cause and central message. Religious beliefs do nothing but divide members of the human family. It's time to give love and peace a chance! Some of what Jesus said and did can be useful in moving us toward the harmonious relationships so desperately needed in our world today. Anything in Jesus' message that does not move us in that direction should be discarded as unhelpful.

• **LUNATIC: Jesus was out of touch with reality.** Some people during Jesus' lifetime—including family and friends—thought he had gone off the deep end. Maybe he did. The question isn't whether Jesus was sincere. But was he misguided, out of touch, or at times excessively full of himself?

• **LIAR: Jesus didn't really believe what he said.** When people lie long enough to themselves, they start lying to others as well. Is it possible that Jesus intentionally misrepresented the truth and led people astray? Or maybe the deception was not directly of his own doing. Maybe, as many Muslims believe, it was Jesus' followers who were the ones responsible for corrupting the texts concerning Jesus, altering the story, and handing on misinformation about what Jesus really said and did.

Maybe It's Time to Take Another Look at Jesus

Every one of the questions raised above deserves attention, and many of them have in fact been engaged in a wide range of publications, some of which appear in the bibliography at the end of this book. It has been the conviction, however, of the writing team contributing to the sixteen essays in this volume that the time has come to take another look at Jesus, to return to the biblical text, our primary written source for encountering him, to listen

once again to the captivating narrative that unfolds within its pages, and to remind ourselves anew of the remarkable relevance of Jesus to our twenty-first-century circumstances.

Such an exercise does not necessarily answer all the questions we might have. Yet as we explore the biblical story and

The time has come to take another look at Jesus, to return to the biblical text, to listen once again to the captivating narrative that unfolds within its pages, and to remind ourselves anew of the remarkable relevance of Jesus to our twenty-first-century circumstances.

learn more about the passionate convictions of the first New Testament faith communities presented there, we find ourselves intrigued and strangely drawn to this Jesus for whom they abandoned all and for whose cause they were willing to die. In the process, we begin to discover that this carpenter from Nazareth is as disturbingly relevant for us in our North American world today as he was for Palestinian peasants and villagers living two millennia ago.

The picture of Jesus presented to us by these early witnesses is not an exact *photograph* in high definition detail. Neither is it an indistinct *abstract painting*, offering us a distorted Jesus, unrecognizable from the Galilean carpenter in whom the Word "became flesh and made his dwelling among us."[5] Rather, we believe, it is more like a *portrait*, reliable and trustworthy in its representation, with more than enough detail for us to ask serious questions and find life-giving answers about who this Jesus was and is and how, hailing from a dumpy, back-water town in northern Palestine, he has become the most famous, transformative person in all of human history.[6]

In many ways it comes down to something as simple as this: If Jesus is non-existent, unworthy, inaccessible, or unreliable in any way, then nothing much about him ultimately matters. If, on the other hand, Jesus is what he said, said what he meant, and meant what he said, then he could well be—in our lives and in the world—the *only* reality that ultimately matters! Nothing, of course, is more counter-intuitive to most people in our world today, yet these issues remain central to the journey we are on—a journey we as writers invite you to join in the pages to follow.

> If Jesus is what he said, said what he meant, and meant what he said, then he could well be—in our lives and in the world—the *only* reality that ultimately matters!

The Beginning, Not the End, of a Journey

"It's a fairly embarrassing situation," writes Bruce H. Hargon, astrophysicist at the University of Washington, "to admit that we can't find 90 percent of the universe." That is the kind of humility it takes when you're writing a book about Jesus.

The fact is there is much about the earthly Jesus and, even more, about the Christ of faith that we don't fully comprehend. As one of the New Testament writers, the apostle Paul tells us, Christ is "God's great mystery" through whom "all things hold together" and in whom "all the richest treasures of wisdom and knowledge are embedded."[7]

> The portrait of Jesus presented here is based on the Scriptures and in particular on the four Gospel accounts of Matthew, Mark, Luke and John.

If it is true that all of reality is somehow comprehended in and by Jesus Christ, there is then, as George R. McDermott reminds us, "an infinite number of aspects or vantage points from which to see the idea of Christ, each of which will show something new and unique about what it means for God to be in Christ. This also means that as a church," McDermott adds, "we may have only begun the journey of understanding Christ, that there may be far more to Christ that the church will learn as it reflects on Scriptures and tradition—and perhaps other religions—with the help of the Holy Spirit."[8]

Our journey with Jesus in this book is characterized by the following features and commitments:

• **Biblical.** The portrait of Jesus presented here is based on the Scriptures and in particular on the four Gospel accounts of Matthew, Mark, Luke and John, though other parts of the Bible are also cited. We have followed the narratives of Jesus as they are presented in the New Testament, beginning with the birth accounts and moving from Jesus' announcement of the kingdom and confrontation with the powers through various aspects of his teaching and ministry, his death and resurrection, and on to his role in the future of God's purposes for the world. Scripture references appear in footnotes for readers interested in looking more closely at the biblical texts that have inspired the writers' comments.

• **Popular.** We have tried to avoid the use of technical terms, expressions and scholarly debates that are accessible only to a small group of initiated readers. In certain instances, definitions of less well-known terms are offered in either the text or in footnotes to provide clarity for the reader. Though the content of these chapters is not driven primarily by the hot-button issues of contemporary culture, the reader will find frequent connections being made by the writers between the good-news message of Jesus and the socio-cultural, economic, environmental, and religious challenges of the twenty-first century.

• **Conversational.** Each chapter has a primary writer, many of whom are pastors, authors or professors in Mennonite colleges and seminaries throughout North America. Each chapter is also, however, a conversation between the writer and one or several younger companions of the authors' choosing. Most of these are young adults in their twenties, some a bit older, a few in their late teens. Several writers chose to work on this assignment with their own children, grandchildren, or other members of their immediate families.

The conversation between members of the writing teams took place in a variety of ways, around twenty-inch pizzas, through email and letter exchanges, by phone conversations, and in face-to-face chats. Participants in this project did not always agree, and some of those unresolved issues are reflected in the chapters presented here.

It was a deliberate choice not to make this collection of essays an international forum but to focus on North America as a context for the conversation. There are nonetheless insights shared in these chapters by people with personal connections to Kenya, Japan, Colombia, Ecuador, Lithuania, South Africa, and many other places around the world where writers have lived or traveled throughout the course of their lifetimes. These internationalist insights are helpful, we believe, in broadening our perspectives on Jesus and in helping us to avoid the pitfalls of a North American-centered worldview.

The themes in this book are relevant to life as we experience it. In that spirit each chapter invites reflection, exploration, discussion, discernment, and commitment.

• **Reflective.** The themes in this book are relevant to life as we experience it. In that spirit each chapter invites reflection, exploration, discussion, discernment, and commitment. A biblical narrative introduces each chapter inviting engagement with a Scripture text especially pertinent to the theme of the chapter. Questions are included at the end of each chapter. These are intended to encourage further probing of the meanings of the narratives and the relevance of the material for the journey of life today. Most chapters include extensive Scripture endnotes for those who wish to explore the biblical passages that inspire the various themes developed. The bibliography at the end of the book introduces pertinent publications for further reflective reading.

We commend this book to the casual reader who wants to become better acquainted with Jesus. The book is also written for young-adult study groups, Sunday school or neighborhood Bible study groups, and college or high-school classes. The writers were committed to writing in a style that can be understood and appreciated by those who are unacquainted with Jesus' narratives of the New Testament as well as those who may be well-acquainted with Jesus but want to further explore his life and teachings.

Virtually all of the writers, both older and younger, have been shaped by long-standing connections or more recent adherence to the Anabaptist-Mennonite stream of Christian history.

• **Anabaptist-Mennonite.** Virtually all of the writers, both older and younger, have been shaped by long-standing connections or more recent adherence to the Anabaptist-Mennonite stream of Christian history. Central to that perspective is the firm conviction that Jesus is and must remain at the very heart of all matters related to the faith, life, and practice of those who would call themselves Christian. The favorite preaching text of Menno Simons, the sixteenth-century Dutch reformer from whom the movement got its name, was found in 1 Corinthians 3:11, "For no one can lay any foundation other than the one already laid, which is Jesus Christ."

Many North American Mennonites today struggle as much as any other fellow Christians with the enticing impulses and demands of our pluralistic culture. We would be the last to say we have found easy answers to the enormous challenges we face in attempting to follow Jesus—all the more reason to engage with a sense of critical urgency the conversation taking place in the pages of this book. Happily for all who believe in and follow Jesus, he himself promises to go before us on the journey. We do not, therefore, journey alone but rather in joyous obedience to the call of the One who leads the way.

• **Invitational.** Without claiming to understand the full implication of the title we have chosen for this collection of essays—*Jesus Matters*—we are of the conviction, nonetheless, that God has done, is doing, and will do something in Jesus that is good news not only for Mennonites, nor only for North Americans, but for all people of the world.

Lesslie Newbigin, a life-long missionary and former bishop in the Church of South India, takes this conviction to another level when he writes:

> If, in fact, it is true that almighty God, creator and sustainer of all that exists in heaven or on earth, has—at a known time and place in human history—so humbled himself as to become part of our sinful humanity and to suffer and die a shameful death to take away our sin and to rise from the dead as the first-fruit of a new creation; if this is a fact, then to affirm it is not arrogance. To remain quiet about it is treason to our fellow human beings.[9]

Though it might be that not all writers enlisted in this project would necessarily want to state the alternatives we face in such stark terms, Newbigin's bold affirmation does urgently invite us to ask hard questions about what, finally, we will do with Jesus—this same Jesus who reaches out his nail-pierced hand to each of us with a warm and engaging call of invitation, "Believe in me and follow!"

James R. Krabill
David W. Shenk
February 2009

Notes

1. Acts 2:17; Joel 2:28.

2. Robert N. Bellah, et. al., *Habits of the Heart: Individualism and Commitment in American Life* (Berkeley, CA: University of California Press, 1985; paperback, Harper & Row, 1986; updated paperback edition with new introduction, "The House Divided," University of California Press, 1996).

3. See Charles Strohmer, *The Gospel and the New Spirituality* (Nashville: Thomas Nelson Publishers, 1996).

4. A new book by Mark Driscoll and Gerry Breshears, *Vintage Jesus: Timeless Answers to Timely Questions* (Wheaton, IL: Crossway Books, 2007), does a particularly brilliant job of exploring the message of Jesus within the context of today's pop culture. Some of the examples referenced here are described more fully in that work.

5. John 1:14.

6. James R. Edwards believes that all views of Jesus can ultimately be reduced to one of these three picture-types—photograph, portrait or painting—and spells out in more detail his understandings of these three views in his book, *Is Jesus the Only Savior?* (Grand Rapids, MI: Eerdmans, 2005): 23-32.

7. Colossians 1:17; 2:2, 3.

8. See Gerald R. McDermott, *Can Evangelicals Learn from World Religions?* (Downers Grove, IL: InterVarsity Press, 2000):16.

9. Taken from "A Sermon Preached at the Thanksgiving Service for the Fiftieth Anniversary of the Tambaram Conference of the International Missionary Council," *International Review of Mission* 78 (1988):328.

Chapter 1

Jesus Calls:
Believe in Me and Follow

April Yamasaki with Peter Sensenig

———————— Narrative: *Jesus calls his first disciples* ————————
(Matthew 4:18-25)

Congratulations! You have won an all inclusive cruise to the Caribbean. To claim your prize, simply press 9. That's the 9 key—press it now. . . .

How do you respond to this telephone message? Are you eager to claim your prize? Do you call your family and friends to share the good news? Do you press the 9 key out of curiosity? Ignore the message? Wonder if it's some kind of scam? Hang up? Wish it were a real person instead of a recording?

Again and again throughout his public ministry, Jesus called people to follow him. In his own way, he was just as persistent as any telephone sales caller—but his call was and is much more significant and life-changing! Instead of leaving a recorded message, Jesus extended a personal invitation—not as some fly-by-night scam, but an invitation to a new way of life that would last forever. The call of Jesus offered a real prize, but in his ministry and teaching, and by his own example, Jesus was also very clear that it carried a real price. More than anything else, his call provoked response—some believed immediately and gladly invited others to follow; some

> Again and again throughout his public ministry, Jesus called people to follow him.

just as quickly lost interest; others reacted with criticism and anger; others refused and simply walked away.

Jesus Calls

From the opening chapter of the Bible and right through to the end, God is one who calls. At creation, God called heaven and earth and everything else into being.[1] God called Abraham and Sarah to a new land, to become a new people that would be a blessing to others.[2] God called the Hebrew people out of slavery in Egypt to a new freedom and to create a new community.[3] God called Isaiah, Jeremiah, and other prophets to speak to the people.

Jesus himself called out that "whoever believes in him shall not perish but have eternal life,"[4] and "if any want to become my followers, let them deny themselves and take up their cross daily and follow me."[5] That call included those who were healthy and active, those who were afflicted and in need of healing, those who were imper-

> While the call of Jesus is for everyone, it is also uniquely personal.

fect and sinful. Jesus still calls today, "Let everyone who is thirsty come. Let anyone who wishes take the water of life as a gift."[6]

While the call of Jesus is for everyone, it is also uniquely personal. To the fishermen Simon Peter, and his brother, Andrew, "'Come, follow me,' Jesus said, 'and I will make you fishers'" of people.[7] With the more philosophical and well-educated Nicodemus, Jesus uses the metaphor, "You must be born again."[8] When he had a conversation with a small-town woman of Samaria at a well, he offers "living water."[9] To a leader of the synagogue, he says, "Don't be afraid; just believe."[10] To a tax collector named Levi, he says simply, "Follow me."[11] To a wealthy young man, he says, "Sell your possessions and give to the poor, and you will have treasure in heaven. Then come, follow me."[12]

In the early fifth century, a man named Patrick received a call in a dream to be a missionary for Christ. He followed his calling to Ireland, where he had formerly been a slave. The monastic movement that emerged out of his work soon became the leading force in spreading the gospel to Britain.

In the late 1940s, a young Albanian nun named Agnes was called by Jesus to Calcutta, India. For more than forty years she ministered to people in poverty and illness, until her death in 1997. Now she is known as Mother Teresa, and her Missionaries of Charity spread the love of Christ in many countries around the world.

Throughout history and even today, the call of Jesus is not just for a few special people, but for every one of us.

Young and old, men and women, people who are active in their jobs and people who are sick and struggling with disease, people who may become household names and those who continue to work in obscurity all their lives, those with extra money in the bank and those with no money left at the end of the month, those with a long string of degrees and others without formal education—throughout history and even today, the call of Jesus is not just for a few special people, but for every one of us.

The People Respond

Matthew 4:18-25 illustrates the initial excitement over Jesus and how the people responded in overwhelming numbers to his call. Simon Peter and his brother, Andrew, and James and his brother, John, all left their work as fishermen to follow Jesus. New followers came from "Galilee, the Decapolis, Jerusalem, Judea, and the region across the Jordan." They left their homes, their jobs, their families (or brought them along), and they lifted those who were sick off their sick beds and brought them too.

Learning to Know Jesus

When I (April) was a young teenager, a friend invited me to a youth rally at her church. I no longer remember who the speaker was or what he said, but when the altar call was given, I went forward in tears, and I still remember the Bible verse that I was given at that time: "But to all who received him, who believed in his name, he gave power to become children of God."[13] I can't say that my life changed radically after that—at least not in any noticeable way. After the youth rally was over, I still went home to my same parents and three sisters; I still had school the next morning; I was still me.

Over time, I came to understand that following Jesus meant more than that one altar call experience—my newly acquired belief was certainly a beginning, for "without faith it is impossible to please God, because anyone who comes to him must believe that he exists and that he rewards those who earnestly seek him."[14] The Scriptures were written that we might believe,[15] and Jesus himself proclaimed, "The time has come. . . . The kingdom of God is near. Repent and believe the good news!"[16]

> Over time, I came to understand that following Jesus meant more than that one altar call experience.

Loving God and Neighbor

But once we believe, following Jesus means loving God with all our heart and soul and strength and mind,[17] loving God so much that it makes a difference—in the way we spend our time; the way we relate to family, friends, strangers, and enemies; the way we live every part of life. It makes a difference in who we are—humble and gentle, patient, bearing with one another in love, kind, compassionate, forgiving, submitting to one another, and other qualities of character.[18] And it makes a difference in whose we are—we are children of God and we belong together with all those who follow Jesus.

Following Jesus means loving our neighbors as ourselves—to want the best for them and to look out for their well-being as we look out for our own. Loving our neighbors includes the homeless panhandler asking for spare change, the well-dressed couple who cross the street to avoid him, the neighbor next door with the yappy dog, the child in a refugee camp halfway around the world, the people on every continent. Following Jesus means loving our neighbors even when—maybe especially when—they are very different from us in personality, language, culture, class, or religion, even when our neighbors treat us as enemies.

To love God and neighbor in such a profound and ongoing way takes more than a moment. It takes more than a lifetime to follow Jesus, and more than a lifetime to receive the great prize that it offers.

> Following Jesus means loving our neighbors even when—maybe especially when—they are very different from us in personality, language, culture, class, or religion, even when our neighbors treat us as enemies.

Receiving the Prize

The Old Testament looked forward to a time of great blessing and joy: the oppressed would hear good news, the brokenhearted would receive healing, the captives would be released, ruined cities would be rebuilt, mourning would turn to gladness, and the Lord's favor would be evident to all.[19] Jesus declared himself to be the fulfillment of all these hopes and dreams.[20] When John the Baptist asked, "Are you the one who is to come, or should we expect someone else?" Jesus replied, "Go back and report to John what you hear and see: The blind receive sight, the lame walk, those who have leprosy are cured, the deaf hear, the dead are raised, and the good news is preached to the poor."[21]

This was the long-awaited "kingdom of God" brought near in the life and ministry of Jesus.[22] In the Gospel of John, Jesus called it eternal life, salvation, abundant life.[23] It was so all-encompassing and so wonderful that it was hard to define exactly, but it meant rest in God, protection from the evil one, abiding in God's love as friends instead of servants, answered prayer, forgiveness from sin, peace, the Holy Spirit, and Jesus' own continuing presence.[24]

If all that weren't reward enough, the rest of the New Testament continues to elaborate on God's glorious grace, forgiveness of sin, peace with God and with others.[25] Through Christ, we have a new identity as God's people—"a chosen race, a royal priesthood, a holy nation, God's own people,"[26] "a kingdom and priests serving our God."[27]

All of this was such good news that it needed to be shared with others! Andrew found his brother, Simon; Philip found Nathaniel; and they passed on Jesus' invitation to "come and see."[28] Jesus himself devoted his own life to proclaiming God's kingdom and sent his disciples out with the same mission: to declare the kingdom and call all people to follow him. As God's new people, all those who follow Jesus are also called to "declare the praises of him who called you out of darkness into his wonderful light."[29]

And yet for all of the nearness of God's kingdom, for all of its rich blessing in this life, the fullness of God's kingdom is still to come. Jesus acknowledged this as he taught his disciples to pray, "Your kingdom come."[30] Yes, there is peace with God in this life—and yet unrest and violence continue in our own hearts and in the world. Yes, there is forgiveness from sin—and yet sin and evil still flourish. This life is only a foretaste of all the fullness of God's kingdom. In the meantime, to use the apostle Paul's words, we "press on toward the goal to win the prize for which God has called (us) heavenward in Christ Jesus."[31]

Counting the Cost

Jesus' first disciples left their homes, their livelihood, and their families to follow him. These were not arbitrary choices to abandon their former lives, nor simply tacked on after the fact like a sales tax might be added to the price of a purchase.

Instead, these very real sacrifices were at the very core of what it meant for them to follow Jesus—it was their way of denying themselves and taking up the cross, just as he had said.[32]

In the Old Testament, God's leading also called for the same risk-taking and sacrifice. In their senior years, Abraham and Sarah took the risk of leaving their home to venture

Jesus' first disciples left their homes, their livelihood, and their families to follow him.

to a new land.[33] During the Exodus, the Hebrew people left the life they knew for an unknown future.[34] The prophet Jeremiah faced opposition and imprisonment.[35]

In the New Testament, Levi left his life as a tax collector. Simon Peter, Andrew, James, and John left their fishing boats and nets behind.[36] Jesus warned of family division, insult, accusation, and persecution, the sacrifice of money and possessions, opposition, and even death as a result of following him.[37] Jesus himself had no home. All four gospels tell the story of his arrest, torture, and execution. The early church faced similar threats of arrest and murder.

The early Anabaptists of the sixteenth century came to believe strongly that following Jesus was something one chooses, not something into which one is born. The authorities of the day were so threatened by this conviction that thousands of Anabaptist believers in Jesus were hunted down, imprisoned, tortured, or killed in Switzerland, Germany, and the Netherlands. Like many believers before them (and still today in some parts of the world), the early Anabaptists paid a great cost for their commitment to follow Jesus.

These very real sacrifices were at the very core of what it meant for them to follow Jesus.

That cost might not be so steep in our own time and place. For the most part, freedom of thought and religion in the West has allowed people to follow Jesus and to gather together in his name without fear of imprisonment, persecution, or death. Yet even though the physical costs may not be paramount, risk-taking and self-sacrifice are still part of what it means to follow Jesus.

When I (Peter) was about twelve, I saw a neighbor boy steal a model car that belonged to me. He refused to admit that he had stolen it, and for several months I felt resentful and bitter toward him and even considered taking something of his. When I finally decided to forgive him, I felt a deep sense of relief. Although he never returned the model, I was able to treat him with respect and friendship because I took the risk of forgiving him.

> The early Anabaptists of the sixteenth century came to believe strongly that following Jesus was something one chooses, not something into which one is born.

When we are wronged, it's a risk to respond with forgiveness instead of seeking revenge. When we speak up for peace in a time of war, we risk ridicule, insult, and opposition. When we do the right thing even when others misunderstand, even when it costs us more money, even when no one else offers us recognition or thanks, that's part of what it means to carry the cross, even if it's only a very small sliver compared to what others must bear. Even today, following Jesus still means giving and living sacrificially.

The Challenge of Following

In spite of the initial interest in Jesus' call, it didn't take long for the enthusiasm of the crowds to wane. Already in John 6:66, many of his followers were unwilling to accept Jesus' teaching to believe and follow. In Matthew 19:22, a rich young man "went away sad, because he had great wealth." Even for Jesus' closest, most faithful disciples, who had given up everything to follow him, the cost of discipleship sometimes seemed too great. On the night he was arrested, when Jesus asked them to watch and pray, they fell asleep. They ran away at his trial and crucifixion, and with few exceptions, left him to die alone.[38]

Like the disciples, sometimes we are too weary or fearful to

take up the challenge of following. If believing in Jesus really
means following him in a radically new life, with all its promise and sacrifice, who can possibly measure up to that? In the

Even for Jesus' closest, most faithful
disciples, who had given up everything
to follow him, the cost of discipleship
sometimes seemed too great.

face of misunderstanding by others, hostility from the world, and
even persecution and death, who would dare to follow him?

Early on, when some of his followers began turning away,
Jesus asked his disciples, "Do you also wish to go away?" In
one of his best moments, Simon Peter replied, "Lord, to whom
shall we go? You have the words of eternal life. We believe and
know that you are the Holy One of God."[39] Although Peter
would later deny Jesus and refuse to admit that he even knew
him, at that point at least, Peter got it right and continued to
follow in spite of all of the obstacles.

Even though our belief and knowledge may be halting,
incomplete, or imperfect, we too can follow Jesus despite our
doubts, questions, and fears. Though we sometimes fail and have
to start over again, God remains faithful even when we are not.
God will carry us through even when we think we can't go on.
Like the desperate father who
had brought his son to Jesus
for healing, we can cry out, "I
believe; help my unbelief."[40]
Like Peter, who wept bitterly
over his betrayal of Jesus,[41]

Even though our belief and knowledge
may be halting, incomplete, or imperfect,
we too can follow Jesus despite our
doubts, questions, and fears.

when we fail, we can be forgiven and restored,[42] recommit ourselves to follow Jesus and invite others to join us.[43] God works in
us and one day will bring that good work to completion.[44]

Anyone starting a business needs to calculate the risks against
the possible gains. Will my investment be rewarded? Will I end
up losing more than I gain? In the same way, when it comes to
Jesus' call, we might also calculate the risks and rewards. Yet paradoxically as Jesus himself points out, those who lose their life

"for my sake will find it,"[45] and when they discover the great treasure of God's kingdom, they gladly give up everything else.[46]

All of those who follow Jesus do so because of who Jesus is, and we learn to know who Jesus is by believing and following. As the early Anabaptist leader Hans Denck wrote: No one can truly *know* Christ unless they *follow* him in life.[47] That was true of the early disciples who learned to know Jesus by spending time with him, listening to his teaching, following his example, and believing in him. Likewise we learn to know Jesus as we believe and follow him with a joyful "yes" in answer to his call.

> All of those who follow Jesus do so because of who Jesus is, and we learn to know who Jesus is by believing and following.

The rest of the chapters in this book explore believing and following Jesus in greater depth. Did Jesus really rise from the dead, and why does that matter? How can we hold on to the uniqueness of Jesus and yet respect people of other faiths? We hope you'll stay with us for the rest of the book to consider these and many other questions of faith. For we are convinced that Jesus *does* truly matter, and that believing and following him is, in the end, the most important matter in all of life!

Congratulations! Jesus is calling you to a radically new way of life that will cost you everything yet make you rich beyond your imagination. To claim your prize and pay the price, believe and follow!

Questions for Discussion

1. Jesus called his first disciples with astounding authority. "Come and follow me!" Why did Jesus have that authority?

2. What did believing and following Jesus mean for the first disciples? What did they need to give up? What did they gain?

3. What does following Jesus mean for personal ethics and daily living—does it really change the way I interact with people, the way I manage my time, how I spend my money, the kind of

work I do? How does it challenge the world around me—the popular culture, and the social, political, and other power structures?

4. What does suffering for Christ look like today?

5. Jesus said that he had come to give abundant life for his disciples. What does that mean?

Notes

1. Genesis 1:1-31.
2. Genesis 12:1-4.
3. Exodus 3:10-12.
4. John 3:16.
5. Luke 9:23 NRSV.
6. Revelation 22:17 NRSV.
7. Matthew 4:19.
8. John 3:7.
9. John 4:10ff.
10. Luke 8:50.
11. Mark 2:13-14.
12. Matthew 19:21.
13. John 1:12 NRSV.
14. Hebrews 11:6.
15. John 20:31.
16. Mark 1:15.
17. Luke 10:27.
18. Ephesians 4:1–5:21.
19. Isaiah 61.
20. Luke 4:18-21.
21. Matthew 11:4-5.
22. Matthew 12:28; Mark 1:15; Luke 8:1.
23. John 3:16-17, 36; 6:40; 10:10.
24. Matthew 11:28-30; 28:19-20; Luke 7:41-50; John 14:13-14, 26-27; 15:1-17; 16:33; 17:13-19; 20:22.
25. Ephesians 1:6-7; 2:14-16.
26. 1 Peter 2:9-10 NRSV.
27. Revelation 5:9-10 NRSV.
28. John 1:35-46 NRSV.
29. 1 Peter 2:9.

30. Matthew 6:10.

31. Philippians 3:14.

32. Matthew 16:24-26; Mark 8:34-35; Luke 9:23-27.

33. Genesis 12.

34. Exodus 12:40ff.

35. Jeremiah 37.

36. Mark 2:13-14; Matthew 4:18-22.

37. Matthew 5:11-12; 6:24; 10:17-25, 34-39; Mark 10:30; Luke 14:25-33; John 9:22; 16:2.

38. Mark 14:32-40; John 19:25-26.

39. John 6:68-69.

40. Mark 9:24 NRSV.

41. Mark 14:72.

42. Mark 16:7.

43. John 21:15-22.

44. Hebrews 13:20-21; Philippians 1:6.

45. Matthew 10:39.

46. Matthew 13:44.

47. Adapted from "The Contention that Scripture Says," in Walter Klaassen, ed., *Anabaptism in Outline: Selected Primary Sources* (Scottdale, PA: Herald Press, 1981), 87.

Chapter 2

Who is Jesus?

John Driver with Daniel Driver

———— Narrative: *Names for Jesus in the birth accounts* ————
(Matthew 1:17–2:23; Mark 1:1; Luke 1:26–2:38)

When a child is born, our first question is, "What is the baby's name?" However, in many societies it might be some weeks until the name is decided because parents and the community want a name that fits the personality of the baby. In some parts of Latin America, parents bless the baby by giving the name of the Catholic saint who was honored on the day the child was born. In the traditional Kekchi society of Guatemala, parents sometimes named the children for the day on the Mayan calendar that the child was born. Each day, it was thought, represented a quality, and the Kekchi expected the child to carry the quality of the day on which they were born.

At the birth of Jesus, those around Jesus all contributed names to be ascribed to him. Here are some of the names in the Gospel prologues and birth narratives: Jesus, the Christ or the Messiah, Lord, Savior, Immanuel, the Word, the Life, the Light, Son of Man, the Son of God, the Son of the Most High, the King of the Jews, David's throne, and the Lamb of God. We will explore only five of these: Jesus, Savior, Messiah, Son of God, and Lord.

> In many societies it might be some weeks until the name is decided because parents and the community want a name that fits the personality of the baby.

Good News

In various ways all the names of Jesus mean good news! Mark opens his Gospel with the words, "The beginning of the good news of Jesus Christ, the Son of God."[1] The angel of the Lord sang the night of his birth, "I bring you good news of great joy that will be for all the people!"[2] This is why the four books of memories of Jesus—Matthew, Mark, Luke, and John—are intentionally called Gospels. The word means good news!

The term *gospel* was widely used to proclaim good news in the Greco-Roman world at the time of Jesus. Gospel was special good news that was for the whole society, like the birth of an heir to the king. In his narrative of the birth of Jesus, Luke sets up a contrast between Jesus and the emperor, Caesar Augustus. First-century readers would have picked up on this contrast right away. "In those days Caesar Augustus issued a decree that a census should be taken of the entire Roman world."[3]

> The Gospels set the dynamics of imperial rule and those of Jesus' reign as very different kinds of kingdoms.

The emperor in the ancient world was held to be divine. News of his birth, his coming of age, his accession to the throne, his acts and his decrees were all held to be "good news." By contrast, Luke claims that the birth of Jesus is "good news." The Gospels set the dynamics of imperial rule and those of Jesus' reign as very different kinds of kingdoms.

The angel choirs proclaimed that the birth of Jesus was good news "for all people." When Jesus began his public ministry, the Gospels introduce his mission as good news. Mark writes that Jesus proclaimed, "The kingdom of God is near. Repent and believe the good news."[4] Luke reports that Jesus announced, "The Spirit of the Lord is upon me, because he has anointed me to bring good news to the poor."[5] All the names of Jesus we explore are about this good news—the kingdom of God is at hand!

Jesus

Jesus is the most common name by which the person at the center of the Christian faith is known. The name Jesus appears more than four hundred times in the Synoptic Gospels (Matthew, Mark, Luke) and about two hundred and fifty times in the Gospel of John. How does the name Jesus help us understand this person?

In Matthew's Gospel, the angel instructed Joseph to name the child Jesus, because "he will save his people from their sins."[6] Luke reports that it was Mary who first heard this angelic voice: "You will name him Jesus. He will be great and will be called the Son of the Most High. . . . His kingdom will never end."[7] The fact that the angelic messengers instructed both Joseph and Mary to name the child Jesus indicates its importance. In that context the name established the child's identity and his role in the ongoing story of their people.

Jesus is the most common name by which the person at the center of the Christian faith is known.

The Hebrew equivalent of Jesus, Joshua, is found in the Old Testament. But the name Jesus was also common during the New Testament period. For example, at the time when Jesus was on trial in the Roman court, Pilate, who was in charge, gave the Jews a choice of prisoners who could be released to them at the Passover: "Jesus Barabbas or Jesus who is called the Messiah."[8] Other examples of persons named Jesus include a helper of Paul and a sorcerer from Cyprus.[9] Josephus, the Jewish historian, listed some twenty persons named Jesus, ten of whom would have been contemporaries of Jesus of Nazareth.

How does the name Jesus help us understand this person?

Mary's child was given a name common, assuring us that Jesus was fully human. Jesus, in sharing a common name, also shares fully our humanity. The New Testament writers refer to the carpenter, Jesus of Nazareth, as the One who shares our human likeness; he is the true model for his followers.[10]

The Hebrew name Joshua means "Yahweh saves," or "Yahweh is our salvation." The name Yahweh was revealed to us when God met Moses at the burning bush, about thirteen hundred years before Jesus was born. At that time the Hebrew people were enslaved by Pharaoh in Egypt. God declared to Moses, "I have come down to rescue them."[11] He told Moses that his name was "I AM." God as I AM who comes down to rescue us is Yahweh. Jesus as "Yahweh saves" must surely underlie the angel's message: "For he will save his people from their sins."[12]

> Mary's child was given a name common, assuring us that Jesus was fully human. Jesus, in sharing a common name, also shares fully our humanity.

Jesus came bringing God's *shalom*, a Hebrew term meaning peace in the fullest sense of the word—wholeness, reconciliation, right relations with God, others and creation, well-being, forgiveness, restorative justice rooted in righteousness, abundant life, and joy. Jesus came to free humanity from the critical oppression of sin with all its devastating consequences and to restore humanity and creation to its intended wholeness and peace. Furthermore, "they will call him Immanuel—which means, 'God with us.'"[13] The message was clear. The community gathered around Jesus saw God present in Jesus, acting to save. That is why his name is Jesus!

Savior

We need to explore more thoroughly the meaning of Jesus as Savior. The angel who appeared to shepherds announcing the birth of Jesus not only proclaimed that his birth was good news but also announced several of his names with this startling message: "Today in the town of David a Savior has been born to you; he is Christ (Messiah) the Lord."[14] The names Savior, Messiah, and Lord are surprising and must have shaken the shepherds and Luke's earliest readers in the emerging churches of Asia, Africa, and Europe.

The early church gave witness that Jesus was Savior within a world that proclaimed many other saviors as well. In ancient

Greece, the gods on whom humans depended for their well-being were called saviors. These included Greek gods such as Zeus, sustainer of world order and human life, or Aesculapian, the god of healing. Gradually savior was also applied to rulers whose policies benefited their subjects. In Rome, emperors, generals, and statesmen were called saviors. Caesar Augustus, under whose reign Jesus was born, was one of these "saviors."

So in what way is Jesus Savior? His ministry as Savior is different than that of a Roman emperor or the gods of the Greek pantheon. One gift of Jesus as Savior is forgiveness of sin. A question that people everywhere ask is how to cope with feelings of guilt, shame, or falling short of one's ideals. In his ministry Jesus occasionally startled people by announcing forgiveness of sins.[15] Sin means "missing the mark" or the goal. At the last supper with his disciples, just before his crucifixion, Jesus broke bread and shared a cup of wine with his disciples saying, "This is my blood of the covenant, which is poured out for many for the forgiveness of sins."[16]

The early church gave witness that Jesus was Savior within a world that proclaimed many other saviors as well.

Jesus as Savior forgives sins! He even cried out in forgiveness for those who crucified him. The Greek gods and Roman emperors represented centers of domineering power, not redemptive forgiveness. But Jesus as Savior has given his life in suffering redemptive love so that we are forgiven. Around the world wherever people believe in Jesus as Savior there is joy as people bear witness, "I know my sins are forgiven!"

Other chapters in this book will explore the rich meanings of the term *salvation*. Chapter 11, in particular, focuses on "Jesus Our Salvation." Here we simply note several other dimensions of the term—abundant and eternal life, freedom from sin, redemption, and reconciliation. Jesus brings about a new creation so that we might live joyously, righteously and abundantly. Jesus called this new creation "born again."[17]

People everywhere ponder the meaning of death. Jesus our Savior has overcome death and offers the gift of eternal life. All believers in Jesus receive the guarantee of eternal life![18] Jesus shared this good news with a Jewish leader saying, "For God so loved the world that he gave his one and only Son, that whoever believes in him shall not perish but have eternal life."[19]

The Greek gods and Roman emperors represented centers of domineering power. But Jesus as Savior has given his life in suffering redemptive love so that we are forgiven.

Jesus saves us from death! He has promised, "I am the resurrection and the life. He who believes in me will live, even though he dies."[20] Jesus promised, "I will come back and take you to be with me that you also may be where I am."[21] For this reason, many Christian funerals are characterized by songs of praise that give thanks for the assurance of eternal life. Physical death is not the end of the journey but the gateway into eternity with Jesus our Savior.

Messiah

The heavenly messenger also described the newborn baby *Christ*, which is the Greek version of the Jewish term Messiah. Messiah and Christ mean "the Anointed One."

In the Old Testament, kings were anointed with oil by prophetic and priestly leaders. For example, the prophet Samuel anointed a young shepherd, David, as the next king of Israel, replacing Saul. This was a symbol of God's action in electing him to kingly service. The anointing was confirmed by the coming of Yahweh's Spirit upon the one anointed.[22]

For many centuries before the birth of Jesus, the prophets of Israel envisioned the appearance of the Messiah who would fulfill God's intention to restore shalom within creation and among humans. The prophet Isaiah is an example of messianic expectations during the centuries before Jesus' birth. He wrote, "Of the increase of his government and peace there will be no end."[23]

But there was also expectation that the Messiah would restore Israel to its national glory by overthrowing its oppressors. This led to nationalist attempts to free the Jewish people from foreign control during the four hundred years between the Old and New Testament period. At the time of Jesus, there were Jewish resistance movements that held keen hopes that the Messiah would free them from Roman oppression.

The heavenly messenger also described the newborn baby Christ, which is the Greek version of the Jewish term Messiah. Messiah and Christ mean "the Anointed One."

Consequently, Jesus faced the decision about what kind of a Messiah he was called to be. The Gospels tell us of this struggle, mainly in narratives of the Devil tempting Jesus to become a typical political king. Jesus rejected those temptations and chose the vision of the prophets who described the Messiah as Suffering Servant.[24] Jesus knew that was God's intention for the mission of the Messiah. Jesus and the New Testament church also knew that his mission was universal, not just for the Jewish people. That is the reason the Greek name *Christ* rather than the Jewish *Messiah* is most often used in the New Testament.

Luke highlights the universal mission of Jesus in his narrative of Jesus' birth. He describes an old man named Simeon, who

Jesus faced the decision about what kind of a Messiah he was called to be.

believed God would restore Gentiles as well as Jews to God's shalom. When Joseph and Mary brought Jesus to the temple to be dedicated to God, Simeon held the child in his arms and exclaimed to God, "My eyes have seen your salvation, which you have prepared in the presence of all people, a light for revelation to the Gentiles, and for glory to your people Israel."[25] Indeed, proclaiming shalom for all peoples was the mission of the Messiah.[26]

Son of God

The angel also told Mary, "So the holy one to be born will be called the Son of God."[27] Throughout Jesus' life, this name persisted. Even at his trial and crucifixion the Jewish leaders got Jesus to confess that he was, "God's Son." The Jewish rulers were infuriated and determined to have him crucified, accusing him of blasphemy.[28]

Many centuries earlier the Psalms declared, "You are my son; today I have become your Father!"[29] This was directed to

> Jesus chose the vision of the prophets who described the Messiah as Suffering Servant.

the king as God's anointed ruler. It also looked forward to the expected Messiah. The vision of the Prophet Isaiah was even clearer. "For to us a child is born, to us a son is given, and the government (authority) will be on his shoulders. And he will be called Wonderful Counselor, Mighty God, Everlasting Father, Prince of Peace."[30] The Son of God was expected to restore God's rule of justice and peace among all peoples. Mary, the Galilean peasant girl and mother-to-be of Jesus, may have had that understanding of the angel's amazing message, "He will be called Son of God."[31]

But the title Son of God carried a very different meaning in the world of many gods that characterized the Roman Empire. Rulers among the ancient Greeks and the Egyptians were commonly called "sons of the gods." In fact, Caesar Augustus was explicitly called "son of God." His devotees proclaimed, "Augustus has been sent to us as a savior . . . the birthday of the god Augustus has been for the whole world the beginning of the gospel."[32] Contrast this with the introductory sentence of Mark's Gospel, "The beginning of the good news of Jesus Christ, the Son of God." Imagine how joyful Gentile Christians scattered throughout the Roman Empire

> The Son of God was expected to restore God's rule of justice and peace among all peoples. Mary may have had that understanding of the angel's amazing message, "He will be called Son of God."

were when they read that Jesus, not a Roman emperor, was the Son of God.

The most striking instance of Jesus' being called God's Son came as he hung dying on the cross. The centurion, along with the military unit under his command, was terrified at the whole experience. The centurion exclaimed of Jesus, "Surely he was the Son of God!"[33] What an irony! Legionnaires who, until then, had held their "commander-in-chief" to be god's son, now acclaimed Jesus, their victim, to be the Son of God. Representatives of Caesar's Legions, charged with "keeping peace" in the Empire, had come to represent, in Matthew's Gospel, the citizens of God's alternative kingdom, wherein Jesus was confessed as truly "the Son of God."

Lord

Finally, the heavenly messenger in Luke's birth narrative affirms that the Messiah (Christ) is Lord.[34] This title is used sparingly for Jesus in the birth narratives, but it soon became the most common title by which Christians everywhere confessed their loyalty to Jesus.

In the Hebrew scriptures, God's name was written as four consonants, JHVH, commonly translated "Yahweh" in modern English Bible versions.[35] Pious Jews avoided pronouncing it out of respect for the sacred character of God's name. In the Greek version of the Old Testament, Yahweh is regularly translated *kyrios*, or Lord. This Greek translation of the Old Testament was most commonly quoted by the New Testament writers and was used by early Christians scattered around the empire.

The heavenly messenger in Luke's birth narrative affirms that the Messiah (Christ) is Lord. This title soon became the most common title by which Christians everywhere confessed their loyalty to Jesus.

What this means is that when Christians confessed that Jesus was Lord, they were proclaiming that he was Yahweh. This was amazing to most of the New Testament writers, who were devout

Jews and believed in the oneness of God. Yet in meeting Jesus they knew they were meeting God. Jesus is Lord, they proclaimed joyously wherever they went.

But the term *kyrios* was also used in ancient Greece to mean someone with power and authority. In Rome, where the emperor held absolute power, *lord* came into common usage. From the time of Caesar Augustus, the term gradually became established for reference to the emperors. For loyal Romans, Caesar as lord usurped the authority of God as Lord.

Christians, sometimes at the cost of their lives, refused the empire's demand that all citizens confess Caesar as lord. They confessed that Jesus was Lord, not Caesar. Christians would gather together often secretly on the "Lord's Day" in the early hours of dawn, or after nightfall when daily activities had ceased. With joy they sang, "Worthy is the Lamb who was slain to receive power and wealth and wisdom and might and honor and glory and praise. . . . The kingdom of this world has become the kingdom of our Lord and of his Christ, and he will reign forever and ever."[36]

> The early church knew that this baby of Bethlehem was Savior, Messiah, Son of God, and Lord. Together with the earliest actors in the Gospel narratives, we too can welcome God's Anointed One into the world.

Conclusion

The early church knew that this baby of Bethlehem was Savior, Messiah, Son of God, and Lord. Together with the earliest actors in the Gospel narratives, we too can welcome God's Anointed One into the world. We too are witnesses to the power of Jesus' self-giving love unto death and God's vindication of his Son by raising him from the dead. We too have experienced the wonders of God's reign and the empowerment of God's Spirit. So we too can say yes to the heavenly messenger's announcement that, "A Savior has been born and he is Jesus Christ the Lord!"

Questions for Discussion

1. List the titles, names and metaphors used to describe Jesus in the nativity stories in Matthew and Luke and the introductory sections of Mark and John. What do they say about who Jesus is? Are there other titles or metaphors for Jesus, either biblical or from the church's tradition, that you also find helpful?

2. Do you think that the gospel message is the same for everybody? Does it say the same thing to the long-established citizens as it says to undocumented immigrants in our midst?

3. What was expected of a savior in the world into which Jesus was born? What is expected of a savior now, in our time and in our neighborhoods? What did the angel mean when he proclaimed that Jesus was Savior?

4. Why do you think that it was so dangerous to confess that Jesus is Lord in the Roman Empire of the first century? What are some expressions of opposition to that confession that North American Christians experience? Think of situations where it is costly to confess that Jesus is Lord. Why is this so?

5. In light of the confession that Jesus is Lord, how does one decide what belongs to God and what belongs to the nation-state?

Notes
1. Mark 1:1 NRSV.
2. Luke 2:10.
3. Luke 2:1.
4. Mark 1:15.
5. Luke 4:18 NRSV.
6. Matthew 1:21.
7. Luke 1:31-33.
8. Matthew 27:17 NRSV.
9. Colossians 4:11; Acts 13:6.
10. Philippians 2:5-11.
11. Exodus 3:8.
12. Matthew 1:21.

13. Matthew 1:21-23.

14. Luke 2:11.

15. For example, Luke 5:23.

16. Matthew 26:28.

17. John 3:3-8.

18. Ephesians 1:13-14.

19. John 3:16.

20. John 11:25.

21. John 14:3.

22. 1 Samuel 16:12-13.

23. Isaiah 9:7.

24. Isaiah 53.

25. Luke 2:30-32.

26. Zechariah 9:9-10.

27. Luke 1:35.

28. Mark 14:61-65.

29. Psalms 2:7.

30. Isaiah 9:6.

31. Luke 1:35.

32. Shane Claiborne, *The Irresistible Revolution: Living as an Ordinary Radical* (Grand Rapids: Zondervan, 2006), 23.

33. Matthew 27:54.

34. Luke 2:11.

35. Willard Swartley has further comments on God as Yahweh in chapter 6. It should be noted that the four consonants (JHVH) are also sometimes spelled out as YHVH or YHWH.

36. Revelation 5:12, 11:15.

Chapter 3

Jesus and the Bible

Tom Yoder Neufeld with David Neufeld

———— Narrative: *Two disciples conversing with Jesus on* ————
the Emmaus Road (Luke 24:13-35)

At the end of Luke's account of Jesus' life there is a remarkable story of Jesus' encounter with two of his followers on the road from Jerusalem to Emmaus.[1] Jesus' violent death by crucifixion has left them in a state of shock. Their dreams of liberation for themselves and their people have ended in catastrophe. They don't know what to make of the claims of some women in their group that they found Jesus' tomb empty and that in a vision angels told them that Jesus is alive.

Jesus the Bible Teacher

They are so blinded by shock and grief that they don't recognize the one walking alongside them. It is only when Jesus takes them up on their invitation to have supper with them that they recognize him—"in the breaking of the bread." In the meantime, Jesus has spent the time with them on the road leading them in a Bible study, laying out for them "beginning with Moses and all the prophets" what all this they have experienced means.

Apart from giving us a tantalizing glimpse of how the followers of Jesus experienced him as risen from the dead, this story speaks very directly to our topic of how Jesus relates to the Bible. The story presents Jesus as teacher of Scriptures, here called

"Moses and all the prophets." Jesus and his contemporaries would have thought of the Bible not as a book, nor as the Old Testament, but as a set of sacred scrolls—Scriptures (plural). These sacred and costly scrolls were not readily available to ordinary people, most of whom could not read in any case. They would have been familiar from hearsay, or from listening to scribes, the literate biblical scholars of the day. These Scriptures were the basis on which Jesus and his fellow Jews worshipped, hoped, and acted. In our story, Jesus shows his disciples how to read "Moses and all the prophets" in such a way that they can understand what he himself is about.

Apart from giving us a tantalizing glimpse of how the followers of Jesus experienced him as risen from the dead, this story speaks very directly to our topic of how Jesus relates to the Bible.

The Story(ies) of Jesus and the Scriptures of Israel

Anyone who pays close attention to how the writers of the New Testament present the story and significance of Jesus will notice that they do so with deep conviction that the events surrounding Jesus, his teachings, and who he is as the Messiah, are all deeply rooted in the Scriptures Jews read as word of God. Often we thus encounter in the New Testament phrases like "according to the Scriptures," or "as it is written." There is nothing surprising about this. Jesus and his followers were Jews, devoted to the God of Israel, who had at one time in the distant past brought their ancestors out of slavery in Egypt, who had accompanied them through the highs and lows of life, including the long dark night of banishment to Babylon—today's Iraq—and who had promised that at some time in the future he would usher in what Jesus called the "kingdom of God." God would do so

Jesus shows his disciples how to read "Moses and all the prophets" in such a way that they can understand what he himself is about.

through an "anointed one," a messiah or king, who would bring an end to oppression, poverty, disease, and alienation from God. That is what their Scriptures led them to anticipate.

We can understand, then, why in our story Jesus' friends were so disheartened. They had heard Jesus call people to prepare for God's reign, even inviting them to call God *Abba* (my father). They had heard his remarkable teaching, amazed at how he healed people, physically and spiritually. They had come to believe that as Messiah or Christ (both mean "anointed one") Jesus would put an end to oppression and captivity, whether at the hands of imperial Rome or of demonic powers. While there was much about the way Jesus taught and acted that bewildered them, the one thing they did not anticipate, despite clear hints, was that their hero, their liberator, would fall victim to state terrorism, tortured to death on a Roman cross.

Even so, when decades later they would put their memories and reflections down in writing, they once again went to the Scriptures, to the psalms and the prophets, to tell and make sense of Jesus' death.[2] As our story of Jesus' encounter with his students on the road to Emmaus illustrates, his resurrection too was seen to fit right in to the long story of God's making peace with humankind. What Christians call the Old Testament provided the lens through which Jesus' followers viewed the familiar and the new in Jesus' work, death, and resurrection. Our story suggests they learned that from Jesus himself.

> Telling, hearing, pondering, and passing things on are the raw materials of the New Testament, including the four Gospels, each of which tells the story of Jesus.

Passing on the Good News

If they already had "Moses and all the prophets," how did Jesus' followers come to write what we now know as the New Testament and add it to their Bible?

The first and most important thing to remember is that they

did not keep their experiences, memories, and insights regarding Jesus to themselves. In our story of the Emmaus road, for example, Cleopas and his companion rush to tell their friends in Jerusalem, only to be told that they had already heard from others of Jesus' resurrection. Telling, hearing, pondering, and passing things on are the raw materials of the New Testament, including the four Gospels, each of which tells the story of Jesus.

Think of what happens when you sit in a circle and share stories of stuff that really matters to you. Often one person's story will spark a memory in another, who then shares a story as well, only to be followed by yet another. If your family is like ours, you might even think you can improve on a family member's story. When talking about the development of the New Testament, we call this "tradition," literally "passing things on." We might also call it "giving witness" or "spreading news," or, in order to catch a sense of the urgency with which that happened, "sharing sacred gossip."

People passed on such "gossip" about Jesus for a number of reasons—to strengthen their sense of connection to Jesus, to help sort out how to live as his followers, and to offer good news to all who would listen. After all, as his followers soon came to realize, Jesus was nothing less than the savior or liberator of the world. Many of their contemporaries, both Jews and non-Jews, thought Jesus' followers were crazy for claiming that the one the Romans tortured to death was the Savior or Liberator. Their claims that God had raised him from the dead made even less sense. That may be one reason his followers were so concerned to show that Jesus' teaching about the kingdom of God, his death, and resurrection, were consistent with the Scriptures. Many others, including many non-Jews, did respond positively to this great but very strange news. In fact, figuring out how to handle the enthusiastic

> There were no professional memory keepers, of course, no historians and archivists, only persons who couldn't keep to themselves what they had seen and heard.

response of non-Jews would be one of the biggest challenges Jesus' first companions would face.

We should not be surprised, then, that the early years of Christianity were turbulent, to say the least. Expansion across cultural and religious borders was rapid and chaotic. Remembering Jesus, his teachings, and why he mattered became an ever growing need. There were no professional memory keepers, of course, no historians and archivists, only persons who couldn't keep to themselves what they had seen and heard. True, there were some—Peter, James, and John, Jesus' brother James, Mary of Magdala, to mention only some of the most famous of Jesus' friends, followers, and students—who could verify stories and teachings. But the diversity of "traditions" we see in the Gospels tells us that a whole lot of folks participated in getting news out, which in turn was passed on by others, and yet others, well before these traditions were put into writing.

There is one crucial factor without which we will not understand this process fully. The early communities of Jesus' followers never thought they were simply remembering a Jesus of the past, however important his memory was to them. They believed Jesus to be alive—now! More, they believed him to be present with them through the Spirit, that is, through the living presence of God in their midst.[3] That does not mean that they did not listen carefully and perhaps even critically to each other as they recalled the sayings and deeds of Jesus, but they did listen

> The early communities of Jesus' followers never thought they were simply remembering a Jesus of the past. They believed Jesus to be alive—now!

for what the Spirit of the living Christ was saying to them through each other.[4] After all, they believed themselves and each other to be in some mysterious way "the body of Christ."[5] That is a very different kind of "re-membering" than simply recalling things from a distant past.

The Birth of the New Testament

This need to stay connected to the Jesus who once announced and enacted God's reign in Palestine grew as the communities of believers spread far and wide and incorporated all kinds of persons with less and less connection to the Jewish community. Moreover, the persons who had known Jesus way back then were quickly passing from the scene. This led to writing down the traditions. That is exactly what we find in the Gospels. Scholars have long noticed that the Gospel texts look very much like pearls of memory, treasured anecdotes, profound teachings, strung along a biographical thread that leads from Jesus' appearance, in the case of Matthew and Luke even from his birth, to his death and resurrection. We should not be surprised if sometimes the Gospel writers remember things much the same way and at other times in dramatically different ways and that they sometimes string those pearls in varying order.

Not all of the accounts of Jesus made it into the New Testament. Numerous attempts were made to collect the recollections and memories and put them into a coherent and trustworthy account.[6] While not all stood the test of time, the communities we now call the church preserved, remarkably, not one but four of these diverse accounts. It is important to note that the accounts were not boiled together; rather, the evangelists were allowed to tell their story, each in their own way. In the case of Matthew and Luke, it looks like they took Mark's account and reshaped it to fit their own needs. We call these three accounts the synoptic Gospels, which means "look-alikes" or perhaps "ones that see things the same way." John's Gospel, in contrast, reads like it had a very different set of files from which to work. It took many decades for these writings to be treated as Scripture, that is, to prove themselves to be trustworthy carriers of the words of God, as reliable testimony to *the* Word, Jesus himself.

The New Testament as Part of a Larger Bible

It is quite obvious that the formation of the Christian Bible, which contains both the Old Testament and the New Testament, came about within a long and exciting history. We must not take the shape of the Christian Bible for granted. For example, a second century leader of the church, Marcion, proposed that Christians—as believers in and followers of Jesus came to be known—abandon the Scriptures inherited from the Jewish community, and replace them with the letters of Paul and an edited version of the Gospel of Luke. In his opinion, the violent God of the Hebrew Scriptures was nothing like the loving God of Jesus Christ. But, as we saw earlier, that was not at all how Jesus or the writers of the New Testament documents thought.

The formation of the Christian Bible, which contains both the Old Testament and the New Testament, came about within a long and exciting history.

Over and over, the New Testament writers wanted to make sure their readers would see that the events related to Jesus' life and teaching happened in accordance with what we call the Old Testament. The oft-quoted words in 2 Timothy 3:16-17, that "all Scripture is God-breathed (or God-inspired)," refer precisely to the Scriptures Marcion wished to eliminate. Readers needed to be reminded that the Scriptures we know as the Old Testament were useful "for teaching, for rebuke, correcting, and training in righteousness." This was so that everyone who belonged to God "may be thoroughly equipped for every good work."

This was a battle for the ages, quite literally. In the end, Marcion's proposal was soundly rejected. The leaders of the church as a whole agreed that the Christian Scriptures should include both the Old Testament as well as the writings that remembered and reflected on the life, death, resurrection, and teachings of Jesus and their implications for communities trying to live that out in real life. That is the reason that the Scriptures accepted by the church came to include not only the New

Testament, but also "Moses and all the prophets," as well as the wisdom literature and the psalms. The New Testament is thus a library of diverse writings that faithfully recount Jesus and all he represents in light of the Scriptures of Israel. To eliminate the Old Testament makes the New Testament completely unintelligible. Worse, it makes Jesus unrecognizable.

> To eliminate the Old Testament makes the New Testament completely unintelligible. Worse, it makes Jesus unrecognizable.

Perhaps not as radically as once did Marcion, many readers of the Bible today still sense a tension between the two testaments, often choosing the New Testament and neglecting the Old. There truly are tensions, many of them difficult to resolve, between depictions of God as a powerful warrior and vengeful judge and the forgiving and reconciling God who chooses to suffer on the cross and turn it into an offer of reconciliation. But mercy, grace, and fathomless love are present throughout the whole of the Bible, as are shocking warnings of the dire consequences of ignoring the will of God—often on the lips of Jesus himself.

However challenging, followers of Jesus read the Bible—the whole of it—as a long complex story of God's relentless effort to save the world, climaxing in the self-giving divine embrace of sinful humanity in and through the birth, ministry, death, and resurrection of Jesus the Son of God.[7] We thus read the Bible through the Jesus lens, we might say. That is how we see most clearly the ways and intentions of God and can listen to the story most attentively. As the two followers on the road to Emmaus remind us, however, as surely as we need Jesus to help us understand the whole of the Bible, we need the whole of the Bible, "Moses and all the prophets," to recognize Jesus and understand why he matters.

Trusting the New Testament on Jesus

Why should we trust those accounts and the people who wrote

and selected them? Many today suspect that the "real" Jesus is very different from the one we encounter in the pages of the New Testament. They view belief in him as Messiah and Son of God, indeed *as* God,[8] as making it difficult if not impossible to reconstruct what Jesus was really like. Some wish to treat writings that are not in the New Testament, such as the Gospel of Thomas, as of equal value in telling us who Jesus was. Or, to turn it around, the Gospels in the New Testament are viewed as having no greater historical value than those that were not included. As a result, some have grown deeply suspicious of the New Testament,

> Many today suspect that the "real" Jesus is very different from the one we encounter in the pages of the New Testament.

while others have taken a hard line defending it as revelation and therefore beyond questioning as history.

Neither skepticism nor trumping history with revelation respects the way we encounter Jesus in the pages of the New Testament. Despite the enormous importance of the Bible for our understanding of the Jesus whom the Gospel of John calls "the Word," John insists that that Word became *flesh*, not paper or scroll.[9] God has always encountered the human community on its own turf, so to speak. In Jesus, God has encountered the human community first and foremost as a human being. This "Word-become-flesh" did not, tellingly, put his thoughts and teachings into writing, but entrusted them to the memories of his excited followers, none of whom were professional record keepers or archivists, and all of whom were eager to get word out. What an astonishing act of love, grace, and trust on God's part. What a way of honoring the skill, the commitment, and the creativity of Jesus' fragile following.[10] But this also means that all the *written* words are at best pointers, testimony, witness, holy "gossip" about the life-giving, life-sustaining, and *living* Word of God—Jesus, the Christ.

> God has always encountered the human community on its own turf.

We might wish it were different. We might wish, for instance, for something much safer, less vulnerable to faulty memory or enthusiastic embellishment, less "biased," and less vulnerable to skepticism, like a DVD of Jesus telling his parables, or whatever a first-century equivalent might have been. It is of course true that "oral" rather than written cultures do a much better job of remembering than we do, who typically commit matters to paper, film, or data files. Furthermore when the oral memory is not only individual memory but community memory, that memory is nurtured with remarkable fidelity.

> We might wish, for instance, for something much safer, less vulnerable to faulty memory or enthusiastic embellishment, like a DVD of Jesus telling his parables.

Even so, the words and deeds of Jesus were entrusted to real people living in a particular time and place. To wish it were different is to question the God who fashioned us as a human community rooted in historical reality and pronounced it good. Being "historical" and thus rooted in a time and place is not a result of falling away from God. To see evidence of real history and historical process all over the accounts of Jesus is not a failing of the New Testament and does not render it untrustworthy. As Paul reminds us, God chose what is weak and foolish—human memory, human communication, rooted in and shaped by history—to bring news of salvation to the world.[11]

The "real" Jesus is encountered through the memories of persons and communities very different from ourselves. Through their diverse testimonies, we today encounter the Spirit of Jesus, the promised exhorter, admonisher, comforter, and advocate,[12] the one who resided in their individual and collective memories as the Holy Spirit does in our circles when we struggle together for insight and faithfulness and who guides us

> To see evidence of real history and historical process all over the accounts of Jesus is not a failing of the New Testament and does not render it untrustworthy.

in our gathered recollections.[13] As the Gospel of John tells it, before his departure, Jesus promised that the Counselor, the Holy Spirit "will teach you all things and will remind you of everything I have said to you."[14] The witnesses, the storytellers, the writers of the New Testament, and their readers knew they were not alone. The Spirit of the living Word was with them, reminding and guiding them in their efforts at faithful remembering and proclaiming.

If God has trusted the human community devoted to confessing Christ in word and deed, we trust God in how we read the New Testament. In the end we do not trust because many of the writers may have been there or known those who were (which is true in many instances), nor because they worked hard at getting it right (which they also did, as Luke makes explicit in 1:1-4), nor because of the long time of testing and sifting leading to the inclusion of these and not other writings in the New Testament, nor, finally, because of a particular theory of inspiration. It is because we trust the God of "Moses and all the prophets" that we trust those early followers when they tell us about Jesus. It is because they trusted God that the early witnesses and storytellers trusted their eyes and ears and hands in their encounter with Jesus.[15] That is the God whose very presence they recognized in Jesus, and whose ongoing empowering presence they called "Holy Spirit." It is why they called Jesus "Lord," "Christ," "Wisdom," "Word," "Immanuel"—"God with us." That Spirit is no less present with us who read the Gospels today, introducing us to Jesus all over again.

> If God has trusted the human community devoted to confessing Christ in word and deed, we trust God in how we read the New Testament.

Reading the Bible Faith-fully

A proper reading of the Bible will thus always be filled with a real, albeit life-giving, tension. On one hand, we are concerned with the *words* of the Bible. We want to know what those ancient writers of Scripture meant to say to their own contemporaries and what that might have to say to us about Jesus. We are followers of a Jesus who knew the Scriptures, and even more importantly, who knew the God of the Scriptures, and who announced that the promises made in the Scriptures were coming true in and through him and his ministry. Text matters; texts matter. On the other hand, we encounter in the text a God, a "Word," who does not want to be locked up on a page or in a scroll, who springs off the page, out of the scroll, to be present as Spirit, infusing memories, tellings, hearings, and discernments, with full respect for the fragile humanness of the witnesses and our equally fragile humanness as hearers, readers, and interpreters.

We come to this encounter with Jesus together with others. And then, as often as not, even after a day-long Bible study with Jesus on our Emmaus road, we recognize him finally in "the breaking of the bread," when we worship together and celebrate the Lord's Supper. We recognize him in our shared practice of faithfulness to his way of peace and reconciliation. And then, we look at each other as members of his body and our eyes are opened, and we "know" in ways that clearly go beyond any simple knowing. We know he has been and is with us. And we can't wait to share it with others, only to find out the same Lord has met them too, in ways that might surprise us.

> We come to this encounter with Jesus together with others. And then, as often as not, even after a day-long Bible study with Jesus on our Emmaus road, we recognize him finally in "the breaking of the bread."

Questions for Discussion

1. Why would some persons wish to distance Jesus from his roots in the history and Scriptures of Israel? What are the consequences of doing so?

2. Can the New Testament be both reliable and trustworthy,

on one hand, and have emerged in real history, on the other? If so, how do you imagine God's work in this process?

3. Do you find it disturbing or exciting that there are four accounts of Jesus' life and ministry?

4. How do you imagine the Holy Spirit's role in the process of remembering and passing on the traditions of Jesus' words and deeds?

Notes
1. Luke 24:13-35.
2. E.g., Isaiah 53 and Psalm 22.
3. John 14:25-27.
4. See 1 Thessalonians 5:19-21.
5. 1 Corinthians 12:27.
6. Luke 1:1-4.
7. Hebrews 1:1-4.
8. John 1:1.
9. John 1:14.
10. Matthew 11:25-27; 1 Corinthians 1:26-30.
11. 1 Corinthians 1:20-25.
12. John 14:25-27.
13. Matthew 18:20.
14. John 14:26.
15. 1 John 1:1-4.

Chapter 4

Jesus and Creation

George Brunk III with Laura Amstutz

———————Narrative: *Feeding of the five thousand*———————
(Mark 6:32-44 and parallels)

J. C. Penney is selling a line of tee shirts imprinted with slogans like "Think Green, Be Cool." Ten years ago this kind of shirt would have only been seen on the edgier websites selling organic cotton and hemp clothing. Now it is part of the mainstream, far from the alternative clothing scene. Wal-Mart now sells organic cotton tee shirts for children. Farmers markets are sprouting up all over the country. Hundreds of books, articles, and films about saving the environment are being produced. Ecology is a center piece of political discourse. "Being Green" is the new catch phrase for everything from oil and buildings to clothing.

Christians are catching the "green" wave too. In our town of Harrisonburg, Virginia, a group of churches sponsored a program called "Less Oil for Lent," in which Christians gave up or significantly reduced the amount of crude oil they consumed during Lent. The Catholic Church has recently added "polluting the environment" to its list of cardinal sins. But are Christians just following a trend by putting their own spin on a secular movement? Or might Christians have even more reason to care for the environment? Does Jesus have anything to say about caring for God's creation?

Creation versus Environment

The language we use is one way to differentiate a Christian view from other positions. Rather than saying just "the environment," "the earth" or "nature," Christians prefer the term *creation*. Our world has been made by a power that is greater than *it* is. It is the intricate work and design of an artist. In the term creation, we are recognizing God's authority over the whole order of creation, including ourselves as created beings. This is ultimately God's world. God is the owner and we are to serve God's purposes for creation.

Rather than saying just "the environment," "the earth" or "nature," Christians prefer the term *creation*.

Thus a primary difference between Christians and many others is the way we view our origins. Some of this gets lost in debates about intelligent design, evolution, and other scientific issues. But regardless of the *process* of creation, Christians believe that God is the world's creator and sustainer. The Genesis accounts do not intend to provide a scientific explanation. They are a proclamation that God created the world rather than a description of how it all happened.

Christians hold diverse views on their interpretation of the creation account in Genesis 1. Some believe that the six days of creation are literal twenty-four hour days. Others believe that "in the beginning" might have been millions of years ago. Whether we believe that God created the world in six days or six million years is really secondary to the proclamation that God created it, be that through instant acts or prolonged processes.

Regardless of the *process* of creation, Christians believe that God is the world's creator and sustainer.

A significant element in the Genesis account of creation is the repeated claim that God sees creation as good. This means that no part of creation is worthless and outside of God's concern. Creation serves in achieving the good purposes of God.

The New Testament agrees: "For everything created by God is good and nothing is to be rejected, provided it is received with thanksgiving."[1] Sin has damaged this good creation, but because the earth is God's good project, God will never give up on it. The Bible consistently holds that one day all of creation will be renewed into a place where peace and righteousness dwell. Some Christians take this to mean that it does not matter what we do to creation, because God will ultimately restore it. However, as we will see, the continued redemption of the created world is not just something that will happen in the future, it is something that is in process now. Christians can take part in this redemptive process.

In the opening paragraphs of the Bible, we learn that human beings are the caretakers of the rest of creation. They are created in the image of God and on that basis are agents of the dominion of God in caring for creation as one cares for a garden. The picture of a garden illustrates that natural creation is neither to be left untouched, nor is it to be abused or misused. It is to be respected as valuable in its own right and used to achieve the goals of blessing and justice for the whole of creation. Like a garden, the whole creation is meant to bring delight, joy, and sustenance to humans. A tall order but an inspiring mandate for the human race!

> The continued redemption of the created world is not just something that will happen in the future, it is something that is in process now.

Understanding that the world was created by God gives Christians the foundation block in the tower of reasons that we should care for the earth. The trend for earth care may fade from secular popularity, but in recognizing that God created the earth we are committed to respect and care for it within the purposes God has set for it.

Jesus and the Creation Event

While it is clear in the Old Testament that God was present at the earth's beginnings, it may be less clear what this has to do with Jesus. How can those who believe in Jesus understand his connection with creation? The answer provides the second block in the tower of understanding a Christian perspective of creation care. While Jesus during his earthly ministry made some allusion to his existence before his human life on earth, he did not make explicit statements about a role for himself in the creation of the world. The early church, however, clearly understood that he occupied a central role in creation. This is affirmed in several places in the New Testament writings.

For example, the first sentence in the Gospel according to John proclaims, "In the beginning was the Word, and the Word was with God, and the Word was God. He was with God in the beginning. Through him all things were made; without him nothing was made that has been made."[2] In these astonishing words the writer identifies the human Jesus with the Word that has existed eternally and shares in the being of God. By starting these verses with the same words as Genesis 1, John linked Jesus into the creation narrative that was familiar to readers. Jesus, in his prehuman state as "the Word," was with God during creation and as an active participant, the agent ("through him") of the creative acts. Not one thing, in fact, came into being without him. Just as the Genesis passages are a declaration that God created the earth, so this passage in John is a declaration that Jesus, as the Eternal Word, shares in the very being of God and is also one who creates.

John is not the only one who links Jesus with God and with the act of creation. Paul in his letter to the Colossians affirms that "he is the image of the invisible God, the firstborn over all creation. For by him all things were created; things in heaven and on earth, visible and invisible, whether thrones or powers or rulers or authorities; all things were created by him and for him. He is before all things and in him all things hold together."[3]

> Jesus, in his prehuman state as "the Word," was with God during creation and as an active participant, the agent of the creative acts.

Again we see that Jesus, now confessed as Christ and Son of God, is linked with creation in a central way, as the one who was the actual agent of creation and the one whose purposes creation serves ("for him").

Paul in his Colossians letter then goes on to describe how this special connection to creation gives Jesus, Son of God, the power to deliver all things from their bondage to evil. Because he was before all things and holds together all things, he is the one in whom all things can be redeemed and reconciled with God. This was the common understanding for early Christians. Other texts make similar claims. See 1 Corinthians 8:6 and Hebrews 1:1-3 for further examples. Both of these texts extend the role of Jesus beyond the beginning of creation to the care and keeping of it throughout history.

Because Jesus is the "heir of all things,"[4] he will have a central role in the future when creation is renewed. Thus the work of Jesus as creator is continuous. He shares with God the Father in the care and guidance of all creation at all times. Since the accounts of Jesus' earthly life don't make this claim explicitly, we might well ask how this soaring belief in Jesus' role in creation came about. We begin with a consideration of Jesus' earthly life and ministry.

Jesus' Life and Creation

The focus of Jesus' ministry was human need and human relationships with God and with others. But the reign (kingdom) of God involves God's interest and claim over all things. (See chapter 5, "Jesus and the Kingdom of God.") Jesus announced that the reign of God was present and at work in his ministry on earth. His acts of healing and blessing had both spiritual and physical dimensions.

We might expect that even the natural world would somehow figure into the ministry of Jesus. And it does. While Jesus makes few statements about his power over creation he demonstrates this power in miracles surrounding the natural order. These are known as the nature miracles of Jesus. The most commonly cited accounts in this category are stilling of the storm,[5] feeding of the five thousand,[6] and walking on the water.[7] In all of these accounts Jesus displays the power to intervene in the natural world and cause change in the state of things. Like God

While Jesus makes few statements about his power over creation he demonstrates this power in miracles surrounding the natural order.

merely had to speak for the world to exist, so Jesus merely has to speak and the material world obeys.

The important point in these miracles is that Jesus sees the realm of nature as significant for his mission and uses it to accomplish divine purposes. Creation is at the service of God's kingdom. At the very least we can see from these miracles that creation has value because of the way Jesus uses it for kingdom purposes.

And there is more. These same events raise the question of who Jesus is. At the end of the story of stilling the storm the disciples ask one another, "Who is this, that even the wind and the sea obey him?"[8] This is indeed the right question! These actions bring to mind Old Testament images of God calming the sea and commanding the elements of nature,[9] images that express the sovereignty of God over

Like God merely had to speak for the world to exist, so Jesus merely has to speak and the material world obeys.

creation. One who has this control over creation must have a particularly close relationship to its maker and sustainer—God. Thus the question of how Jesus relates to creation is put to his listeners and before us.

Jesus also draws our attention to creation in parables. He is constantly using the natural world to illustrate the kingdom of God. In the Sermon on the Mount, Jesus draws our attention to the simplicity of creation and God's care for it. Jesus asks us to consider the lilies of the field and the sparrows, two of the more "lowly" members of creation. God feeds the sparrows and clothes the grass of the fields, the weeds, with splendor. So how much more will God care for us?[10] In taking a lesson from creation for human living, Jesus is also saying something profound about God's care for creation itself. In that same sermon Jesus points to God's love for all persons, good and evil, by giving sunshine and rain to everyone.[11] God uses creation to bring blessing to humanity rather than returning evil for evil. Jesus says that God's children should act in the same way toward friend and foe. Creation can be used to help establish peace in the world. (See chapter 12, "Jesus our Peace.")

> Jesus places creation in the service of the reign of God and uses it with the values of justice and peace as his foremost concern.

From these miracles and parables we see that Jesus values creation in the way that God asks humans to value it in Genesis. Jesus does not value it only for its own beauty or terror, nor does he destroy or harm it only for his own gain. Jesus places creation in the service of the reign of God and uses it with the values of justice and peace as his foremost concern.

Jesus as Exalted Lord of All Creation

The resurrection of Jesus from the dead signaled a major advance in understanding who Jesus was, who he would be, and who he had been before his life on earth. On the one hand, the resurrection confirmed the claims of Jesus to be God's saving agent, the Messiah or Christ. On the other hand it meant that Jesus was alive in a new and perfected form of life. Moreover, God had given him a position of highest authority participating in God's lordship over the world. (See chapter 7, "Jesus and God," and chapter 9, "The Resurrection of Jesus.") All of these momentous effects of the resurrection were reflected in the lofty title used for Jesus by the first Christians—Lord Jesus Christ.

But the early church saw still other implications in this exalted position of Jesus. As Lord over all, this same Jesus was Lord of all history past, present, and future. This became the basis for confessing that Jesus was active in the first creation. It was also the grounds for believing that he would accomplish the *new* creation when the world would be completely transformed and renewed in a manner that had been displayed in Jesus' own resurrection. (See chapter 16, "Jesus and the Future.")

> Everything we do as Christians, therefore, to care for creation is pleasing to God and contributes to the future purposes of a renewed creation.

Followers of Jesus have reason, then, to care for creation because we understand that God's ultimate goal is the redemption and restoration of all creation. A key principle of all Christian living is that once we catch a view of what is coming in God's plan, we want to get in step with the new as much and as soon as possible. While we recognize the imperfections of the present world and the failings of its human inhabitants, we believe that God wills to redeem the whole of creation, not only the human elements. Everything we do as Christians, therefore, to care for creation is pleasing to God and contributes to the future purposes of a renewed creation.

Creation Care as Continuing Jesus' Reign

There is one final building block in a coherent argument for Christians to care for creation, and it is related to Jesus' ministry and our call to continue Jesus' reign on earth. Care for creation, particularly in our modern world is directly related to Jesus' call to act justly toward the poor and the oppressed. Much of Jesus' earthly ministry revolved around caring for the poor and oppressed in Jewish society, feeding, caring for and protecting the poor from the powerful political rulers and religious leaders.

Christians in today's "developed" countries in particular must pay attention to the ways that our use and misuse of the created world harm the less fortunate about whom Jesus was concerned. One primary concern is the resources these countries use at the expense of the poor in other countries. For example, while the United States has only five percent of the world's population, it uses 30 percent the world's resources. This is a gross overuse of resources that we are called to share with the world. Many of the resources that developed countries use are taken from the world's poorest countries at the expense of the world's poorest people. In "The Story of Stuff," an online video, the narrator and author Annie Leonard says that 30 percent of kids in the Congo drop out of school so they can mine coal.[12] The coal in the Congo is used to produce goods consumed in the western world. This is just one example of many one could cite.

> While the United States has only five percent of the world's population, it uses 30 percent of the world's resources. This is a gross overuse of resources that we are called to share with the world.

Jesus was hardest on those who took advantage of the poor. Each time he uttered harsh words in the gospels it was to someone who had power and abused it. Christians in the West have huge amounts of economic and political power in contrast to Christians elsewhere. Our culture and lifestyle of consuming goods and polluting the environment put us in the position of the oppressors of the world's poor.

As Christians we have an opportunity to model a different set of values. We can model the kingdom values of justice and peace by using only those resources we truly need. In doing this, we can participate in the redemptive work of God, who calls us to treat the whole of creation with justice.

A Christian Perspective on Creation Care

Concern for the environment is on the forefront of secular dialogue and discourse. Christians, however, have reason to give *sustained* attention to these concerns, not just at times of environmental crisis.

First and foremost, the world and everything in it belongs to

God. God gave humans a mandate to care for the earth, as a gardener would tend a garden, using the resources in respectful ways.

Second, Christians understand that Jesus has a special relationship to creation, as the one through whom the entire world was created and therefore, through whom the entire world can be redeemed. In his life Jesus displayed his power over the created order by performing miracles, and he showed God's care for the created world, by using the natural world in countless parables as examples of the kingdom of God. By placing the kingdom values of justice and peace ahead of personal gain or desires, Jesus provides the model for how to use the created order in the service of God's kingdom.

Finally, Jesus' resurrection is a preview of the final restoration and redemption of the whole creation and is God's pledge that it can and will be so. As Christians we are enabled to live in the power of the resurrection anticipating the blessings of that new creation in our service to the present creation.

What Can *We* Do?

What can Christians do to be better stewards of the world God created? There are many ways to be personally involved in caring for creation. Walking, biking, or using public transportation will reduce our consumption of oil and gas. Recycling, composting, and growing even a small portion of our own food reduces the amount of trash we put in landfills. Supporting local, organic farmers reduces the amount of toxic chemicals put into the earth and atmosphere by large corporate farms. The ways to be personally involved are endless.

As much as individual participation in creation care practices are important, corporate actions by congregations are that much more important. Imagine if every congregation took seriously the role they played in caring for versus destroying creation. How might our world be different if, for example, at potluck dinners every church had a supply of washable plates, cups and silverware for everyone to use, instead of paper, plastic or Styrofoam products? What if every church used organic, fair trade coffee at coffee breaks instead of coffee harvested by people who aren't getting a fair wage and are exposed to toxic chemicals in the process? What if families who lived close to each other carpooled to church, or if they're within walking or biking distance used those modes of transportation to reduce emissions and the use of oil and gas? Or perhaps it starts with something as simple as preparing a worship service around the Genesis or John passages discussed in this chapter or leading a discussion of how creation care relates to the reconciling work of Jesus and the church.

We are called to care for creation because of the role God played, now plays, and will play in creation. Jesus, the Son of God, through whom creation originates and is sustained, calls his followers to be his representatives in the world to act as caretakers of the earth. True lovers of God also love the whole universe that God has made. They take loving care of it, even in this present time when it is spoiled by sin, because they have glimpsed in Jesus' resurrection a vision of the world as it could be and will be. And they are confident that what they do to benefit creation now will not be lost. They believe that, in light of the resurrection, their present labor on behalf of creation "is not in vain."[13]

Questions for Discussion

1. Can you explain in your own words why the first Christians were so quick to confess the human Jesus as the Creator, with God, of the world?

2. What differences do you see between the Bible's view of the natural world and a secular, materialist view? In what ways should such differences make a difference in our behavior?

3. In the Sermon on the Mount Jesus teaches commitments that relate to creation care (Matthew 5:44-45; 6:25-30). What are those commitments and what steps can we take to abide by them?

4. Name a few practical ways that your congregation can participate in creation care.

Notes

1. 1Timothy 4:4 NRSV.

2. John 1:1-3.

3. Colossians 1:15-17.

4. Hebrews 1:2.

5. Matthew 8:23-27; Mark 4:35-41; Luke 8:22-25.

6. Matthew 14:31-21; Mark 6:30-44; Luke 9:10-17; John 6:1-14.

7. Matthew 14:22-33; Mark 6:45-52; John 6:15-21.

8. Mark 4:41 NRSV.

9. See, for example, Psalm 107:28-29.

10. Matthew 6:25-30.

11. Matthew 5:44-45.

12. See www.storyofstuff.com.

13. 1 Corinthians 15:58.

Chapter 5

JESUS AND THE KINGDOM OF GOD

Stanley W. Green with Sarah Thompson

———— Narrative: *Jesus begins his public ministry in Nazareth* ————
proclaiming good news (Luke 4:16-30)

Nelson Mandela suffered greatly during his twenty-seven-year imprisonment on Robben Island and the Pollsmoor Prison in South Africa. While he was in prison, Hendrik Verwoerd died. Verwoerd had been the architect of the racist apartheid regime that had imprisoned Mr. Mandela and robbed him of the best years of his life. When Mr. Mandela was finally released, one of the first people he visited was Hendrik Verwoerd's widow, Betsie. She received him with open arms in her house in a white suburb, and Mr. Mandela warmly embraced her.

Later, the grandson of Wilhelm and Betsie Verwoerd, Wilhelm, went on to become a member of the African National Congress (ANC), the political party that brought Mr. Mandela to the presidency of South Africa in the country's first free democratic elections. Wilhelm also came to play an important role in South Africa's Truth and Reconciliation process. In that reconciling embrace between Nelson Mandela and Betsie Verwoerd, and in Wilhelm's becoming a member of the

> In that reconciling embrace between Nelson Mandela and Betsie Verwoerd, we are given a glimpse of the reconciliation, justice, peace, and forgiveness that are at the heart of the announcement of the kingdom of God by Jesus.

ANC, which would seek to undo the legacy of apartheid shaped by his grandfather, we are given a glimpse of the reconciliation, justice, peace, and forgiveness that are at the heart of the announcement of the kingdom of God by Jesus.

Different Ideas about the Kingdom of God

In Jesus' preaching, there are important themes such as peace, justice, salvation, and eternal life. There is one theme, however, that Jesus repeats so often that it is without doubt at the *very core* of his ministry and message: the kingdom of God—a theme that provides content and meaning to all other things that Jesus talked about.

> There is one theme that Jesus repeats so often that it is without doubt at the *very core* of his ministry and message: the kingdom of God.

The concept of the kingdom of God has been used in many ways throughout history. It has been identified with the Holy Roman Empire, the brutal Inquisition, the bloody Conquista, the global Colonial project, the Holocaust of the Third Reich, the genocide of the indigenous peoples in the Americas, and the horrors of the transatlantic slave trade. These tragic distortions make it critical for us to understand the meaning that Jesus gave to the kingdom of God.

The Kingdom of God as the Activity of God

Jesus declared, "I must proclaim the Good News of the kingdom of God."[1] The distortions noted above are hardly good news! But the kingdom of God in Jesus *is* good news. The expression *the kingdom of God* from the Hebrew *malkuth*, or the Greek *basileia tou theou*, is used sixty-eight times in the New Testament. The expression *the kingdom of Heaven* is used thirty-one times, all in the book of Matthew. A variation of this expression, *the kingdom of Christ*, is used once. These phrases seem to be used interchangeably and, taken together, they suggest that the kingdom of God has to do with the *purposes* of God. Indeed, our very identity as disciples of Jesus requires that we discover, as best we can, what Jesus meant by *basileia tou theou*.

The kingdom is experienced in the triumph of God over those who oppose his righteous rule and in God's victory over evil, death, and distortion, the conferral of God's blessings on God's people, and the fulfillment of God's intended purpose for the created order. The kingdom is God acting in power for the salvation of humanity and the restoration of creation.[2] The kingdom is God's doing; it is God who brings the kingdom. It is the activity of God!

> The kingdom is God acting in power for the salvation of humanity and the restoration of creation. The kingdom is God's doing; it is God who brings the kingdom.

The Kingdom of God: Good News in Jesus

The synoptic gospels (Matthew, Mark, and Luke) bear witness to three ways that Jesus inaugurated the kingdom.

- *Preaching* the kingdom—"The time is fulfilled, and the kingdom of God has come near; repent and believe in the good news."[3]
- *Teaching* the kingdom in the parables.
- *Performing acts of healing and exorcisms* that demonstrate the powerful impact of the kingdom.

Jesus made the claim to his listeners that these acts were evidence of the kingdom of God in their midst. According to the witness of Matthew, Mark, Luke, and the Acts of the Apostles, the good news that Jesus proclaimed was realized in his announcement of the kingdom. For Jesus, the in-breaking kingdom of God *is* the gospel! The evangelist Luke twice declares that the kingdom *is* the gospel message.[4] The Gospel writers believe and proclaim that God in Jesus has broken into history to redeem all of life and inaugurate a new order. That is great news.

The good news of the kingdom is embodied in the life and witness, words and deeds, death and resurrection of Jesus. When Jesus cures a leper or a woman with an issue of blood and exorcises a demon-possessed victim, he establishes healing and wholeness as the essence of the kingdom. When Jesus fellowships with prostitutes and extortionary tax-collectors, he reveals that forgiveness and pardon are at the heart of the kingdom. When Jesus feeds the hungry and binds up the brokenhearted, when he upholds the importance of clothing the naked and visiting those in prison, he asserts that compassion and care for the vulnerable are at the very core of the kingdom.

> The good news of the kingdom is embodied in the life and witness, words and deeds, death and resurrection of Jesus.

When Jesus chooses to fellowship with ostracized women, like the woman at the well in John 4, and to enjoy the dinner company of sinners, he illuminates grace, welcome, and hospitality as fundamental to the nature of the kingdom. When Jesus loves the unlovely or touches the untouchable, when he engages the marginalized and reintegrates the outcast, when he highlights the welcome extended to the wayward (the prodigal son in Luke 15), lauds the generosity of the stranger (the good Samaritan in Luke 10), shows concern for the children and invites us to love our enemies or pray for our persecutors, Jesus is pointing to the radical newness of the in-breaking kingdom.

Jesus announces that the old ways of an eye for an eye, of neglecting justice and oppressing the poor, of disregarding the vulnerable and ignoring the hurting, of condemning the weak and caring only about self and status are in opposition to the kingdom.

The whole life of Jesus and all his works provide meaning and content to the announcement of the kingdom. Therefore, to declare Jesus is to declare the gospel. Jesus does not bring the gospel, he is the gospel—the good news that in him the kingdom of God has broken into history and accomplished everything necessary for the restoration and healing of our world.

Jesus taught about the kingdom of God in parables. He describes the kingdom as something that is near.[5] It is something that should be sought.[6] We may enter the kingdom;[7] however,

> To declare Jesus is to declare the gospel. Jesus does not bring the gospel, he *is* the gospel.

it can be shut up and taken away.[8] It is preached.[9] It is forcefully advancing.[10] It comes secretly.[11] It will come in power.[12] It is to be looked forward to.[13] And yet, it is already "among you."[14] It is only for the committed.[15] It is for children and those who are like children.[16] It is for the poor in spirit and the persecuted.[17] The poor disciple possesses it, but the rich man enters it only with great difficulty.[18] It is above all a mystery, and it may, thus, take people unawares.[19]

The kingdom is about right, joyous, and reconciled relationships. Developing that theme, a Latin American womanist theologian, Ada María Isai Díaz, observes that rather than an invitation to be God's subjects, simply substituting the earthly hierarchy for a heavenly one, the experience of God's "kindom" (her intentional spelling to reference the family-like relationship between all those who are followers of Jesus) is like an invitation to join God's extended family, where everyone counts equally and reciprocity is encouraged.[20] The "kindom"—kingdom—is a family, the family of the people of God!

Jesus describes the kingdom as a tiny mustard seed that becomes a tree where the birds live; it is like yeast that permeates and changes the bread dough.[21] The unobtrusive, powerful and transforming growth of the kingdom in our lives often surprises us. For example, when tough Roy became a member of the local church, he said, "I am here because when I was a teenager hanging out with my buddies on the street, a kind woman invited us into her basement on cold winter nights for hot chocolate. We knew her love for us had to do with Jesus. That is why after these many years, I also want to believe in and follow Jesus."[22] That woman had planted mustard seeds of the kingdom among some teenage guys that in time became a pungent garden shrub!

Obviously the kingdom of God as revealed in Jesus is rich and varied; it is God's good news movement. The kingdom is not static; it is dynamic![23] To do justice to all that Jesus intended we must seriously explore the rich spectrum of meanings embedded in the kingdom as expressed in Jesus. In this way we will expand our understanding of the broad range of blessings we receive in the announcement of the good news.

Should We Wait Awhile or Start the Party Now?

Should we celebrate that the kingdom of God has come, or should we wait because it is yet to come? Jesus used the kingdom of God to describe the new reality of God's reign, which *was being fulfilled* in his ministry.[24] He also used the concept to describe *the final goal* of human history.

Jesus understood himself to be inaugurating the kingdom of God in the present. He reveals the presence of the kingdom in such diverse and humble ministries as conversations at meals with his disciples or with outcast sinners, in his exorcisms of demons, and in his offer of hope to the poor, hungry, and weeping. This is the meaning of Jesus' announcement that the kingdom is "among you."[25]

He proclaims that the kingdom of God has already broken in, since he himself with the Holy Spirit is indeed already repulsing death by healing the sick and raising the dead.[26] These acts anticipate the victory over death which Jesus obtains in his own death and resurrection. Jesus announced, "But if it is by the finger of God that I cast out demons then the kingdom of God has come upon you."[27]

At other times Jesus observes that the kingdom of God is not yet completely fulfilled even though it is imminent. He teaches the disciples to pray for the "coming" of the kingdom, suggesting that though the kingdom is dawning, it has not yet fully arrived. Jesus does not seem to need to resolve this tension of the kingdom *present* and the kingdom *not yet fulfilled*.

Because the kingdom is God's self-revelation in Jesus, we can embrace a multifaceted interpretation that includes many amazing dimensions of the kingdom. This means that we see the kingdom of God acting now and as not yet fulfilled but moving toward a future irresistible climax. The integrating center to the kingdom is divine personality. In Jesus, and in his life and preaching, we have the principal witness to God's reconciling act both now and in the future.

> Jesus does not seem to need to resolve this tension of the kingdom *present* and the kingdom *not yet fulfilled*.

Worship and Discipleship: Our Response to the Kingdom

What does the announcement of the kingdom mean for the followers of Jesus in the present context? The kingdom embodies two poles. The one pole represents *divine performance*, that is, what God has done. God has acted decisively in Jesus to overcome death and evil, liberating creation from the distortion of God's purposes. God's breaking into human history to effect our salvation through Jesus infuses the created order and all dimensions of life with hope and invites us to worship and celebration.

The other pole represents *human performance*. It is our response to what God has done that leads us into an engagement with the created order and all of society for the purpose of transforming it in the direction of God's purposes. Our response presumes the establishment of alternative communities that are formed by and for God's purposes. These communities incarnate the values modeled and proclaimed by Jesus.

The kingdom, thus, is realized at the creative interface between *promise* (divine performance) and *action* (human response). The human response is repentance and commitment to Jesus Christ. Our calling is to be humble and energetic witnesses in pointing to the in-breaking of God's reign as we allow the kingdom values of love and forgiveness, justice and peace to form us and our communities. We share the good news of God's intent for the world as it was embodied in Jesus and invite people everywhere to believe, repent, and become participants in the kingdom.

> The kingdom is realized at the creative interface between *promise* (divine performance) and *action* (human response).

Communities of the Kingdom

Disciples of Jesus are privileged to become participants in communities of the kingdom, the church. (Chapter 6, "Jesus Triumphs over the Powers" and Chapter 13, "Jesus and the Church" explore this theme more fully.) The church is the community or the creation of the kingdom, but it is never the kingdom itself. Believers in Jesus belong to the kingdom, but in their sinfulness they are not the fullness of the kingdom that Jesus demonstrated.

The kingdom is the reign of God that Jesus fully demonstrated in his life and teachings. By contrast, the church is a fellowship of forgiven and redeemed sinners. The church is comprised of broken and fallible humans who are often out of alignment with God's reign. Nevertheless, the church is the only community of believers who confess that Jesus is Lord. That confession when expressed in repentance and sincerity is a commitment to becoming kingdom people through the empowerment of the Holy Spirit.

> The church is the community or the creation of the kingdom, but it is never the kingdom itself.

Communities of Transformation

The church is not an end in itself. It exists for the kingdom that is its goal. However, the church is called to engagement with the world for the sake of the kingdom. Jesus was committed to bring good news to the poor, for the captives to receive their release, for the blind to see again and for those who were oppressed to receive their liberty.[28] This mission of Jesus as good news for the poor and freedom for the captives was an extension of the Year of Jubilee that Moses proclaimed for the Hebrew people many centuries before Jesus Christ lived among us.[29]

Wherever the church in its life and ministry reflects these commitments that Jesus inaugurated, it becomes a transforming community within societies. For example, as the world approached the year 2000, many church communities in wealthier countries such as the United States urged governments and global banking systems to work in concert to forgive the debts of poorer nations.

This debt relief movement, as flawed as it was, developed in part as churches, as flawed as they were, gave witness to the jubilee themes of God's kingdom!

That plea was heard! As many regions of the world celebrated the two-thousandth anniversary of the coming of Jesus, a number of governments and global financial institutions such as the World Bank worked together to forgive the international debt of countries that met the criteria of integrity and responsible government. That forgiveness was an enormous encouragement to these countries and has contributed in many cases to economic progress. This debt relief movement, as flawed as it was, developed in part as churches, as flawed as they were, gave witness to the jubilee themes of God's kingdom!

Church members and leaders are called to model kingdom ethics, even when it means taking risks. In the 1980s, when the apartheid system in South Africa segregated people into neighborhoods by race, a white church leader named Nico Smith came to the realization that the Bible didn't teach apartheid and that thus he could no longer accept this unjust system. Uncertain about his future, yet sure about his newfound beliefs, he began to take a prophetic stance against apartheid and preached a message of reconciliation for whites and blacks. Troubled by his conscience, he was forced to resign a university professorship and, in violation of the country's laws, became the first white to move his family into a black neighborhood where he pastored an all-black congregation.

His actions risked the rage of his white compatriots and put his family's safety in jeopardy because of the anger of many in the black community toward the oppressive realities of apartheid. Smith believed that Jesus called his followers into a new kind of family, one in which race and ethnicity no longer divide and separate. The attention that Smith's witness received led to many church-based Koinonia reconciliation groups across the country which, in turn, contributed to the downfall of apartheid. Smith understood that Jesus' followers were called to a different kind of ethics and often to a courageous witness that ran counter to the cultural norms.

Good News Ethics

No one is surprised about the Ten Commandments that God revealed to the prophet Moses at Mount Sinai. Most religions affirm in various ways the ethics of these commandments, which provide guidelines on matters related to honoring the deity, respect for elders, proper sexuality, honesty, avoiding jealousy, not stealing or killing, and rest days.

> The Sermon on the Mount describes the ethical life style of the church, the good-news-kingdom-people.

The Sermon on the Mount, on the other hand, *is* surprising.[30] Jesus begins this sermon by proclaiming blessings upon the poor in spirit, those who mourn, the meek, those who hunger and thirst for righteousness, the merciful, the pure in heart, peacemakers, and those persecuted for righteousness. Jesus calls for inner transformation that produces the fruit of genuine sexual chastity, integrity, forgiving and loving the enemy, giving to the needy, and embracing the kingdom rather than pursuing earthly wealth. The Sermon on the Mount describes the ethical life style of the church, the good-news-kingdom-people.

When a Chinese pastor was visiting North America she was asked, "Why is your church growing so rapidly?" She responded:

> We seek to live as Jesus taught in the Sermon on the Mount. For example, one member of my church is a poor vegetable vendor in the local market. One day she over-charged a customer. When she discovered her mistake, she left her stand and ran hither and yon through the aisles until she found the customer she had overcharged. The customer was astonished and asked the vendor why she had returned the money. The vendor replied simply, "I am a believer in Jesus." The next Sunday, the customer was in church with her neighbors and friends who came to learn about Jesus who creates such integrity![31]

Like the members of the Chinese pastor's church, we are called as the church to follow Jesus in fulfilling the mandate for which the Spirit equipped him and for which the Spirit seeks to equip the church. We are called to be a community of the king-dom, a people shaped by the kingdom's alternative values. When the church lives by these values, we grow in our capacity to fulfill Jesus' mandate. Like Jesus, we are empowered by the Holy Spirit.

Do Not Be Surprised by the Opposition

Jesus' commitment to the kingdom brought much joy and rich-ness into his life, but it also resulted in constant opposition and ultimately his crucifixion. In fact, when he began his public ministry in his home town synagogue in Nazareth and made the declaration that the good news for the poor is being fulfilled, within minutes the congregation took him to a cliff intending to hurl him to his death.[32] Why? Because he declared that even Israel's enemy neighbors would be included in this good news. From that time until his crucifixion three years later, opposition never ceased.

Beware! Kingdom living does invite opposition, for our modern and postmodern societies do not live by kingdom values. When the church lives as a kingdom people, that church and its individual members will, like Jesus, experience opposition from time to time. At this very moment, there are thousands of believers around the world who are persecuted because of their faithful commitment to Jesus and the kingdom he inaugurated.

> Beware! Kingdom living does invite opposition, for our modern and postmodern societies do not live by kingdom values.

Jesus said, "Blessed are you when people insult you, persecute you and falsely say all kinds of evil against you because of me. Rejoice and be glad, because great is your reward in heaven."[33]

Conclusion: A 'Kingdom Come' Prayer

Jesus' disciples often saw him in prayer, and so they asked him to teach them to pray. He instructed them to intercede that the kingdom would happen on earth as in heaven! This prayer that God's kingdom might happen in our lives and churches and among the nations pulls together the major themes of the kingdom—the grace of knowing God as our loving heavenly Father, receiving his kingdom, food for the hungry, extending and receiving forgiveness, victory over evil, and glorifying God now and eternally!

Let's together join in that fervent prayer of hope and expectancy:

Our Father in heaven,
    hallowed be your name,
your kingdom come,
    your will be done

on earth as it is in heaven.
    Give us today our daily bread.
Forgive us our debts,
    as we forgive our debtors.
And lead us not into temptation,
    but deliver us from the evil one.
For yours is the kingdom and the power and the glory for-
ever. Amen![34]

Questions for Reflection

1. You have just read the prayer that we call "the Lord's Prayer." What transformations would you anticipate in your community as God moves in response to this prayer?

2. What transformations would take place in your church and in your own life as God's kingdom comes "on earth as in heaven"?

3. In what ways do you and your church demonstrate signs of the presence of the kingdom of God?

4. Share with others your observations about the kingdom of God. In what ways do you observe people opposing the kingdom? In what ways do you see the transforming power of the kingdom bringing new life and hope?

5. Hope is a precious gift of the kingdom of God. In what ways does the church reveal and celebrate hope? In what ways do you celebrate the hope of the kingdom in your own experience?

Notes

1. Luke 4:43 NRSV.
2. Cf. Bruce Chilton, *God in Strength: Jesus' Announcement of the Kingdom* (Freistadt: Plöchl, 1979).
3. Mark. 1:15 NRSV.
4. Luke 4:43; 16:16.
5. Mark 1:15; Luke 10:9, 11.
6. Matthew 6:33.

7. Matthew 5:20; 7:21; Mark 9:47; John 3:5.

8. Matthew 16:19; 23:13.

9. Matthew 24:14; Luke 4:43; 9:60.

10. Matthew 11:12.

11. Luke 17:20.

12. Mark 9:1.

13. Matthew 6:10; Luke 19:11.

14. Luke 17:21 NRSV.

15. Luke 9:62.

16. Mark 10:14.

17. Matthew 5:3, 10.

18. Mark 10:23-25; Luke 6:20.

19. Matthew 12:28; Mark 4:11.

20. Ada María Isai Díaz, *Mujerista Theology* (Maryknoll: Orbis Books, 1996).

21. Matthew 13:31-33.

22. Reported by David W. Shenk, former pastor, Mountville (Pa.) Mennonite Church.

23. Norman Perrin, *Jesus and the Language of the Kingdom: Symbol and Metaphor in New Testament Interpretation* (London: Fortress Press, 1976).

24. Luke 4:21.

25. Luke 17:21 NRSV.

26. Matthew 11:3ff.; 12:28; Luke 10:18.

27. Luke 11:20 NRSV.

28. Luke 4:18-19.

29. Leviticus 25:8-54.

30. See Matthew chapters 5–7.

31. Hong He, pastor Beishi Church, Shenyang, China, in a testimonial given at the Lancaster Mennonite Conference annual meeting, March 1994.

32. Luke 4:24-30.

33. Matthew 5:11-12.

34. Matthew 5:9-13 NRSV.

Chapter 6

Jesus Triumphs over the Powers

Willard Swartley with Michael Fecher

———Narrative: *Jesus triumphs over nature, demonic power,*———
sickness and death (Mark 4:35–5:43)

Two stories, one here and one at the end of this chapter, illustrate God's mighty power over evil and Jesus Christ's victory over the powers.

The first story takes place in East Germany, where for nearly half a century the oppressed population longed for freedom from Communist rule. During 1989 increasing numbers of believers and unbelievers came together to pray for God's help and protection. As one East German-born Christian told it to me, with tears, people who had never come to church came and called upon God for help—in simple and earnest prayers. Many began to meet regularly on Monday nights at the *Nikolaikirche* (Nicholas Church) in Leipzig.

Communist troops threatened to halt their gatherings by force. The church called on both the government and the people to refrain from violence. A petition not to resort to violence was read from every pulpit in the city and broadcast over the municipal public address system. The petition invited people to come to the church and pray Monday night. Seventy thousand people

> When the secret police felt the power of the faith movement, they left. The people, weeping with joy, praised God for this divine intervention.

showed up. When the secret police felt the power of the faith movement, they left. The people, weeping with joy, praised God for this divine intervention. This was a new biblical Red Sea miracle as when God delivered Israel from Pharaoh's oppression in Egypt.[1] We read, "The LORD said, 'I have indeed seen the misery of my people in Egypt; I have heard them crying out because of their slave drivers, and I am concerned about their suffering. So I have come down to rescue them from the hand of the Egyptians.'"[2]

Old Testament Foundations

God's deliverance of Israel from the great Egyptian power formed Israel's identity. The drama of the ten plagues highlights the contest between Pharaoh's power and the LORD God's power. God acted so "that they may know that I am the LORD." *YHWH* (LORD)[3] reveals himself to Moses so as to empower him to confront the mighty Pharaoh. Israel is called to trust God for defense against enemy onslaughts. Numerous "Lament Psalms" speak of "the enemy" from whom God delivers.[4] God protects the covenant people under the shelter of divine wings.[5]

Israel was not to put trust in chariots, swords, and armies. Many Psalm texts echo God's prototype-promise to Moses to defend Israel.

The Old Testament is replete with accounts portraying wars and God as a God of war.[6] However, there are many nonresistant peacemaking accounts, such as Abraham and Isaac settling quarrels over wells[7] and Elisha healing the Syrian enemy captain, Naaman, from leprosy, then throwing a banquet for the invading Syrian army rather than killing them.[8] Others are absurd stories in which victory over the stronger powers is won miraculously: Gideon, with only three hundred men, wins with torches inside jars;[9] Jericho's walls fall when Joshua's troops march around the city, the priests blow trumpets and the warriors shout;[10] and David overcomes Goliath with a pebble from a sling-shot.[11] God defeats the huge Assyrian army under Sennacherib by an angel of the LORD who "annihilated all the [Assyrian] fighting men and the leaders and officers."[12] God protects and rescues Daniel from the the lions' den and his friends from the fiery furnace.[13]

These are marvelous accounts of God's victory and call to trust and not to be afraid. Indeed Israel was not to put trust in chariots, swords, and armies.[14] Many Psalm texts echo God's prototype-promise to Moses to defend Israel. Moses said to the people, "Do not be afraid. Stand firm and you will see the deliverance the LORD will bring you today. The Egyptians you see today, you will never see again. The LORD will fight for you; you need only to be still."[15] Israel, however, often reverted to trust in the military, wealth, sorcery, divination, and worshipping idols—gods and goddesses. In idol worship, "they sacrificed their sons and their daughters to demons."[16] Thus on the day of God's judgment the people will throw away their idols. "In that day" also God will punish and exile Israel. And, as we know, what happened to Israel, the northern kingdom, was repeated in the southern kingdom of Judah as well.[17]

> The prophets thus looked beyond national Israel to a new covenant and to a messianic figure to bring deliverance, the gospel of peace—shalom.

Jesus Messiah

The prophets thus looked beyond national Israel to a new covenant[18] and to a messianic figure to bring deliverance, the gospel of peace—shalom, for "God reigns"[19] when "all the ends of the earth will see the salvation of our God."[20]

This promise is fulfilled in Jesus the Messiah who comes to save the people "from their sins."[21] Anointed by the Spirit, Jesus comes proclaiming the gospel of God, the gospel of peace.[22] God's jubilee reign dawns now in Jesus' ministry. Jubilee was the year when the people of Israel were to forgive all debts and free all slaves![23]

The vast stream of prophetic justice is now *incarnated* in Jesus:[24]

• He denounces substituting laws of religion for love of humanity.
• He rebukes Peter for identifying messiahship with oppressive power.
• He calls his followers to take up a cross, not a sword.
• He cleanses the temple, defending the rights of the Gentiles.
• He sets before his disciples the images of cross, child, and servant.

Jesus' way differs from that of the Zealots, Sadducees, Pharisees, and Essenes in their strategies to free Israel from oppressive Roman occupation. Jesus teaches love of enemy and nonresistance, seeking to turn the enemy into a friend and restore human dignity to both the oppressor and oppressed.[25] He creates an alternative community whose LORD God empowers disciples with freedom to love enemies and be peacemakers. This is God's new community of love with humble service that challenges conventional political, economic, and social norms.

Jesus' kingdom is a power greater than all other powers, portrayed graphically in Jesus' economic teaching,[26] accepting and healing social outcasts (leper, prostitute, even rich Zacchaeus, a hated tax collector). At Jesus' trial Pilate asks him if he is a king.[27] Jesus declares that his kingdom is greater than Pilate's for God's *power* is greater than Pilate's.[28] Jesus incarnates power greater than all earthly powers. He stills the stormy sea chaos, heals the sick, and casts out demons—signs of his power over nature, illness, and death.[29]

As king, Jesus rides into Jerusalem, humbly on a donkey.[30] He forgives those who crucified him.[31] Thus Jesus' dying manifests his and God's love for the world. The cross, the instrument of torture for political subversives, becomes a symbol of peacemaking through Jesus. The gospel of peace does not kill the enemy, but kills the enmity.[32] Jesus welcomes enemy Samaritans and Gentiles into the new community that he gathers, nurtures, and re-forms.[33]

Jesus sends out his apostles to inaugurate the peace gospel of God's kingdom. "When Jesus had called the Twelve together, he gave them power and authority to drive out all demons and to cure diseases, and he sent them out to preach the kingdom of God and to heal the sick."[34] Jesus also sends out seventy-two to proclaim the gospel of peace, heal the sick and announce that the reign of God has come upon them.

> Jesus' dying manifests his and God's love for the world. The cross, the instrument of torture for political subversives, becomes a symbol of peacemaking through Jesus.

Jesus *sees* Satan *falling*.[35] The Greek verb the evangelist Luke uses is imperfect tense, with Jesus saying, "As you went about announcing the kingdom, I was *seeing* Satan falling like lightning from heaven." Here is the video of Satan's dethronement. A new world has come, and people are invited, entreated to embrace it, through submitting to Jesus as Savior and LORD of all. Luke's summary of Jesus' ministry in Acts 10:34-38 accentuates Jesus' peace gospel and deliverance, a liberating message that releases people from the oppression holding them captive. A new reality dawns!

What in this extraordinary ministry of Jesus destined his crucifixion? The essay "Jesus Crucified" (chapter 8) shows how Jesus' death on the cross fulfills God's purpose to love, forgive, and save in the face of hostility and crucifixion. Certain events in Jesus' ministry provoked the animosity of the religious leaders against him. Many scholars regard the cleansing of the temple as the event that most infuriated the authorities. The narrative concludes, saying, "The chief priests and the teachers of the law . . . began looking for a way to kill him."[36] But a similar destiny looms earlier, already when Jesus violates Pharisaic Sabbath laws, in which Pharisees collude with Herodians, the party supportive of Herod as deputy of Rome—an unusual political coalition indeed!—to scheme a way to kill Jesus. In the trial narrative Jesus' temple confrontation and blasphemy in claiming to be the Son of God join as causes to condemn him to death.[37]

Also, Jesus' healings lead to popularity that threatened the religious establishment, turning them against Jesus. The authorities even fear the Romans will come and destroy the nation if they do not destroy Jesus. In Luke the Jews bring three charges against Jesus— perverting the nation, forbidding payment of taxes to Caesar, and claiming to be the Messiah king. Jesus' kingdom vision, teachings, and actions provoke opposition from the powers, in religion, economics, social class, and politics. Jesus dies on the cross because he exposes human sin in structures and practices of oppression. He sides with the poor and the outcast. Jesus dies for his commitment to God's kingdom. Jesus dies to save us from our sin, revealed graphically in people's rejection of his ministry. This happens in accord with God's plan, to show God's and Jesus' undying love for us. Jesus dies that we might be forgiven, transformed, and freed from sin and bondage.

Jesus' victory over death in the cross and resurrection releases us from fearing death and assures us that the devil's power over us is broken. The epistle to the Hebrews says, "Since the children have flesh and blood, he too shared in their humanity so that by his death he might destroy him who holds the power of death— that is, the devil—and free those who all their lives were held in slavery by their fear of death."[38]

The New Testament celebrates the Messiah's victory over Satan and the powers. Jesus' ministry continues in the early church, stirring the powers to opposition.[39] Evangelism and exorcism of demons are often intertwined.[40] As the gospel of

Christ's salvation and lordship is received by grace through faith, Satan's power is broken.

Paul's Witness to Jesus' Victory over the Powers

Paul proclaims God's victory in and through Jesus Christ as power and gift that deliver us from the works of Satan so we can know the peace of Christ ruling in our hearts, uniting us in the bond of peace.[41] Hear

The New Testament celebrates the Messiah's victory over Satan and the powers. Jesus' ministry continues in the early church. Evangelism and exorcism of demons are often intertwined.

the promise: "The God of peace will soon crush Satan under your feet!"[42]

Paul proclaims Jesus Christ's victory over the powers:

1) And having disarmed *the powers and authorities*,
2) HE MADE A PUBLIC SPECTACLE OF THEM,
3) Triumphing over them by the cross.[43]

Not only are the powers defeated but they are put on public spectacle, just as the Romans put captors on public display, dragging them through the streets. Christ leads those who believe as victors over evil "in triumphal procession."[44] Paul's missionary zeal is rooted not only in his Damascus Road conversion encounter with Jesus but also in being transformed from a "violent man"[45] into a herald of Jesus Christ making peace.[46] The peace gospel Paul proclaimed

Not only are the powers defeated but they are put on public spectacle, just as the Romans put captors on public display, dragging them through the streets.

subverts Rome's peacemaking claim in its so-called Pax Romana, which was really a regime of much oppression and violence.[47] Christ's death and resurrection are God's and Christ's gift for human redemption, dethroning the principalities and powers, and indeed Satan, who colludes with them to foment sin, evil, oppression and violence.[48]

God's intention is that political authorities function in a way that rightfully orders the world so as to curb evil. In fact all powers have been created by God through Jesus Christ to function in ways that glorify God.[49] Recall chapter 4 of this book, which describes Jesus as Lord of creation. However the powers have rebelled against God, notably in crucifying Jesus Christ.[50]

> Christ's death and resurrection are God's and Christ's gift for human redemption, dethroning the principalities and powers, and indeed Satan, who colludes with them to foment sin, evil, oppression and violence.

Jesus' victory over the powers includes release from *nature* powers, what Paul calls the *stoicheia*, often translated as "the elemental spirits of the universe."[51] These powers manifest themselves in the ordering structures and rituals of pagan religions and philosophies, controlling humans through astrological fate, fortune, and magical practices.[52] In traditional pagan religions a hill and/or a tree is often held to be the abode of evil spirit-power. Jesus' *crucifixion* on a *tree*[53] has double symbolic significance—the *means* of death, ultimate political power, and the *place* of death, ultimate nature power. Jesus' death by crucifixion on a tree was from all appearances the triumph of the pagan political and nature powers. Jesus' death in this manner

> God's resurrection of Jesus "trumps" the power of the powers, proclaiming victory over these powers even in their utmost effort to destroy the truth and light of God in Jesus.

exposes—for all to see—the evil empowering these powers. But God's resurrection of Jesus "trumps" the power of the powers, proclaiming victory over these powers even in their utmost effort to destroy the truth and light of God in Jesus who reveals God's love and power in fullness.[54] The powers act out their rebellion, killing the revealer of the true God of the universe. The cross thus exposes their ignorance, evil, and futility.[55] But Jesus cannot be held by death's power, for God raises him from the dead, and exalts him to eternal power at God's right hand.[56]

Numerous texts announce and declare the victory of Christ over the powers:

- **1 Corinthians 15:24-27.** Every authority, rule, and power has been disempowered, subjected to Christ. When Jesus hands over the kingdom to the Father, the powers will be stripped completely of their power.
- **Ephesians 1:19-23; 3:16-19.** The exalted LORD Jesus Christ reigns, far above all rule and authority, power and dominion. All such powers are subject to Christ for the sake of the church, to enable it to spread the knowledge of God and radiate his love to all.
- **Ephesians 3:9-10.** The church witnesses to the powers of the manifold wisdom of God in uniting formerly hostile parties, Jews and Gentiles, in Christ.
- **Ephesians 6:12-18.** Believers stand against the strategies of the powers to trick, deceive, and defeat us. The armor to resist is *God's* in conquering evil.
- **Romans 8:35-39.** Nothing in all God's creation, not even the powers (demons) can separate believers from the love of God that is in Christ Jesus our LORD.
- **1 Peter 3:22.** All angels, authorities, and powers are subject to Jesus Christ, who is in heaven, at the right hand of God.
- **Revelation 18:2b, 10c.** "Fallen, fallen is Babylon the great. . . . In one hour your doom has come."

In his letter to the Ephesians, Paul celebrates Jesus Christ's victory, which even unites into one body former enemies; this miracle-church fellowship is witness of God's manifold wisdom to the powers.[57]

Then in his letter to the Colossians he envisions ultimate reconciliation of the powers to God! "For God was pleased to have all his fullness dwell in him (Christ), and through him to reconcile to himself all things, whether things on earth or things in heaven, by making peace through his blood, shed on the cross."[58]

A later chapter in this book describes Jesus' triumph over

death (chapter 9). Paul's resurrection discourse in his letter to the Corinthians proclaims, "Death has been swallowed up in victory!" "But thanks be to God! He gives us the victory through our LORD Jesus Christ."[59]

The Authority of the Believer

Jesus' victory over Satan releases believers from Satan's power in all realms of life—personal, political, economic, and social. Paul's epistles speak of Satan's efforts to deceive and mislead believers. He masks himself as an angel of light, seeking with deceitful designs to get an advantage over believers. Believers must resist Satan.[60] We are warned to give no place to the devil, by not letting the sun go down on our anger.

The believer seeks to follow in Christ's footsteps, both in proclaiming Christ's death and resurrection as victory over evil, and in steadfast testimony to deliverance from demonic powers. Believers position themselves "in Christ" and draw from Christ the power to free from sin and evil. We do not attack or fight the powers; God has done that in Christ on and by the cross on our behalf. (See chapter 12, "Jesus Our Peace.") Jesus' cross is victory over evil by bearing the sin of all humanity and by God's defeat of the sinful powers crucifying Jesus. We proclaim Christ's victory over sin, evil, death, and the powers. We seek to live the new way of love that overcomes evil with good. We confront evil victoriously only in the name and power of Jesus Christ, praying for protection of loved ones and our church body.

The beginning of this chapter described the church united in prayer for deliverance from political oppression. I conclude with an account of prayer for deliverance from demonic oppression:

One afternoon a colleague in deliverance ministry called asking me to pray and bind the demon of murder in a man who had just threatened to come to his church and murder the pastor. My colleague, I, and the pastor began praying where we were. The man came into the church parking lot and started toward the church with a gun, then suddenly stopped, got back into his pickup, tore out of the church lot, went home, called the pastor on the phone, and said, "I need help. I am overcome with evil to murder you." The pastor arranged a meeting for the same evening and invited several of us to come and assist.

During my twelve-mile drive to the church, I struggled with how a nonresistant Mennonite handles violence. I cried to God for help. Several times the verse came to me, "Jesus said: 'Love your enemies.'" How does this figure when one is confronted with violence, I agonized? Not long into the evening session, I thought I was a "goner." The man, much bigger than me, lunged toward me with his fist aimed at my head. The words I heard from God in the car burst out of my mouth, "Jesus said, 'Love your enemies.'" The man collapsed to the floor, with swinging arm gone limp.

Then we learned from the demon, when commanded to speak the truth, that someone had murdered this man's father when the man was twelve years old, and that he had sought to kill the man who had killed his father these twenty-five-plus years. We told this to the man when he had come out from the demonic spell, to test it as truth. The man broke down and said, "How do you know this? I've told no one. It's true. I am overcome with the spirit of murder." He then confessed his sin and asked God's forgiveness. From then on, we knew what we were dealing with. Expulsion of that demon from the man came quickly in the next round of command-confrontation. The spirit of murder cannot withstand being confronted with Jesus' "enemy-love" command.[61]

Jesus, the humble, king servant in his obedience unto death, even death on a cross, is the exalted, triumphant one. All powers, now subjected to him, will one day "bend the knee and confess him as LORD." Let us have the mind of Christ, who emptied and humbled himself, and trust in him from whom nothing in all creation, not even the powers, can separate us.[62] Jesus is LORD. He is LORD!

Jesus, the humble, king servant in his obedience unto death, even death on a cross, is the exalted, triumphant one. All powers, now subjected to him, will one day "bend the knee and confess him as LORD."

Questions for Discussion

1. What is it about human nature that keeps us from trusting God to protect us and save us from the powers of evil?

2. Are we on the side of those who collude with the powers and perpetrate oppression or are we the victims of oppressive powers? Or are we some of both?

3. Do you ever feel that the powers block your prayers? When we prevail in prayer, do we sense release from the powers, with freedom and joy in the Spirit?

4. Jesus gathered a community to continue his mission in this world. What roles might we as individuals and our church community play in witnessing to Christ's victory over the powers?

Notes

1. Jürgen Moltmann says three hundred thousand people came with candles and prayers for the reunification of Germany on these Monday nights during a six-week period. Read his account in *Politics of Discipleship and Discipleship in Politics: Lectures and Dialogue with Mennonite Scholars*, ed. Willard M. Swartley (Eugene, OR: Cascade Books, 2006), xiii-xiv. This event, together with other factors, led to the astonishing collapse of the communist regime.

2. Exodus 3:7-8a.

3. See chapter 2 discussion on Yahweh and Lord. In this chapter I use Lord for God as Yahweh (or YHWH, written in Hebrew without vowels). I capitalize the word (LORD) throughout this chapter to remind us of the sacred, "awesome" quality this divine title held for the Hebrew people.

4. Psalms 5, 7, 9, 10, etc.

5. Psalms 5:11; 36:7; 61:4; 91:1-6.

6. Since the Hebrew lacks a verb, the Greek Septuagint translators rendered the verse, "The Lord crushes war" (cf. Psalms 46:9). NT writers generally used the Greek Septuagint.

7. Genesis 21:25-33; 26:17-33.

8. 2 Kings 5 and 6.

9. Judges 7.

10. Joshua 6.

11. 1 Samuel 17.

12. 2 Chronicles 32:21.

13. Daniel 3 and 6.

14. Psalms 20:7; 33:16-17; 44:3-6; 46, esp. verse 9; 76:3; 147:10.

15. Exodus 14:13b-14.

16. Psalm 106:37.

17. Isaiah 2:20; 7:17-25; 2 Chronicles 36.

18. Jeremiah 31:31-34.

19. Isaiah 52:7.

20. Isaiah 52:10.

21. Matthew 1:21.

22. Mark 1:14-15; Luke 10:5-6; Acts 10:36.

23. Leviticus 25:8-55.

24. See multiple texts in Mark that present the themes listed here: 2:28–3:6; 8:27-38; 9:33-37; 10:42-45; 11:15-19.

25. Matthew 5:38-48.

26. Luke 12-16.

27. John 18:36-38.

28. John 19:10-12.

29. Mark 4:35–5:34.

30. Zechariah 9:9–10; Matthew 21:5.

31. Luke 23:34.

32. Ephesians 2:14c.

33. Mark 3:13-19; 8:27–10:52; John 4 and 21; Acts 10.

34. Luke 9:1-2.

35. Luke 10:17-20.

36. Mark 11:18.

37. Mark 3:6; 14:58-65.

38. Hebrews 2:14-15.

39. Acts 3-5, 8, 13, 16 and 19.

40. Robert E. Webber, *Celebrating Our Faith: Evangelism through Worship* (San Francisco: Harper & Row, 1986), 35-37.

41. Colossians 3:15; Ephesians 4:3.

42. Romans 16:20.

43. Colossians 2:15 (emphasis added). See here Ernest Martens' chiastic analyses of verses 13-15 in *Colossians and Philemon Believers Church Bible Commentary* (Scottdale, PA: Herald Press, 1995), 113.

44. 2 Corinthians 2:14.

45. 1 Timothy 1:13.

46. See Ephesians 2:14-18, where *peace* is used four times.

47. Willard Swartley, *Covenant of Peace: The Missing Peace in New Testament Theology and Ethics* (Grand Rapids, MI: Eerdmans, 2006), 38-40, 164-70, 245-53.

48. See Swartley (2006), chapter 8, for an extended discussion of evil and Christ's victory over the powers.

49. John 1:3; Colossians 1:15-16; Hebrews 1:3.

50. It is unclear in Scripture just how and when some powers fell from their original state. (See Jude 6; Isaiah 14:12-15.) First Corinthians 2:6-8 and the Gospels' trial narratives attest to the rebellion of the powers against God.

51. Galatians 4:3, 8-9; Colossians 2:8, 18-23.

52. Swartley (2006), 226-27.

53. Galatians 3:13.

54. Colossians 2:9-10; Hebrews 1:3; John 1:18.

55. 1 Corinthians 2:6-8; Acts 4:27.

56. Acts 2:24, 32-36; 4:5-10.

57. Ephesians 2:14-18; 3:9-10.

58. Colossians 1:19-20.

59. 1 Corinthians 15:54b, 57.

60. 1 Corinthians 7:5; 2 Corinthians 2:11; 11:14; 12:7; 1 Thessalonians 2:18; Ephesians 4:26f.

61. Willard Swartley, "Reflections on Deliverance Ministry," in

Even the Demons Submit: Continuing Jesus' Ministry of Deliverance, Loren L. Johns and James R. Krabill, eds., (Scottdale, PA: Herald Press, 2006), 110-11.

62. Philippians 2:6-11; Romans 8:37-39.

Chapter 7

Jesus and God

Lois Barrett with Susanna Barrett Mierau

Narrative: *Jesus' last conversation with his disciples before his arrest and crucifixion* (John 14:8-10)

How can we know what God is like? At some point, we all wonder. If God is not a "person," and particularly not an old man with a long white beard sitting up in the sky somewhere, is God personal? Does God love me, as a person might—or *better* than some people do? Or is God an abstract force of the universe—just there, like gravity? Is God real, or is talk about God just a massive fraud perpetrated on unsuspecting folks? Does God act in the world today, or did God set the world in motion and then withdraw to observe the world from some icily neutral vantage point? If we have a spiritual experience, how can we know whether it is from God or from some other spirit? Is it even possible to *know* God, not just know *about* God?

Show Us God!

We're not alone in wondering about God. "Show us the Father" was the request of Philip, one of Jesus' twelve apostles. In the Gospel of John, Jesus was having a final conversation with his disciples, doing a bit of teaching at their last meal before his arrest and crucifixion.

Philip said to him, "Lord, show us the Father, and we will be satisfied." Jesus said to him, "Have I been with you all this time, Philip, and you still do not know me? Whoever has seen me has seen the Father. . . . Do you not believe that I am in the Father and the Father is in me? The words that I say to you I do not speak on my own; but the Father who dwells in me does his works."[1]

Often in the Gospels, the disciples are shown as having a hard time understanding Jesus. They just don't get it. So Jesus tries to make it clear to them. Jesus tells them that whenever they look at him, they are seeing God. Earlier in the Gospel of John, its writer claims that no one has ever seen God, but Jesus has made God known.[2] Through Jesus we can know God.

How is it that we learn about people whom we have never met? We read about them. We ask mutual friends about them. The friends might say, "Well, she is about Brittany's height. She talks fast like John. She has a sense of humor like Sarah." We often describe people by comparing them to someone the person already knows. That is the way it is with describing God. Since we can't see or touch God, we can learn about God by comparison with Jesus. In the Gospels we have a record of Jesus—who people said he was, what he said, how he acted. So what is God like? God is like Jesus.

Jesus Shows Us God

How does Jesus show us God? Can we look at this human being and see God? Yes, according to Jesus' own teachings and the witness of the early church. And there are a number of ways in which this happens.

Jesus Speaks God's Word and Does God's Will

The Gospels tell us that Jesus is the Messiah, or the Christ. These two words mean the same thing; *Messiah* is taken from the Hebrew, and *Christ* from the Greek, for "anointed." Jesus is God's anointed one. In the Old Testament, prophets or priests or kings were anointed as a sign of a special assignment from God. Jesus was also anointed by God. In his first sermon at the synagogue in his hometown, Nazareth, Jesus preached from the writings of the Prophet Isaiah: "The Spirit of the Lord is upon me, because he has anointed me to bring good news to the poor."[3]

> Jesus was sent out on God's mission in the world. Jesus was on assignment from God.

At his baptism, God's Spirit rested on Jesus. Jesus was so connected with God that he spoke God's word to the people. Jesus said, "I have not spoken on my own, but the Father who sent me has himself given me a commandment about what to say and what to speak."[4] Jesus was sent out on God's mission in the world. Jesus was on assignment from God.

After the resurrection, Jesus gave that assignment also to his disciples. He told them, "Peace be with you. As the Father has sent me, so I send you."[5] Through Jesus, we participate in God's mission in the world.

> Through Jesus, we participate in God's mission in the world.

Jesus Preaches, Teaches, and Heals in the Context of God's Reign

Jesus made God's reign—God's rule over all creation, present, past, and future—the center of his preaching.[6] He taught about the reign, or kingdom, of God in the Sermon on the Mount.[7] He performed "signs and wonders" through the power of God. These miracles included healing of people and forgiveness of sins. Others recognized that "no one can do these signs that you do apart from the presence of God."[8] Jesus himself was a sign of God's activity in the world.

We too are called to be instruments of God's reign, continuing Jesus' ministry of preaching, teaching, and healing.

Jesus Is the Son of God

In Hebrew idiom, "son of" something or someone means "like" that thing or person. In the Bible, we see terms like "sons of thunder,"[9] "children of light,"[10] and "children of God."[11] "Sons of thunder" does not mean that the disciples James and John had thunder as a parent; it is a figure of speech to describe their personalities.

So when the New Testament calls Jesus "the Son of God," it could be interpreted in various ways. Is this talking about genetics? Or is it talking about Jesus' character? Or does it refer to the relationship Jesus had with God? We do know that Jesus had a close relationship with God, so close that Jesus called God *Abba*, "Daddy." Jesus shared the character of God in judgment, forgiveness, compassion, and love, even of enemies.

But is Jesus the Son of God in a way that goes beyond the figure of speech? The New Testament sometimes calls Jesus the "only begotten" Son of God. Jesus is a child of God in a sense that others cannot claim. Jesus is the first of those raised from the dead, and according to Romans 8:29, the "firstborn among many brothers and sisters" (TNIV). Jesus is God's Son in a way we cannot claim.

> Jesus had a close relationship with God, so close that Jesus called God *Abba*, "Daddy." Jesus shared the character of God in judgment, forgiveness, compassion, and love, even of enemies.

At the same time, Jesus as the pioneer of our faith makes it possible for us to be adopted as sons and daughters of God, brothers and sisters of Jesus. We are invited into relationship with God and into right relationship with other people, even enemies. In this way, says Jesus, we are like God who also loves and blesses enemies.[12]

Jesus Is the Image of God

"Image of God" is another way of talking about how Jesus is like God. Colossians 1:15-20 is an ancient hymn of the church that describes Jesus' special relationship to God:

He is the image of the invisible God, the firstborn of all creation. . . . He himself is before all things, and in him all things hold together. He is the head of the body, the church; he is the beginning, the firstborn from the dead, so that he might come to have first place in everything. For in him all the fullness of God was pleased to dwell, and through him God was pleased to reconcile to himself all things, whether on earth or in heaven, by making peace through the blood of the cross.

Hebrews 1:3 says it another way. Jesus "is the reflection of God's glory and the exact imprint of God's very being." How is this being "in the image of God" different from all of humanity being created "in the image of God"?[13] Although the first human beings sinned, marring the image of God in which they had been created, Jesus has the "fullness of God." He is the "exact imprint" of God. And he is the pattern for our lives. As disciples of Jesus, we are to be in Jesus' image. According to the apostle Paul, through Christ, we are being transformed into the image of Christ.[14]

Jesus was both fully human and fully divine. He wasn't half man and half God; he was completely *human and* completely *divine.*

Jesus Is Fully Human and Fully Divine

One of the ways that the early church explained the relationship between Jesus and God was to say that Jesus was both fully human and fully divine. He wasn't half man and half God; he was *completely* human and *completely* divine. The early church said that Jesus had two "natures." Jesus was a real human being. He was born. He really suffered on the cross. He died. But he was also completely filled with the divine Spirit. God raised him from the dead and lifted him up to be ruler of everything on earth and in the spiritual realm. This is a paradox, but it is an important way to understand who Jesus is.

The apostle Peter speaks of Christ's divine power. This power completely infused the life and being of Jesus Christ. Through this power, Christ has given us everything needed for living a godly life, so that we may become "participants of the divine nature."[15] Because of Jesus, we also as human beings can share something of the divine nature.

The Anabaptists, radical reformers of sixteenth-century Europe, believed that Christians really could participate in the divine nature. Other reformers thought that it wasn't really possible to live like Jesus—or that Jesus' teaching was there only to give us a sense of our own unworthiness in the face of such a high standard and thus encourage us to depend on God's mercy. The Anabaptists, on the other hand, thought that conversion did actually change people. Jesus' commandments were meant to be obeyed. The Sermon on the Mount was meant to be lived. Christians could risk their lives for the sake of the gospel, as Jesus did. Christians could hope in the resurrection, just as Jesus trusted God to raise him from the dead. Christians could be on the path of participating in the divine nature. The Holy Spirit could work in the lives of Christians as it had worked in Jesus' life.

> The Anabaptists, on the other hand, thought that conversion did actually change people. Jesus' commandments were meant to be obeyed. The Sermon on the Mount was meant to be lived.

Jesus Is Part of the Trinity

The Trinity is a concept that the church developed to express the unity of Father, Son, and Holy Spirit—and at the same time their separate identities. The Trinity is not explicitly mentioned in the New Testament. Sometimes Father, Son, and Holy Spirit are mentioned.[16] Sometimes it is the Lord Jesus Christ, God, and the Holy Spirit.[17] Other times only two of the three are mentioned together—Jesus Christ and God the Father.[18] Both testaments refer to God's Spirit in various contexts.

> The Trinity is a concept that the church developed to express the unity of Father, Son, and Holy Spirit—and at the same time their separate identities.

The issue of the Trinity arose in the early centuries of the church as it grew in Greek-Roman culture. From an early time, the church worshipped Jesus Christ. The martyr Stephen prayed to Jesus just before his death.[19] Christians called Jesus "Lord," the same word they used for God. Did this mean there was more than one God?

No, said the church. God is still one. But there are three ways that we can perceive God:

• Father,[20] the Ruler of the universe, the One whose face we cannot see directly;
• Jesus Christ, the Son, fully human and fully divine, who shows us completely the character of God; and
• the Holy Spirit, God's activity in the world and among human beings, the animator of life, the breath of God, who empowered Jesus and continues to empower the church.

Sometimes the church has talked about God in three "persons." But these are not persons in the sense of three separate beings. *Persona* in Latin referred to masks or roles, ways that we perceive a character in a drama. God is both three and one. The three persons of the Trinity are so closely connected that Christians cannot think of one without the others. One way to think about the Trinity is to imagine the three dancing in a circle, with separate identities, but as one community of love—or as particles in an atom, revolving around one another, different yet one. Or we can think of the Trinity as three ways that we experience God.

The three persons of the Trinity are so closely connected that Christians cannot think of one without the others.

Christians sometimes run into problems when they try to separate the parts of the Trinity. Many churches have ignored the Holy Spirit because the Spirit is often unpredictable. The Spirit goes where it wants to go, surprising us or leading us into new places. So churches that like order and regularity can be uncomfortable with the Holy Spirit. The danger in doing that is legalism.

The gospel is hardened into a list of rules and regulations. God's grace and power are not noticed. People forget that the Spirit that worked through Jesus for forgiveness and healing can also work through the church today.

Other churches have a different problem. They recognize the gifts of the Spirit, but they don't know how to distinguish between God's Spirit and some other spirit. One pastor told me about his congregation's quandary. The congregation believed that the Holy Spirit still spoke to people today, and several people in the congregation were prophesying, saying, "This is God's word for us." The problem was that not all this prophecy was saying the same thing. How is a congregation to discern whether a prophecy is really from God? What eventually helped this congregation in their dilemma was to read the words of Jesus in John 14:26: "But the Advocate, the Holy Spirit, whom the Father will send in my name, will teach you everything, and remind you of all that I have said to you." In other words, we can discern whether a message is from God by comparing it with what we know that Jesus said. The Holy Spirit does new things, but they are always aligned with what Jesus said and did. The Holy Spirit is not going to send us in some direction other than the way of Jesus.

So we need to pay attention to the whole Trinity. The three persons of the Trinity are in complete harmony with each other. They act as one.

If You Want To Know What God Is Like, Look at Jesus

Jesus is so closely connected with God, so filled with God, so in tune with God's will, that God is what we see when we look at Jesus. We don't need to wonder about God's character because we can read the stories of Jesus in the Gospels. Does God's mercy trump God's judgment? Read the story of the woman caught in adultery, where Jesus says, "Neither do I condemn you. Go your way, and from now on do not sin again."[21] Does God become indignant with the unjust exploitation of the poor and extend righteous judgment upon those unrepentant who neglect the oppressed? Read the accounts of the cleansing of the temple[22] or Jesus' warning of final judgment and the great separation of the sheep who care for the oppressed and goats who neglect the poor.[23] Can God forgive even those who kill? Read the story of Jesus' forgiveness of his executioners as he hung dying on the cross.[24] Is God more powerful than evil or death? Read the Gospel accounts of Jesus' resurrection.[25]

> Jesus is our picture of the God who cannot be seen. Jesus is the body of the God who is Spirit and cannot be touched.

Jesus is our picture of the God who cannot be seen. Jesus is the body of the God who is Spirit and cannot be touched. Jesus is one in whom God's Spirit lives and who anoints the church with that same Spirit, so that we can give others a glimpse of God's reign on earth as it is in heaven.

Questions for Discussion

1. What have been your images of God through the years?

2. How is Jesus a prophet speaking God's word—and more than a prophet?

3. Skim the Gospel of Mark. What words and actions of Jesus give us a picture of what God is like?

4. What is the difference between thinking of Jesus as fully human and fully divine, versus half human and half divine?

5. Many hymns of the church sing praise to the Trinity. Why is it important to consider all three persons of the Trinity? What happens when we concentrate only on one?

Notes

1. John 14:8-10 NRSV. Bible citations in this chapter are NRSV.
2. John 1:18.
3. Luke 4:18; Isaiah 61:1.
4. John 12:49.
5. John 20:21.
6. Mark 1:15.
7. Matthew 5–7.
8. John 3:2.
9. Mark 3:17.
10. 1 Thessalonians 5:5.
11. John 1:12.
12. Matthew 5:43-48.
13. Genesis 1:27.
14. 2 Corinthians 3:18.
15. 2 Peter 1:4.
16. Matthew 28:19.
17. 2 Corinthians 13:13.
18. Galatians 1:1.
19. Acts 7:59.

20. Although Jesus referred to God as "Father," he also used mother-like expressions in describing God, such as a mother hen. In Genesis 1:27 we read that humankind, male and female, is created in God's image. The character of God contains both male and female qualities. Since God is not a human being, neither male nor female images of God can completely describe God.

21. John 8:1-11.

22. Matthew 21:12-13; Mark 11:15-17; Luke 19:45-46; John 2:14-17.

23. Matthew 25:31-46.

24. Luke 23:32-34.

25. Matthew 28:1-10, Mark 16:1-8, Luke 24:1-12, John 20:1-18.

Chapter 8

Jesus Crucified

Mark Thiessen Nation with Nelson Okanya

———— Narrative: *Jesus breaking bread and sharing the cup* ————
with his disciples (Luke 22:14-20)

Heidi Neumark, a Lutheran pastor in the South Bronx, is accustomed to celebrating communion in the weekly worship service. She and her congregation regularly hear the words, "this is my body, which is for you" and "this cup is the new covenant in my blood." Together these phrases remind them that in celebrating the eucharist, Christians "proclaim the Lord's death until he comes."[1] Neumark assumed that these words were repeated in all Christian churches during the celebration of the Lord's Supper. Then she visited a megachurch in Las Vegas.

'A Power Stronger Than Any Wounding Force'

Neumark visited this Las Vegas church when they were observing communion. However, it was a bloodless communion; no mention of blood or death. The pastor explained to Neumark that this omission reflected their attempt to

Pastor Heidi Neumark visited this Las Vegas church when they were observing communion. However, it was a bloodless communion; no mention of blood or death.

be culturally relevant, to be inviting to "seekers." He didn't need to convince Neumark of the importance of being contextually appropriate. In the South Bronx, Neumark was committed to relevance. But then she wondered:

Is bloodless Communion really so culturally relevant?
What culture would that be? People in Las Vegas don't
bleed? I know that most of the architecture is fake, but it
seems an insult to imply that the people are, too. . . . I
think bad theology—and I put bloodless Communion in
that category—can carry with it an edge of pathology,
however well-intentioned it may be. Communion is not
about wearing a smile on the outside when you're dying
inside, like the decals plastered on broken buildings. It's
about finding life in a power that has proven to be
stronger than any wounding force.[2]

The God Who Suffers with Us

My wife and I recently watched the film *Slumdog Millionaire*. It's
a powerful and painful film if you allow yourself to be transported
into the world created by this cinematic story. The world of dire
poverty and violence it portrays offers little hope of escape. As we
sat watching it together, on February 14 of all days, we turned to
each other in the midst of the pain and jointly quipped, "Happy
Valentine's Day." A romantic comedy would have seemed more
appropriate.

I wonder if a bloodless communion reflects our desire for
worship services, and the elements like communion, to be a religious
version of a romantic comedy, an escape from real life. Perhaps we
resist being reminded of our connection to the pain and suffering

> Perhaps we primarily see church as an experience that should make us feel good and remind us that there is always a happy ending.

of the world by the words "proclaiming the Lord's death until he
comes." Perhaps we primarily see church as an experience that
should make us feel good and remind us that there is always a
happy ending. It seems we will never understand the centrality of
the cross in the New Testament if we fail to realize that the con-
ditions behind this cross are the suffering and pain of the world,
a world wracked by sin in all of its particular manifestations. To

be sure, the cross is now empty. Christ rose from the dead. He has conquered death in all of its forms. Victory is assured. But the resurrection does not silence the message of the cross.

My wife and I are a part of a new Mennonite church in the heart of the relatively small city of Harrisonburg, Virginia. We worship in a community center where many of our members work and play with our neighbors who have fallen through society's cracks. When we gather for worship we are visibly reminded of the pain and suffering and the sin in our world. And we're made aware of our own sin as well. There's no artificial architecture. It is basic and functional. The setting makes it at least a bit more difficult to wear plastic smiles—as if all is well in the world. When we sing of salvation, when we sing of the coming reign of God, we know that we need to find "life in a power . . . stronger than any wounding force." The cross of Christ offers this strong power. The death of Christ embodies and communicates the love of God for a hurting world. Yes, the cross is central to the way in which the New Testament describes God's love in summary form.

> We must not valorize victimization for its own sake.

The Cross and Victimization

Neumark goes on to mention one of the contemporary concerns about how we portray the death of Jesus, about how we name the significance, the efficacy, of the crucifixion of Jesus:

> Some feel that lifting up the cross implies the elevation of victimization and abuse. Tragically, it is all too true that many women have suffered, and even died, as victims of domestic violence under the rubric of "bearing their cross." But that is a twisted use of the cross.[3]

I confess that I have felt this concern for many years now. Having experienced domestic violence in the home of my childhood and having been a child protective services social worker, I am sensitive to this concern. We must not valorize victimization for its own sake. Pastors and friends should be sensitive in helping those in painful situations discern when they are in unhealthy ways submitting themselves to abuse. However, in the midst of these concerns, we must also know that as followers of Jesus we are called to pick up our cross daily.[4]

What distinguishes martyrdom from victimization? What distinguishes embracing the cross from unhealthy submission to abuse?

Each one of us is called to serious discipleship. Embodying Christlike love in a sinful world will be costly, sometimes very costly. So what distinguishes martyrdom from victimization? What distinguishes embracing the cross from unhealthy submission to abuse?[5] A lot, Neumark writes:

> When we sing about "power in the blood" here in the Bronx, we're not glorifying suffering and advocating victimhood. We're taking life seriously. Blood is not just death. From the womb, life and blood are inseparable. My babies came out shining with my blood. Burnice's were born bright with hers. I'm sure it is also true in Las Vegas. I bleed every month. My heart bleeds with pain when blood is spilled. This doesn't make me a victim. It makes me a woman. It makes me human. Jesus' blood made him human. Without it, he's no better than a molded action figure. Our faith is that he died in the fight for life—and that he didn't die in vain. He didn't die as a passive victim. He died because of his powerful passion for us, resisting all dehumanizing powers. His blood doesn't call us to lie down and rest in peace, but to rise in strength.[6]

For God so Loved the World that He Sent his Son

Anyone who is reading through the Gospels cannot help but notice that Jesus treasures life—offering new and abundant life to those who were helpless and hopeless. We will never understand the centrality of the cross in the New Testament if we do not notice the importance of the life and love at the root of it. In the Gospels and in the Epistles, we are repeatedly and in various ways reminded that the life of Jesus that culminates in the cross is an expression of the love of God for the world.[7]

But of course Jesus crucified and risen is also about the power of God that overcomes the sin of the world. Paul begins his first letter to the Corinthian church by devoting two chapters singularly to "Jesus Christ, and him crucified."[8] In the beginning of this letter and elsewhere Paul reminds the churches that in the cross there is "wisdom," "power," "strength," "life," "right-eousness," "justice," "redemption," "reconciliation," "forgive-ness" and "sanctification." Moreover, the power available through the life, death and resurrection of Jesus is made possible because the love of God the Father was made known through the love and faithfulness of Jesus the Son.[9]

I was not brought up in a Christian home. My father, and then later my step-father, both abused alcohol. During some years of my childhood, violence, drunkenness and unfaith-fulness plagued my life at home. Lone-liness, lack of direction, and youthful temptations led me down a treacherous path. Then at age seventeen I was powerfully encoun-tered by the transforming power of God. The love of God—the extraordinary power of this love—was made visible to me through the cross. The cross, in all its horror and beauty, conveyed in ways that words never could the depth and breadth of the wondrous love of God. For this God became flesh in Jesus and was willing to love even to the point of death on the cross.

Jesus willingly died at the hands of evil people, people who even in their villainy were forgiven by this compassionate One. This God loved me in this way. This Lord redeemed my life, brought healing to my woundedness, and set me on the road to salvation. Having been made new through the Spirit, within the body of Christ, I was being enabled to live the righteous, just, and holy life to which my Lord called me. I knew almost immediately that this salvation was not just for me, it was for the sake of the world. Thus I was called to witness in word and deed. The cross of Christ taught me what it meant to love my neighbors as myself and to love even my enemies.

Christ Crucified—the Power of God

The cross as an expression of the power of God the Father and our Lord Jesus Christ speaks in life-transforming ways to many. One last word from Heidi Neumark:

> This is what drew me back to Christianity, knowing a God who could bleed to death and yet live. We who bleed in the Bronx want to live, too. We want "power in the blood." . . . I simply don't know a context on the face of the earth where bloodless Communion is relevant to human life. It is precisely that cup that Jesus agonized over on the Mount of Olives. The anemic Eucharistic prayer of a bloodless church dishonors Gethsemane where Jesus struggled and Golgotha where Jesus died. It dishonors those who have died in the fight for justice and truth. And it fails to take our own wounds seriously, whatever zip code we live in.[10]

I have attempted to live with the various Scriptures that convey a sense of the redemptive power and mystery of the cross over the years. Additionally, I have heard numerous testimonies to the many ways in which God in Christ has wrought transformation in people's lives. The mystery and meaning of the cross is like a multi-strand rope: no single description can capture the fullness of what has happened in the crucifixion of Jesus who is "the Lamb that was slain from the creation of the world."[11] The New Testament writers present an array of richly intertwined threads such as triumph over the powers and over death, reconciliation, redemption, the one who has borne our sins and our punishment, forgiveness, suffering with us and the ultimate revelation of the love of God. Theologies rooted in these multiple images keep reaching for the textured language adequate to describe the mystery and the wonder of it all.[12]

> The mystery and meaning of the cross is like a multi-strand rope: no single description can capture the fullness of what has happened in the crucifixion of Jesus.

Seeing the love of God made visible in the life, ministry, death, and resurrection of Jesus is foundational to such a portrayal of God's love and grace extended to us. Knowing the huge sacrifice this represents to the God who became flesh in Jesus speaks powerfully; knowing that the self-sacrifice is for the world and for each of us; knowing that then the redemption wrought within the body of Christ is to enable us to live holy, righteous and just lives for the sake of the world; and knowing that we live in hope of the final redemption of the world within which we now witness to this coming Kingdom—all of this leads us to sing praises to the God and Father of our Lord Jesus Christ for all that He has done and is doing.[13]

> Knowing the huge sacrifice this represents to the God who became flesh in Jesus speaks powerfully.

Response by Nelson Okanya

I could not argue with the words my dad has just spoken to me in a brief phone call from Nairobi, but I could not accept them either. My sister had died suddenly in childbirth, but her baby boy had survived. Death had come to my family, and its sting had made its way deep inside my whole being. I wrestled with this reality, which was complicated by distance and a lack of details. My consolation came from Scripture as I remembered my crucified Lord and Savior. I was reminded that he too had been stung by death and had wept at a friend's grave.

In that moment of deep grief, I knew that he understood what I was going through. At the cross, Jesus identifies with us in our pain, suffering, and brokenness. By submitting himself to death, he exposed death for what it is and triumphed over it through the cross and resurrection. I knew that death did not speak the last word over my sister, who was a believer in the Lord Jesus—the one who defeated death. I wait in hope, for Jesus our Savior has tasted the sting of death and triumphed over the grave.[14]

> Death had come to my family, and its sting had made its way deep inside my whole being.

Mark has written that the first Christians believed that the crucifixion of Jesus was integral to the Gospel message.[15] They proclaimed Jesus crucified even though their cultural context rejected the notion that a crucified man could be a savior. The cross did not fit their philosophical or religious categories.

The idea of a suffering savior also didn't fit within the world view of the traditional African religions that my forefathers practiced. Neither does the cross fit twenty-first-century North American cultural and philosophical sensibilities. It is therefore not surprising that Paul asserts that the world considers the cross to be foolish. Nevertheless the early church confronted the objections to that message instead of trying to reduce it to suit the culture of the day, as Paul does in 1 Corinthians:

> It is therefore not surprising that Paul asserts that the world considers the cross to be foolish.

> For Jews demand signs and Greeks desire wisdom, but we proclaim Christ crucified, a stumbling block to the Jews and foolishness to Gentiles, but to those who are the called, both Jews and Greeks, Christ the power of God and the wisdom of God. For God's foolishness is wiser than human wisdom, and God's weakness is stronger than human strength.[16]

Paul writes elsewhere, "Before your very eyes Jesus Christ was clearly portrayed as crucified."[17]

The first Christians believed there was no such thing as good news without the cross. In Christ's death, our sins are forgiven; in his life and teachings we are provided guidance for faithful living;[18] and in his resurrection and promised return we are enabled to live in hope of restoration.[19]

The first Christians believed there was no such thing as good news without the cross.

N. T. Wright points out that Jesus viewed his pending crucifixion as redemptive and relevant within his own first century Jewish world. He writes:

> "Jesus . . . believed himself called by God to announce Israel's imminent judgment and to inaugurate in and around himself Israel's reconstitution. He continued to pursue his vocation even when it was more than apparent where it would lead, believing that if Israel's death could be died by her representative she might not need to die it herself. This . . . was in line . . . with the pattern of significant actions which marked his public career as a whole, in which he constantly shared the uncleanness or stigma of the physically or socially handicapped, in order to heal and restore (or, as the evangelists often say, "save") them."[20]

Mark has likewise described the cross as redemptive and transformational in his own experience. I also saw the crucified and risen Jesus redeeming and transforming members of my family. My younger uncle was not a Christian. The way he treated us and his family was completely different from the way my father and my older uncle, who had discovered the power of the cross, treated us. My younger uncle regarded women and children as property and treated us as such. He would not allow us to sit on chairs, for example, because he believed that if we did we would grow up to be arrogant. Even at meals, we had to kneel rather than sit on chairs. He beat his wife and whipped us frequently, even for a small mistake. My dad and my older uncle, on the other hand, repeatedly referenced the cross as the place where they confessed their own brokenness and yet as transparent and repentant men were enabled to live the life exemplified by the crucified One.

I agree with Mark that the New Testament reveals a profound and multifaceted meaning of Jesus' sacrificial death.[21] In his crucifixion and resurrection, Jesus frees us from bondage to powers that control and hold us captive, such as addictions, raging anger, hatred, gluttony, selfishness. In addition to Christ dying for us, we in our sinful nature in turn died with him.[22] Through faith in him, we participate in his death and resurrection. Such participation in his death leaves us no room for abuse or victimization. The cross offers redemption, deliverance and healing for both the abuser and the victim.[23] I witnessed this reality in my own home; testimonies around the world bear witness that this is true wherever people believe in and are committed to Jesus crucified and risen.

> The cross offers redemption, deliverance and healing for both the abuser and the victim. I witnessed this reality in my own home; testimonies around the world bear witness that this is true.

Our alienation from God has a momentum that works itself out; as the Scripture says, "The wages of sin is death."[24] Sin injected poison into the world. Its mechanisms, such as violence, get embedded into social systems that need to be undone. This undoing cannot be dealt with at its roots by anything or anyone or any other power, for that matter, except by God absorbing the consequences of sin through the person of Jesus, the truly superior power. The cross undoes the mechanism; it both judges and heals sin. The condemnation that should have been ours was absorbed by Jesus through the cross.

At the time of Moses, poisonous desert snakes bit and killed Israelites who were traversing the desert. Moses put a copper image of a snake on a pole, and by gazing on the snake, people were healed of the poison snake bites.[25] This was a sign pointing to Jesus who many centuries later was also placed upon a pole (cross). The lifting of Jesus upon a cross heals us.[26] The judgment that was passed on him was not for his sin but for ours:

> There was nothing attractive about him,
>> nothing to cause us to take a second look.
> He was looked down on and passed over,
>> a man who suffered, who knew pain firsthand.
> One look at him and people turned away.
>> We looked down on him, thought he was scum.
> But the fact is, it was our pains he carried—
>> our disfigurements, all the things wrong with us.
> We thought he brought it on himself,
>> that God was punishing him for his own failures.
> But it was our sins that did that to him,
>> that ripped and tore and crushed him—our sins!
> He took the punishment, and that made us whole.
>> Through his bruises we get healed.
> We're all like sheep who've wandered off and gotten lost.
>> We've all done our own thing, gone our own way.
> And God has piled all our sins, everything we've done wrong,
>> on him, on him.[27]

The church is the fellowship of sinners who have been redeemed and forgiven through what Jesus has accomplished on the cross. In word and deed the church embodies the good news of the life, death, and resurrection of Jesus Christ in the power of the Spirit. This worshipping framework defines the church's identity as it understands itself within the entire history of Jesus Christ—his past, present, and future. The church cannot be the church without the entire story of Jesus. Just as the first Christians did not attempt to change the story in light of opposition, the church today ought to proclaim Jesus Christ crucified and risen as good news to all creation.

> The church cannot be the church without the entire story of Jesus.

Questions for Discussion

1. What does Philippians 2:5-11 tell us about God becoming human and a servant in the person of Jesus? And what does it tell us about who we are to be?

2. What does the author of Hebrews mean that Jesus learned obedience through suffering?

3. How do we make the cross central in relation to Jesus and ourselves without "glorifying suffering"? (See, e.g., 1 Corinthians 1:18-31; 2 Corinthians 4:7-12.)

4. How do you experience Jesus crucified to be "the power of God"?

5. Explore the various meanings and images of Jesus crucified that the New Testament presents. How do they deepen our understanding of the multifaceted significance of the cross in our personal lives and the life of the church?

Notes

1. 1 Corinthians 11:23-26.

2. Heidi B. Neumark, *Breathing Space: A Spiritual Journey in the South Bronx* (Boston: Beacon Press, 2003), 257-58.

3. Ibid., 258.

4. Matthew 16:21-28; Mark 8:31-38.

5. For a brief discussion of this see: Nicola Hoggard Creegan and Christine D. Pohl, *Living on the Boundaries: Evangelical Women, Feminism and the Theological Academy* (Downers Grove, IL: InterVarsity Press, 2005), 135-39.

6. Neumark, 258.

7. John 3:16; Romans 5:8.

8. 1 Corinthians 2:2.

9. Romans 5:8; 8:32.

10. Neumark, 258-59.

11. Revelation 13:8.

12. Editors' note: The cross in the mission of Jesus is interwoven within the chapters of this book. We highlight several. In chapter 5, "The Kingdom of God," we meet the ethical implications

of the way of the cross. Then chapter 6, "Jesus Triumphs over the Powers," describes the powers colluding against Jesus. In his crucifixion and resurrection he unmasks and triumphs over the powers. Also pertinent is chapter 9, "The Resurrection of Jesus," and chapter 12, "Jesus our Peace." Jesus enters the realms of death, brokenness and violence, absorbing the bitter fruit of human rebellion and triumphs over it all in his life-giving resurrection. Chapter 12 also develops the themes of forgiveness and reconciliation that are central to the peace of the cross. Then there is a concluding epilogue on meeting Jesus at the communion table wherein the broken bread and cup commemorate that Jesus has borne our sins offering us the grace of forgiveness and new life.

13. John 3:16; Philippians 2:6-11; Revelation 21:1-8.

14. 1 Corinthians 15.

15. Acts 2:22-23; 4:8-10; 5:29-30; 10:39; 13:26-31.

16. 1 Corinthians 1:22-25.

17. Galatians 3:1.

18. Matthew 5:13-20.

19. Revelation 21.

20. Wright, N. T., "Jesus, Israel and the Cross," http://www.ntwrightpage.com/Wright_Jesus_Israel_Cross.pdf, accessed Feb. 24, 2009. (Originally published in *SBL 1985 Seminar Papers*, ed. K. H. Richards. Chico, CA: Scholars Press, 75-95.)

21. Romans 5:6-8; 1 Corinthians 15:3; 2 Corinthians 5:14; Galatians 1:4; 1 Thessalonians 5:10; 1 Peter 2:24; 3:18.

22. Romans 6:3-8.

23. 2 Corinthians 4:7-12.

24. Romans 6:23.

25. Numbers 21:6-9.

26. John 3:14-15.

27. Isaiah 53:3-6, *The Message*. For some very helpful, brief reflections on this passage, see chapter 12 in this book. For more extended reflections, see: Mark Thiessen Nation, "Who Has Believed What We Have Heard?" *Conrad Grebel Review* (Spring 2009).

Chapter 9

The Resurrection of Jesus

Michele Hershberger with Daniel Moya Urueña, along with five students who met occasionally with the writing team: Erica Stoltzfus, Matt Boyts, Grant Sprunger, Zach Hurst, and Hope Weaver

———— Narrative: *The resurrected Jesus appears to his disciples* ————
(John 20:1-18)

Florence looked deathly pale, her breathing erratic. I was relatively new at this, a young pastor sitting next to a dying friend, but I sensed intuitively that the end was near. She and I had talked about this before—what the end would be like. It's not so much a fear of death, she would say, but the transition. What would that be like? I told her that she would not be alone, that we would talk her through it and give her permission to let go—that it would be okay. We talked about her new body, a body free from the cancer that now ravaged her. When we talked about these things, Florence would smile. It was going to be okay.

Florence has not been the only person to face these questions. Her story is different from the stories of Christian martyrs who went bravely and even triumphantly to their deaths, different from countless others who today risk their lives working to build God's kingdom. Yet there is a common thread—the thread of radical hope. Where does this hope come from? Florence would say from the resurrection of Jesus.

Jesus is Risen!

Paul and the gospels give us a resounding anthem of hope that springs from Jesus coming back to life, for as he was raised, so also shall we.[1] The storyline goes like this: Jesus' body was laid in a borrowed tomb, complete with a heavy stone rolled over the opening and guarded by Roman soldiers. Some women came to the tomb very early Sunday morning to put spices on the body, in full expectation of finding a body. But the stone was rolled away and upon inspection, the tomb empty. Then these believers saw Jesus, which terrified them. Gathering their wits, they ran to tell the disciples.

"Christ is risen; he is risen indeed!" This statement is central to the preaching and teaching of the early church. The resurrection is key for several reasons. First, it demonstrates that Jesus did the right thing. God vindicated Jesus, stating clearly through the resurrection that the way Jesus defeated evil—through suffering love—was the right way. Through the resurrection, Jesus, the Suffering Servant, becomes Lord of the entire universe.

> "Christ is risen; he is risen indeed!" This statement is central to the preaching and teaching of the early church.

Revelation 5 shows that the only one worthy to open the scroll, that is, to make history unfold as it should, is precisely the Lamb who is both slain *and* standing. This same resurrected Lamb is the Lion, the conqueror. Jesus conquers evil by obeying God in nonviolent love, even when he is tortured and put to death. So God raised him up and put all things—all powers—under his command. God highly exalted Jesus, giving him the name above every name, because he humbled himself and became obedient, even to the point of death.[2] Resurrection is key to that triumph, that exaltation.

The resurrection of Jesus is also a fulfillment of scripture. On the road to Emmaus, Cleopas and his friend talk with Jesus, although they don't recognize him at first.[3] Jesus opens their minds to see the Old Testament connections that had previously escaped them. Peter has a similar experience. Devastated at the crucifixion, hopeless in the days afterward, Peter sees the risen Lord, and then it all comes together. Jesus is Messiah![4] He then works to make Old Testament connections for Jews who were looking for the Messiah. He refers, for example, to Scriptures like Psalm 16:8-11, in which God promises that he will not abandon his servant to the grave or to decay. Likewise Paul, after seeing the resurrected Jesus in a vision, changes dramatically from persecuting Christians to becoming one of them. From this point on he too makes the connection and fills his letters with Old Testament echoes of the resurrection.

> Through the resurrection, Jesus, the Suffering Servant, becomes Lord of the entire universe.

So What Exactly *Did* Happen?

In interactions with several young adults, Daniel Moya Urueña and I encountered a variety of opinions about exactly what *did* happen. Some believed Jesus' spirit or ghost came back to life, and if the right tomb were found, we would see Jesus' bones today. Others believed that Jesus came back to life, body and all. Still others had never really thought about the issue and wondered out loud if it really mattered.

The writers of the New Testament did not embrace this diversity. They confidently bore witness that Jesus was raised again as a whole person. Paul's letter to the Romans states this central belief clearly, "If the Spirit of him who raised Jesus from the dead dwells in you, he who raised Christ from the dead will *give life to your mortal bodies* also."[5] New Testament writers believed the resurrection, though they certainly hadn't expected it!

Differing Responses to the Resurrection

The resurrection was indeed an astounding surprise. Some Jewish parties like the Sadducees didn't believe in resurrection at all, and while the Pharisees did believe in a bodily rising from the dead, they understood that it would happen corporately at the end of the ages.[6] No one expected a single person to come back to life in "regular time" like Jesus did. There was little motive to *lie* about the resurrection, since no one anticipated it to begin with.

Just as in our world today, not every Christian in the early church was convinced. Paul tackled the issue in his letter to the Corinthian church. In Corinth, two worldviews apparently competed for dominance. The Greek worldview, albeit with some variation, saw the world as Plato did—in a dichotomy of physical and spiritual. The physical was bad and unredeemable and the spiritual was good and the only part of creation that the gods—or God—cared about. For the Christians who grew up in this worldview, the resurrection of the dead—literally the rising of corpses—was repugnant. Salvation meant escaping from the physical world, not reanimating it.[7]

> The resurrection was indeed an astounding surprise. There was little motive to *lie* about the resurrection, since no one anticipated it to begin with.

The Jewish worldview, on the other hand, had no such dichotomy. God created the world, including human flesh, as good. There was no sharp division between the physical and the spiritual. People were whole beings, as the Hebrew word *nefesh* implies. In this worldview, the bodily resurrection made sense. God was in the business of doing to all creation what God did for Jesus. But in Corinth, and elsewhere, these two worldviews clashed.

Debate about the Resurrection

In our day too the resurrection of Jesus remains hotly debated. There is first of all the issue of the empty tomb. While the Gospels are clear that it was empty, many today still wonder what exactly that means. Perhaps the body was stolen, but why would anyone do that? The disciples weren't expecting the resurrection. The Jewish officials and Romans alike only stood to lose in the face of a risen Messiah. Death was their best weapon. And if the women accidentally went to the wrong tomb, as some have argued, then wasn't that fairly easy to check?

It is interesting that the four Gospel accounts reveal some diversity in regard to the details. Some observers use this as evidence that the story was made up.[8] Others argue that this proves there was no collusion between writers and thus the story is true. If the story is a fabrication, it's strange that in each gospel, women were the first ones at the tomb. In first-century Jewish culture, women were not considered reliable witnesses and their testimony didn't stand up in a court of law.[9] If the writers of the Gospel accounts were inventing the story, they would not have chosen women as the first witnesses!

In our day too the resurrection of Jesus remains hotly debated.

The Gospels and Paul do record many appearances of Jesus between the resurrection and his ascension. Jesus appeared to Cephas (Peter), then to the other disciples, then to more than five hundred other believers, James, and finally Paul.[10] Jesus walked on the road to Emmaus with Cleopas and his friend. He invited Thomas to put his hand into the pierced hole in his side. And of course Jesus appeared to Mary Magdalene and the other women at the tomb itself. There are at least a dozen appearances recorded between Jesus' resurrection and ascension.[11]

Second, the Gospels and Paul allude to a physicality that is unique to the resurrected body. Luke and John seem intentional in their efforts to show both continuity and discontinuity between Jesus' body before and after resurrection.[12] Jesus eats fish and can be touched, and then a few verses later, he walks through walls! Are Luke and John bad writers, or are they trying to describe a complex truth? Likewise, Paul compares the differences between our present bodies and our resurrected bodies to a seed and a plant.[13] They

If the writers of the Gospel accounts were inventing the story, they would not have chosen women as the first witnesses!

are both physical, but at the same time radically different from each other. Our resurrected bodies are "imperishable" as Paul writes,[14] not so much in that they aren't physical, but that they are free from decay and disease, free to be more strong and healthy than we can even imagine.[15]

A third consideration is the continuation and growth of the early church. The Jesus movement didn't die. In Jesus' day, there were many others who claimed to be Messiah, and after they met the similar fate of execution, their followers dispersed or found another Messiah to follow. Not so with the followers of Jesus. The believers did not disperse, nor did they proclaim some likely candidate like Jesus' brother James as the new Messiah. Instead, the movement only grew, with the consistent proclamation that Jesus had indeed been raised back from the dead.[16]

Finally, we must consider how the resurrection conquers death. Does resurrection have to mean a bodily resurrection in order for death to truly be conquered? Physical death is a part of all of our lives. No one escapes.

And while we can speak of spiritual death, we also know that in the garden of Eden when our first parents, Adam and Eve, turned away from God they experienced the curse of both spiritual and physical death.[17] Paul compares Adam and Christ: through Adam we all die, and then through Christ we all find life. Since Adam's death was both a spiritual and a physical death, does the resurrection life need to be new spiritual *and* physical life as well? Indeed, yes! That is Paul's exuberant claim in his letter to the Corinthians who were finding it hard to imagine a bodily resurrection of the dead.[18]

From Debate to Belief

In my discussions with young adults about the resurrection, the historical evidence didn't seem that important. They were intrigued with the movement from disbelief to belief. The disciples weren't expecting Jesus to rise again, and so they were devastated by the crucifixion. Did they forget what he had said earlier?[19] My young adult friends could especially relate to Thomas, who struggled to believe even after three years of being with Jesus. They were impressed with the "Doubter" for his courage to ask, for his honesty about his own confusion. Perhaps, even with historical evidence, it is not until we personally meet Jesus ourselves that we can know he is risen indeed. Like Mary who did not recognize Jesus in the garden until he said her name, we too must experience the risen Christ; we too must hear Jesus call our names to really believe.

> Perhaps, even with historical evidence, it is not until we personally meet Jesus ourselves that we can know he is risen indeed.

The Awesome Significance of the Resurrection

The Christian faith is grounded in the most unexpected surprise of the bodily resurrection of Jesus. None of us can scientifically prove the exact nature of the resurrection of Christ. But when the early Christians claimed a bodily resurrection, they claimed a truth that was opposite from all expectations. They had to change their worldview. If there was any expectation of resurrection at all, they would have anticipated Jesus to "shine like the brightness of the heavens," as described by the prophet Daniel.[20] But he didn't. Or they would have expected a corporate resurrection of all humanity, but never a single person rising from the dead. And no one dreamed of a Messiah who would be killed, only to rise again. They looked for a strong Messiah who would fight God's victorious battle for them.[21] Jesus did everything wrong "Messiah-wise." Yet, in an overwhelming chorus of agreement, the early church said, "Jesus rose from the dead—in bodily form. He is the Messiah."

While the proclamation, "Christ is risen; he is risen indeed," was a key doctrine in the early church, some wonder how essential the proclamation is today. "Why does it matter what we believe about the resurrection?" Florence's story helps us remember the first reason—our resurrection will mirror the resurrection of Jesus. But there are even more compelling reasons for wrangling with this difficult issue. Our beliefs affect our ethics, and this issue is no exception. What we believe about the resurrection directly impacts how we live our lives as followers of Jesus.[22]

> Our beliefs affect our ethics. What we believe about the resurrection directly impacts how we live our lives as followers of Jesus.

The Resurrection and Creation Ethics

The bodily resurrection of Jesus is a truth that says no to the Greek dualism of physical and spiritual, and it says yes to the Jewish affirmation of a beloved creation. Growing up in the western world so heavily influenced by the Greek view, we dichotomize the world not only in our minds but in our actions as well. The Greek worldview believed that the spiritual was good and the physical world was inferior. Therefore, if God doesn't care about the physical world, then neither should we. Why not trash the earth, because God will destroy it in the end anyway? Why not overeat or overwork, since only our souls will ascend to the heavenly realms? But if we believe God affirms our bodies and creation in general, then we are more likely to take care of our bodies and be good stewards of the earth.

Paul was adamant about this point in 1 Corinthians. The Corinthian church, a congregation divided on the resurrection issue, was also a church where some struggled with "body" ethics. Some committed sexual sins—incest and using prostitutes—while others were denying sex to their spouses.[23] In the middle of the discussion, Paul writes this as the theological center of his argument: "By his power God raised the Lord from the dead, and he will raise us also."[24] Paul makes a case against these practices and all sins against one's body, based on the belief in the bodily resurrection of Jesus.

A healthy relationship with the physical world is part of salvation. Three of the four fall stories of Genesis 3–11—Adam and Eve, Cain and Abel and Noah and the ark—each demonstrate how sin breaks not only our relationship with God, each other, and our inner selves, but also with all of creation. In the garden story, the ground is cursed because of sin.[25] It is cursed again after Cain kills his brother.[26] Finally the sin of humankind is so great that the entire world is flooded.[27] The pattern is clear. Sin affects creation.

Sin brings physical decay and death. And if that is true, then salvation, the healing of these relationships, must include the created world. Likewise, our faithfulness to Jesus must include a "body" ethic, a creation ethic. Salvation is more than getting a ticket to heaven or even restoring our relationship with God. All the relationships must be healed and every evil power, including death, be destroyed. We must work for justice for all. Salvation starts now, and it includes God's beautiful creation.

This point was crucial for Daniel and other young adults who were part of our conversation. As Daniel wrote, "The resurrection is necessary to explain that the project of life defeats the project of death. Death doesn't have the last word when it comes to bringing God's kingdom, which means bringing justice and reconciliation to a world where the voice of the marginalized and oppressed is easily shot by threats of death and hunger."

> Salvation is more than getting a ticket to heaven or even restoring our relationship with God. All the relationships must be healed and every evil power, including death, be destroyed.

The Resurrection and Our Future Destiny

And what began in Genesis, at the beginning of time, finds its culmination at the end. Fuzzy beliefs about the resurrection go hand in hand with the misguided belief that heaven in a far away beyond is the end point of our existence. The book of Revelation says otherwise. The New Jerusalem comes down to earth. The earth is restored. God doesn't scrap the physical world for the better deal called heaven. No, the wonderful presence of God and the active reign of Jesus are happening right now.[28] That's what we call for every time we pray the Lord's Prayer. "Your kingdom come *on earth* as it is in heaven" (italics added). The day will come when that world—which some would call heaven—and earth will be fully joined together. The bodily resurrection of Jesus is the guarantee from God that we will likewise rise from death and that all creation will be redeemed and restored!

> Our bodies are redeemable, so we had better take care of them. God has promised to redeem and renew all creation, so we need to do our part to care for it too.

Our bodies are redeemable, so we had better take care of them. God has promised to redeem and renew all creation, so we need to do our part to care for it too. We need to live in relation to our bodies and the physical world in ways that are consistent with God's grand plan for their redemption.

Empowerment for Abundant Living

Belief in the resurrection not only impacts our ethics; it also promises the power to live those ethics out. Paul prays that we will know God's "incomparably great power for us who believe. That power is like the working of his mighty strength, which he exerted in Christ when he raised him from the dead and seated him at his right hand in the heavenly realms."[29] The same power that brought physical life back to Jesus is the power available to us to use in the challenges of day-by-day living as we seek to live as faithful disciples of Jesus.

> The same power that brought physical life back to Jesus is the power available to us to use in the challenges of day-by-day living as we seek to live as faithful disciples of Jesus.

In conversations with Daniel and others, this power was important. We all expressed a desire to make the world a better place, to bring justice and reconciliation—this is what energized our discussions about resurrection. And we all sensed the impossibility of such a task. We longed for a miracle. Could that miracle, that power, be connected to the same power of the resurrection? There was concern that focusing on the bodily resurrection of Jesus would lead us to also focus on "just spiritual things." Nobody wanted to be "so heavenly minded they're no earthly good." But the other ditch was equally troubling—trying to bring God's shalom by our own power. Because the bodily resurrection is both miraculous transformation and a transformation that is itself something physical, both concerns are resolved. We use God's resurrection power as partners with God in caring for and healing the physical world and human society.

A true understanding of resurrection and an embrace of the power it assures lead us toward mission and work in God's kingdom. And we know our work is not in vain.[30] We know that our efforts here to bring justice, protect the earth, and foster reconciliation between people groups—all of this and more won't simply be tossed one day in some cosmic garbage dump. Our work here matters; God will redeem it.

A true understanding of resurrection and an embrace of the power it assures lead us toward mission and work in God's kingdom.

Jesus is Lord of All

And, finally, there is one more point to make about the resurrection. Namely, that God has given Jesus, crucified and risen, all authority in heaven and on earth. In his ascension Jesus promised to come back again in power and judgment to fulfill his kingdom. There will be a general resurrection of the dead. And on that day every knee will bow and every tongue will confess that Jesus is Lord.[31]

Life after Death?

But what does all of this really have to do with each of us when we actually die? What happens between our death and the general resurrection when Jesus returns? Jesus rose from the dead within three days. But, as some of my young adult friends would argue, for all the talk of a resurrection of Jesus after three days, it isn't true for us. If we would dig up the grave of a person we knew to be a committed Christian, we would find her bones. Where's the bodily resurrection in that?

Resurrection is, as N. T. Wright puts it, "life after life after death."[32] The worldview of the Pharisees—that there would be a corporate resurrection of the righteous at the end of the ages—holds true. So say the souls who wait under the altar in the book of Revelation,[33] crying for Jesus to finish the fight and bring final justice to the world. And that's what Paul means when he says that Jesus is the first fruits of the resurrection.[34] Jesus went first—before the expected time—and when the time comes for heaven and earth to join together, then full salvation will come to everything, the physical world and our mortal bodies included.

When death drew near, Florence lost her ability to speak or move. Her hand reached up to grasp an unseen hand. And then she died—at peace and with hope.

So where do we go after we die? Toward the end of her life, Florence and I talked about this. We looked at each other in the eyes and said, "Wow, it's a mystery." But we do know this—all is well for those who believe in the One who is the Resurrection. And that made us smile. We both knew that we would meet again!

When death drew near, Florence lost her ability to speak or move. But at the very end, as we gently gave her permission to let go, her eyes opened and she gave a wide smile. Her hand reached up to grasp an unseen hand. And then she died—at peace and with hope.

Questions for Discussion

1. What do you think happens to you after you die? What kind of a body, if any, do you believe you'll have?

2. Do you think your beliefs regarding Jesus' resurrection affect your ethics? How might those beliefs impact you personally and our society in general?

3. Daniel Moya wrote, "The resurrection is necessary to explain that the project of life defeats the project of death. Death doesn't have the last word when it comes to bringing God's kingdom, which means bringing justice and reconciliation to a world where the voice of the marginalized and oppressed are easily shot by threats of death and hunger." Do you think your beliefs regarding Jesus' resurrection affect how you face injustice? How so?

4. Have you seen "resurrection power" at work? How difficult is it for you to believe that you have the same power to help build the kingdom that God used to raise Christ from the dead? What needs to happen for you to utilize this power more?

Notes

1. 1 Corinthians 6:14.

2. Revelation 5; Colossians 1:15-20; Philippians 2:6-11.

3. Luke 24:13-35.

4. Acts 2:24-36.

5. Romans 8:11 NRSV (italics added).

6. John 11:24. See also Marcus Borg and N. T. Wright, *The Meaning of Jesus: Two Visions* (San Francisco: HarperSanFrancisco, 1999), 112.

7. Richard Hays, *I Corinthians, Interpretation: A Bible Commentary for Teaching and Preaching* (Louisville, KY: John Knox Press, 1997), 259-60.

8. Borg and Wright, 122-23.

9. N. T. Wright, *Surprised by Hope: Rethinking Heaven, the Resurrection, and the Mission of the Church* (New York: HarperOne, 2008), 55.

10. 1 Corinthians 15:3-7.

11. The Gospel of Mark, in its earliest form, doesn't specifically mention actual appearances. However, Mark speaks of the resurrection (8:31, 9:31, and 10:34) and some scholars think that Mark didn't include appearances because the resurrection was so well known. See Luke Timothy Johnson, *Living Jesus: Learning the Heart of the Gospel* (San Francisco: HarperSanFrancisco, 1999), 135.

12. See Luke 24:36-42 and John 20:26-29.

13. 1 Corinthians 15:35-38.

14. 1 Corinthians 15:42.

15. Johnson, 18-20.

16. Borg and Wright, 111.

17. Genesis 3:16-19.

18. 1 Corinthians 15:20-28.

19. Mark 8:31; 9:31; 10:34.

20. See Daniel 12:3.

21. Wright, 47.

22. 1 Corinthians 15:32.

23. 1 Corinthians 5:1; 6:15; 7.

24. 1 Corinthians 6:14.

25. Genesis 3:17.

26. Genesis 4:12.

27. Genesis 6.

28. Revelation 5.

29. Ephesians 1:19-20.

30. 1 Corinthians 15:58.

31. Philippians 2:11.

32. Wright, 169. See also Hays, 259-60.

33. Revelation 6:9-11.

34. 1 Corinthians 15:20.

Chapter 10

Jesus and the Sending of the Spirit

Steve Dintaman
with Gintare Giraityte and Daumantas Ivanauskas

Narrative: *The coming of the Holy Spirit at Pentecost*
(Luke 3:15-18; Acts 2:1-41)

Spirituality has made a huge comeback in contemporary culture. Many people who were supposedly on their way to becoming totally secular have discovered the importance of finding a vital connection to a spiritual power beyond themselves. This spiritual power is experienced and named in a wide variety of ways. Some refer to it as "the life force," others call it "creative energy." In popular spirituality this reality is encountered in many ways—in nature, in holy objects, or through meditation. Contemporary spirituality tends to be vague, diffuse, and tailored to the needs and tastes of the individual.

The Bible also speaks of a powerful creative spiritual energy. It is there in the very beginning. Genesis 1:1 says the world was "a formless void and darkness covered the face of the deep, while the wind of God swept over the face of the waters." In the New Testament, this mysterious wind blowing over our world is called the Holy Spirit. In fact, the biblical word for the Spirit of God is not a religious term; it is simply the common word for wind in both Hebrew (*ruach*) and Greek (*pneuma*).

> The biblical word for the Spirit of God is not a religious term; it is simply the common word for wind in both Hebrew and Greek.

143

Jesus' life and work was intimately tied up with this creative wind of God. When John the Baptist introduces Jesus at the beginning of his ministry, John proclaims, "I baptize you with water. But one more powerful than I will come, the thongs of whose sandals I am not worthy to untie. He will baptize you with the Holy Spirit and with fire."[1]

What if we were to take this statement seriously? What if, instead of quickly passing over what John says, we read it as a real clue to what Jesus' ministry is all about? There are many ways to describe Jesus' mission and purpose. Certainly Christians have always said that he came to die on the cross to save us from our sins. Or we say he came to bring us the kingdom of God and introduce us to a new way of living. These are both true, but it is also important to recognize that he came to live and die among us so that we could be baptized with God's Spirit! I want to try to read the story of Jesus in a way that highlights Jesus as the giver of the Holy Spirit.

> The story of Jesus' birth in the Gospel of Luke is saturated with references to the Holy Spirit.

Jesus and the Sending of the Spirit—In Luke-Acts

The story of Jesus' birth in the Gospel of Luke is saturated with references to the Holy Spirit. The Spirit opens the mouth of the dumb, inspires songs of praise[2] and creates new life.[3] The same divine Spirit that was active in the *creation* of the world is the ultimate source of this new life that is coming to *recreate* the world.

The beginning of Jesus' ministry is also filled with references to the Spirit. At his baptism, "heaven was opened and the Holy Spirit descended on him in bodily form like a dove."[4] At his baptism, Jesus receives a divine blessing and public endorsement, empowering him for his work. Next Luke relates that, "Jesus, full of the Holy Spirit, returned from the Jordan and was led by the Spirit in the desert."[5] And then, "Jesus returned to Galilee in the power of the Spirit."[6] From there he goes to the synagogue in Nazareth where he inaugurates his public ministry by taking the scroll of Isaiah and reading, "The Spirit of the Lord is on me."[7]

Jesus Promises the Coming of the Spirit

But Luke also makes it abundantly clear that Jesus is not only filled with the Spirit, his purpose in life was to give this same power and presence of God to us. Luke has a twist on a key saying of Jesus: "If you, then, though you are evil, know how to give good gifts to your children,

> Jesus is not only filled with the Spirit, his purpose in life was to give this same power and presence of God to us.

how much more will your Father in heaven give good gifts to those who ask him!" (Matthew 7:11). But in Luke 11:13, the text reads, "If you then, though you are evil, know how to give good gifts to your children, how much more will your Father in heaven *give the Holy Spirit* to those who ask him" (italics added). Luke makes it clear that the good gift we are to seek and expect from our gracious heavenly Father is the Holy Spirit!

Luke's emphasis on Jesus as the giver of the Holy Spirit comes to its fullest expression in the opening chapters of Acts. After his resurrection, Jesus instructs his disciples to stay in Jerusalem and "wait there for the promise of the Father."[8]

At this point it seems the disciples are confused about what to expect next. They ask Jesus, "Lord, are you at this time going to restore the kingdom to Israel?"[9] They are still expecting from Jesus what they always had expected, the restoration of the Davidic kingdom to Israel through political power. But Jesus gives them a whole new agenda and purpose—"It is not for you to know the times or dates that the Father has set by his own authority. But you will receive power when the Holy Spirit has come upon you; and you will be my witnesses in Jerusalem, and in all Judea and Samaria, and to the ends of the earth."[10] What Jesus gives his disciples is not a program of action to be carried out by their own will and power, but the gift of his own power and presence.

Pentecost and the Coming of the Spirit

In Acts 2, we have the story of the amazing events of the day of Pentecost. As the new believers in the Messiah are together they experience "a sound like the blowing of a violent wind," which fills the house. They see "what seemed to be tongues of fire" that dance above each of them. And finally, "all of them were filled with the Holy Spirit and began to speak in other tongues as the Spirit enabled them."[11] Wind and fire are symbols of the mysterious power of God entering the world, and at Pentecost this mysterious power that comes upon them enables them to speak in other languages.

> What Jesus gives his disciples is not a program of action to be carried out by their own will and power, but the gift of his own power and presence.

Other Jews who had traveled to Jerusalem for the observation of Pentecost heard this commotion and are amazed to hear the mighty acts of God declared in their own languages. As with any crowd that witnesses an unusual event, people search for an explanation of what they are seeing and hearing. At least some in the crowd came up with what seemed like a good explanation—they are drunk![12]

The Holy Spirit and the First Christian Sermon

But then Peter stands up to give a counter-explanation of these events. This is the first published sermon of a believer in Jesus Christ in the New Testament, and quite remarkably it begins, "These men are not drunk!" Peter's explanation of these events names them as the fulfillment of a prophecy from Joel, "In the last days, God says, I will pour out my Spirit on all people."[13]

Whenever you see "the last days" in the Bible, you know you are dealing with something monumentally important. The term points to the fulfillment of God's work and a time that will be a dramatic turning-point in salvation history. You could paraphrase Peter by saying, "What you have just seen is the turning point, the beginning of a whole new era in God's dealing with people."

Having explained the world-changing significance of

Pentecost, Peter goes on to tell the story of Jesus in a special way. He describes Jesus' life, how he was put to death on the cross, and that God raised him from the dead. Then in a key text, verses 32-33, he declares, "God has raised this Jesus to life, and we are all witnesses of the fact. Exalted to the right hand of God, *he has received from the Father the promised Holy Spirit and has poured out what you now see and hear*" (italics added). Peter makes it clear that the outpouring of the Spirit is the fulfillment and the purpose of Jesus' life mission.

Upon hearing this message the people "are cut to the heart." If Peter's words are true, then they have rejected and killed the Messiah! They ask, "Brothers, what shall we do?" Peter says to them, "Repent, and be baptized, every one of you, in the name of Jesus Christ for the forgiveness of your sins. And you will receive the gift of the Holy Spirit."[14] They obviously feared a terrible judgment, but Peter proclaims the graciousness of God. All they need do is repent, be baptized in Jesus' name for the forgiveness of sins, and they too would receive this same Holy Spirit.

Let's look at this simple declaration more closely. What is it that Peter is offering the people? What is the gift and promise of God that we are offered through repentance, baptism, and faith in Jesus? Most believers would say the forgiveness of sins. But that is really an incomplete answer. There is no period in the sentence after the forgiveness of sins. Neither the sentence nor the thought is complete until you add, "and you will receive the gift of the Holy Spirit." Just as we are taught to say Jesus died and was raised so our sins could be forgiven, we must also say he died and was raised so that we could receive the gift of the Holy Spirit.

> God's forgiveness is not in and of itself a complete thought or action; it is simply a step on the way to the main point—life in the Spirit.

The image I like to use is that the forgiveness of sins is the door that opens so that you can go into the banquet of life that is the Holy Spirit. But wouldn't it be strange to stop at this open door and spend the rest of our lives saying, "Hallelujah, the door is open!"? At some point we would want to pass through the door and enjoy the feast! God's forgiveness is not in and of itself a complete thought or action; it is simply a step (a hugely important one!) on the way to the main point—life in the Spirit.

Jesus and the Sending of the Spirit—In John's Gospel

The Gospel of John also makes it clear that the imparting of the Spirit is basic to Jesus' redemptive work. In answer to Nicodemus' famous question, "Can one enter a second time into the mother's womb and be born?" Jesus replies, "No one can enter the kingdom of God without being born of water and the Spirit."[15] The kingdom is not simply a new set of ideals and moral principles; it requires a new birth through the creative Spirit of God.

John seems to suggest that the most immediate, direct outcome of Jesus' life, death, and resurrection is the sending of the Spirit. When the risen Jesus appears to the disciples who are cowering behind a locked door, "He breathed on them and said to them, 'Receive the Holy Spirit. If you forgive the sins of any, they have been forgiven them.'"[16] The payoff of Jesus' death and resurrection is that he imparts to his disciples the same Spirit of new life that had empowered *him*. The Spirit, in turn, empowers the disciples to continue the work of forgiveness.

> The payoff of Jesus' death and resurrection is that he imparts to his disciples the same Spirit of new life that had empowered *him*.

What, then, does the risen Christ do? It is clear in John's Gospel that he imparts the Holy Spirit!

The Work of the Spirit

When my adult son was little, he mentioned on the way home from church one day he had learned that "Jesus lives in your heart." So I asked him, "And what does Jesus do there?" My son answered, "I'm not sure. Maybe watches what you eat." So if it is true that the sending of the Spirit is a vital dimension of what Jesus came to do, then we also need to ask: What does the Spirit do? What is the "work" of the Spirit?

Empowers for Mission

In Acts, the work of the Spirit is focused on empowerment for mission. "You will receive power," Jesus told his disciples, "when the Holy Spirit comes on you; and you will be my witnesses."[17] In the original Pentecostal event the Spirit empowered the disciples to proclaim the good news in many languages. The gospel is meant to be translated and take root in all languages and cultures. A vital role of the Spirit is to enable culture-bound people to transcend cultural divides and build cross-cultural fellowship.

> A vital role of the Spirit is to enable culture-bound people to transcend cultural divides and build cross-cultural fellowship.

Provides Living Link to the Risen Christ

In John 14–17, Jesus prepares his disciples for his leaving them. He assures them that he will not leave them orphaned. He is going to the Father, and when he does he will send the Comforter to be with them. The Spirit, thus, is the living link that unites believers with the risen Christ and makes him present with them.

Enables Us to Continue the Work of Christ

In fact, Jesus even said that it was a good thing that he should go away, because if he didn't, he could not send the Spirit.[18] The Spirit is not only our living link to the risen Jesus, the Spirit also enables us to continue the work of Christ on earth. In fact, we will be able to do even greater things than Jesus himself did![19] Through the Spirit we are empowered to continue and extend Jesus' own work of healing and setting people free from the powers of darkness.

> The Spirit is not only our living link to the risen Jesus, the Spirit also enables us to continue the work of Christ on earth.

Reminds Believers of What Jesus Said and Teaches New Truths

The Spirit is also our teacher. He reminds of everything that Jesus said,[20] but even more than that, he teaches us new truth. Jesus said, "I still have much more to say to you, more than you can now bear. But when he, the Spirit of truth, comes, he will guide you into all truth. He will not speak on his own. . . . He will bring glory to me by taking from what is mine and making it known to you."[21]

The disciples, says Jesus, are not yet ready for all that he has to say. The full implications of his teachings and saving work cannot be immediately comprehended. So the Spirit will lead them into new truth.

But note, the Spirit is not a freelance teacher making up new truths at will. Jesus says, "[The Spirit] will take what is mine and make it known to you." New truth needs to be tested. Is it in continuity with the teachings and spirit of Jesus? Does it take the truth of the gospel and extend it, or is it somehow at odds with who Jesus is? Any spirit at odds with Jesus is not the Holy Spirit and should be rejected.[22]

> The Spirit is not a freelance teacher making up new truths at will. New truth needs to be tested. Is it in continuity with the teachings and spirit of Jesus?

Reveals Jesus, Convicts of Guilt, and Leads to Repentance

The Holy Spirit reveals Jesus and convicts of guilt, which leads to repentance. Without the Holy Spirit we are inclined to feel that we are basically good and have no guilt. But in the light of Jesus, the Holy Spirit enables us to understand that we have fallen short of God's righteous intentions. Recall that when Peter preached his sermon at Pentecost, the Holy Spirit convicted people. They were "cut to the heart,"[23] and three thousand people repented. Jesus promised that the Holy Spirit would convict the world of guilt in regard to sin, righteousness, and judgment.[24]

Assures Us We Are God's Children

The work of the Spirit is both profoundly personal and deeply corporate. The personal character of the work of the Spirit is evident in Romans 8, in which Paul writes, "When we cry 'Abba! Father!' it is that very Spirit bearing witness with our spirit that we are children of God."[25] It is the experience of the Spirit that empowers us to cry out to God with the same boldness and intimacy as Jesus did. The Spirit gives us a deep assurance that we are children of God.

Fills Believers with Power to Lead New Lives

But Paul's experience of the Spirit also has a deep moral transformational aspect. Throughout Romans 8, Paul affirms that the believer has been set free from the law of sin and death and is now empowered to new life through the Spirit. He states very bluntly that, "Anyone who does not have the Spirit of Christ does not belong to him."[26] Paul knows nothing of a Christian life that is not a Spirit-filled life, and this Spirit of God that raised Jesus from the dead will impart new life.

Builds up the Body of Christ

The experience of the Spirit is also corporate. Partly in response to the divisive, competitive spirituality of the Corinthian community, Paul develops in 1 Corinthians 12 and 14 the beautiful image of the church as the body of Christ. This body consists of many members, each of which has received from the Spirit a gift of grace that enables them to contribute to the building up of the whole body. Each member has a gift of the Spirit, and those gifts are not primarily for personal enjoyment but for giving something of value to others. No member has all of the gifts of the Spirit, so we can only experience the fullness of God's Spirit as we open ourselves to receive the gifts God has given others.

> No member has all of the gifts of the Spirit, so we can only experience the fullness of God's Spirit as we open ourselves to receive the gifts God has given others.

Key Theological Conclusions

1. Pentecost is a part of the gospel. One vital dimension of the saving work of Christ is that his death and resurrection open up a new era in the God-human relationship. The Holy Spirit is sent from God the Father and from the crucified and risen Jesus to dwell in and work through us. A gospel that is only about the forgiveness of sins is incomplete and lifeless. Likewise, any discussion of discipleship that is only about Jesus' teachings and our efforts to follow his way is incomplete and deeply flawed. Remember that Jesus' disciples never quite grasped what he was all about. They eventually failed the test, abandoning or even denying Jesus when he went to the cross. Only after the Spirit has been poured out do we see truly transformed, energized disciples engaged in fruitful mission and discipleship. The Spirit has been present and active in the world since the very beginning, but in a unique and special way God's Holy Spirit is poured into our lives because of the transforming event of the crucified and risen Jesus. It is at this key point that the creative power of God comes pouring into our lives, filling our sails and sending us in a new direction.

2. **The Holy Spirit has an identity that is directly derived from Jesus and the cross.** The problem with talking about the Spirit of God is that *Spirit* is so vague. What is the Spirit of God like? What does the Spirit do? How do you recognize the Spirit? The Holy Spirit as presented to us in the Bible is not a vague "something or other." The Spirit has a form and identity, most clearly reflected in the life and ministry of Jesus. Interestingly, this Spirit is given to believers only after Jesus has completed his life and the work of salvation on the cross. There are two reasons for this: First, the Spirit cannot be poured into a broken relationship. Only after Jesus has healed the God-human relationship on the cross, can the vital life-giving link between God and humans be established.

Second, it is through the cross that we see the true form and identity of the life-giving Spirit. Where this linkage to the cross is lost, the Spirit loses any moral identity and simply becomes a source of personal power or self-fulfillment that can be distorted in self-serving ways.

The Holy Spirit as presented to us in the Bible is not a vague "something or other." The Spirit has a form and identity, most clearly reflected in the life and ministry of Jesus.

3. **The Holy Spirit is the living personal God present and active in our world and in our lives.** The Spirit is the person of God, not simply an impersonal spiritual force. The Spirit penetrates the depths of our spirit. The Holy Spirit touches our inner being and non-coercively convicts, persuades, empowers, and guides us. The Spirit is powerful but also very gentle. The Spirit can be resisted and ignored. By our attitudes and actions we can "grieve the Holy Spirit," the Scriptures say. The Spirit knocks on the door of our lives, as it were, but never breaks the door down. He honors and works in and through our freedom. But when we welcome the Spirit we find ourselves renewed and transformed. The Spirit is God present and active in our lives, but it is also important to say that God is more than this. God is also the transcendent creator who exists prior to and beyond us. God is also the communicating God who has spoken and revealed himself through the Word that was incarnate in Jesus Christ.

The Spirit knocks on the door of our lives, as it were, but never breaks the door down. He honors and works in and through our freedom.

Christians around the world refer to the three-fold oneness of God as Trinity—Father, Son, and Holy Spirit. Chapter 7 on "Jesus and God" explores this mystery more thoroughly.

Receive the Holy Spirit

Today it is very popular to practice various forms of "spirituality" that have no clear form or identity. The individual simply declares anything that fulfills and satisfies them to be "spiritual." But followers of Jesus can discern the spirits. Not everything that is powerful or feels good is of God. The New Testament affirms that the Spirit always speaks, moves, and looks like Jesus. He calls people to repentance and commitment to Christ.

The New Testament affirms that the Spirit always speaks, moves, and looks like Jesus. He calls people to repentance and commitment to Christ.

From Jesus' life, death, and resurrection, the Scriptures proclaim that a new and transformational life force has entered into our world and into our lives. This wind of God empowers and fills us full of the same kind of life energy we see in Jesus, enabling us to share in the mission of God in the world. The gospel is an invitation to receive this wind of God into our lives.

Questions for Discussion

1. Is it true that we sometimes read the story of Jesus as though the sending of the Holy Spirit is not a part of the gospel? If so, how does that affect our Christian life and faith?

2. What do you think are the signs that someone has received the Spirit? How do you know today that someone has received the Spirit of God?

3. Why is it important to maintain a clear link between the crucified and risen Jesus and the work of the Holy Spirit? What happens when that identifying link is broken?

4. What are some of the truths that the Holy Spirit has led us into in the past? What are some that the Spirit might be leading us into today? How do you know if new ideas or movements are of the Spirit?

5. Do we stress both the deeply personal dimensions of the Holy Spirit's work and the corporate nature of our experience of the Spirit, or do we tend to stress one at the expense of the other?

Notes

1. Luke 3:16.
2. Luke 1:67.
3. Luke 1:35.
4. Luke 3:21-22.
5. Luke 4:1.
6. Luke 4:14.
7. Luke 4:18.
8. Acts 1:4 NRSV.
9. Acts 1:6.
10. Acts 1:7-8.
11. Acts 2:1-4.
12. Acts 2:13.
13. Acts 2:15-17.
14. Acts 2:38.
15. John 3:4-5 NRSV.
16. John 20:22-23 NASB.
17. Acts 1:8.
18. John 16:7.
19. John 14:12.
20. John 14:26.
21. John 16:12-14.
22. 1 John 4:1-6.
23. Acts 2:37.
24. John 16:8.
25. Romans 8 NRSV.
26. Romans 8:9 NRSV.

Chapter 11

Jesus Our Salvation

Mary H. Schertz with Luke, Sam, and Ben Jacobs

Narrative: *Jesus' encounter with Zacchaeus* (Luke 19:1-10) *and six other "quest stories" from Luke*

The whole Bible is about salvation, not just the part about Jesus. From the beginning to the end, from the garden of Eden in Genesis to the new heaven and earth in Revelation, the story of faith is a story of God on a quest, God seeking relationship with these odd, wayward creatures molded from the dust of the earth. The logic of salvation is in many ways absurd. God creates creatures with minds and wills of their own and then spends eons loving them, courting them, wooing them, wanting their love, but wanting their love voluntarily—not because they have to love.

The people of Israel, Jonah, Job, those to whom Jesus ministered, humanity down through the

> From the beginning to the end, the story of faith is a story of God on a quest, God seeking relationship with these odd, wayward creatures molded from the dust of the earth.

ages, even we are those pursued by the love of God. Salvation is the story of that love and how we respond to it. It is a love story that is as old as time and that also becomes most intimate in the life, ministry, death, and resurrection of Jesus Christ. Salvation as love story is that account of a relationship between God and humanity that forever changes us and our reality.[1]

Good News, Bad News, Best News

Because salvation is relational, it is, from a Gospels perspective, a good news/bad news story. The *good news* is that salvation is simple and free; salvation is a relationship with Jesus Christ. It is a relationship that is there and waiting for us. Furthermore, Jesus wants us more than we can possibly want him. The *bad news* is that, as we all know, no relationship is simple. The truth is that being saved, living a life of faith, is as messy as anything else we humans experience. The best news, however, is that this bad news is really good—in fact, the very best—news. Out of the muddle of our relating to Jesus, as individuals and in the company of others, in the moment and over a lifetime, we live in hope and not in despair. Living in hope and not despair, we live for others rather than ourselves, and yet, paradoxically, we live our own truest selves and our own truest lives, individually and collectively. This life is a risky one, fraught with challenges and few guarantees. At the same time, ironically, we are also completely safe. We are harbored; we are saved.

The Good News

Salvation is not rocket science. It is not hard. It is free; it does not cost a cent. Everybody can have it. In that sense, it is more democratic than democracy is. It in no way at all depends on our sophistication, our popularity, our intelligence, our finances, or anything else we may value or that might set us apart from any other human being on the face of this earth.

Coming to faith, believing in Jesus, changing our allegiance to put God first in our lives—these acts are not that hard to understand, and they are not that hard to do. Is it sometimes a struggle? Sure, some of us struggle with the initial decision to turn our lives over to God and take up with Jesus. What classes to register for, what major to pursue, who to date and marry can also be struggles. But signing up for a class or a major, asking someone out on a date, and even walking down the aisle are not in themselves difficult tasks. Ordinary people do them every day.

Luke's "quest stories" are seven stories in which people approach Jesus with some pressing human need for which they are seeking relief—or, as it turns out, *salvation*. In the course of presenting their quests to Jesus, the "questers" face obstacles that must be overcome before they find what they are seeking. Sometimes what they really want is not what they thought they wanted when they first approached Jesus.

> Luke's "quest stories" are seven stories in which people approach Jesus with some pressing human need for which they are seeking relief—or, as it turns out, *salvation*.

Three of these stories are in the first part of Luke's Gospel, at the beginning of Jesus' ministry in Galilee—the stories of the paralytic,[2] the centurion with the sick slave,[3] and the woman who anoints Jesus' feet.[4] Three more quests occur as Jesus comes into Jerusalem. Here the tone of the Gospel turns ominous, as opposition to Jesus builds and his execution looms. These stories are those of the ten lepers,[5] the rich ruler,[6] and Zacchaeus.[7] Finally, embedded in the story of Jesus' crucifixion and death is the most poignant quest story of all, that of the thief on the cross who dies with Jesus.[8]

Although these questers face different obstacles to succeeding in their quest, and although each quest has its own complexity, every story begins with desire. Our most important reason for coming to Jesus, salvation, likewise begins with desire.

Like Zacchaeus, we come to God because we want to do so. We do not know exactly what motivated Zacchaeus to leave aside his daily obligations and go climb a tree that day when he knew that Jesus was passing by. The story does not spell it out. We do know that his need to see Jesus was compelling, perhaps even overwhelming. Like Zacchaeus, we have in our hearts that glimmer of passion that, no matter how deeply buried in other—ultimately less satisfying—longings, is part of being human.

That glimmer of passion, that first longing for God may involve acknowledgment of pain or dissatisfaction with our lives and the way we have chosen to live them thus far. It may involve simply wanting to be closer to God, to have the kind of inner peace we witness in a friend or mentor. Acting on those longings is what the church calls confession.

Of course, when we confess to God our passion for God, what we find is that our passion meets God's infinitely greater passion and longing for us. That great passion—grace—is part of being divine. Whatever longing compelled Zacchaeus up that tree that day was met with Jesus' ever so much greater longing for Zacchaeus, dubious and alienated tax-collector that he was.

For Christians, the great passion of God for humanity is fundamentally present and active in the incarnation, life and ministry, death and resurrection of Jesus. Salvation does not "begin" with Jesus, or even with the cross, as so many have assumed. From the earliest pages of Scripture, God has been in the business of offering salvation, though it is in Jesus that we finally meet the fulfillment of that divine initiative. The cross is, in turn, vital for Jesus' saving mission and crucial for his proclamation of the kingdom of God and of the whole of salvation God was offering through him to the world.

If our relationship to Jesus begins in much the same way most other relationships do, with desire, there is nevertheless a sense in which this relationship is different from many others. Many human relationships begin with a degree of pretension. We want to make a good first impression, so we dress and act our best. If the relationship goes somewhere, the mask slips, and we start revealing who we really are. Then we see whether the relationship is strong enough to handle the reality.

But God knows exactly who we are and still loves us unconditionally. Good first impressions are not only impossible, they are useless. Repentance is acknowledging that Jesus sees through us, just as he saw through the woman who anointed his feet, Simon the Pharisee, and Zacchaeus. Repentance is dropping the pointless pretensions and all the false hopes that led us to put our effort into those pretensions in the first place. Repentance is turning toward Jesus and everything that a life of discipleship has in store for us.

> For Christians, the great passion of God for humanity is fundamentally present and active in the incarnation, life and ministry, death and resurrection of Jesus.

In Luke's quest stories, all but one of the quests is successful. The paralytic, the centurion, the sinful woman of the city, the ten lepers, Zacchaeus, and the thief on the cross all find salvation. That salvation may be different from the solution they thought they were seeking when they went looking for Jesus. But they all find wholeness and integrity, and so much more, in relationship with Jesus.

The quester who is unsuccessful is the rich ruler in Luke 18. It is no coincidence that this quester cannot face the truth about who he is apart from his many possessions. His relationship with Jesus never quite gets off the ground because he cannot let go of his pretension that who he *is* depends on what he *has*.

The Bad News

The problem with salvation is that, like in any other relationship, beginning it may be simple, but maintaining it is often anything but that. Anyone can walk down the aisle and say "I do." But a loving marriage that lasts a lifetime, through thick and thin, takes work. Getting to know Jesus and letting oneself be known by him is also hard work. It is a different kind of hard work than we have sometimes been led to believe the Christian life will be.

We have sometimes reduced the hard work of being a Christian to a list of "dos" and "don'ts"—go to church, feed the hungry, tithe, don't swear, practice contemplation, march in peace demonstrations, take an anti-abortion stance, recite the Nicene Creed, etc. The list is endless, and the items are good, and we might want to do them. But they may be irrelevant, and they will certainly be irrelevant if we do not keep front and center the real hard work of being Christian, which is simply to relate to Jesus, whatever that takes and wherever it leads.

Anyone can walk down the aisle and say "I do." But a loving marriage that lasts a lifetime, through thick and thin, takes work.

We ought to know how to relate to Jesus, because we know how to relate to each other—in all the joy and difficulty of being alive in company with others. Relating means being present, taking time, hanging out, and caring. Luke's questers paid attention. The paralytic and his friends knew Jesus could heal the man's paralysis because they were paying attention to where Jesus was and what he was doing. The centurion knew what kind of authority Jesus had because he was observing carefully. The woman who anointed his feet knew he was in Simon the Pharisee's house because she was keeping track of Jesus' itinerary. Like these long-ago companions in the faith, we have to take notice of where Jesus is and what he is doing.

Moreover, we have to get ourselves to where he is, just as the questers took trouble to get themselves to where Jesus was. They made the effort. The paralytic found some hardworking and creative friends to take him to the house where Jesus was teaching and then find a way to get him near enough to attract Jesus' attention. In order to see Jesus, the woman who anointed his feet braved the disapproving crowd at Simon's house. Zacchaeus threw caution to the wind and ditched his dignity when he ran down the street and climbed a tree.

Where Will Jesus Be?

Part of working out our salvation, Paul's phrase in Philippians 2:12–13, is getting ourselves to the places where Jesus is hanging out. Fortunately, we have some surefire information about where to find him. We know where Jesus has promised to be.

In the Gathering of Believers

We have some promises. One promise is that Jesus is present wherever two or three are gathered in his name.[9] It would be so much simpler if salvation really were just an individual matter. But it isn't. Sure, we have to make our own personal decision at first. But being saved is a lifelong matter, and we do not do it by ourselves. Or more accurately, God does not accomplish salvation in us one by one. Like it or not, salvation is a team sport, and if you're a member of the team, being present in the gatherings of Jesus' friends is as essential as attending basketball practice for those who want to play. Some skills you can practice by yourself, but you can't learn the game by practicing skills solo day in and day out. You need the team. In fact, the team needs other teams.

So too Christians need a congregation. In fact, we need lots of congregations. Church is a primary place where people gather in Jesus' name. Communion, or Eucharist, is an important way the church remembers and celebrates two things: that we are in this strange thing called faith *together* and that Jesus is truly and really present with us when we gather in his name. When we participate in communion, we acknowledge visually and with our bodies that our salvation is not an object but a web of interactions, both divine and human, that sustains us.

With the Poor, Alien, and Orphan

Another promise is that we know Jesus is present with those who are hungry, thirsty, lonely, naked, sick, or in prison.[10] These words from Matthew 25 echo an Old Testament teaching that God's ear is bent toward the poor, the alien, and the orphan.[11] This is not a romantic view of the poor. Nothing about poverty or hunger or illness or any other human need makes one a better person. The point is that Jesus attends to human misery, and when we join him there we become one with him. In the same way that it makes sense to practice with the band if you want to go on the road, it makes sense to go where God is bending God's ear.

The catch here is that serving a Thanksgiving meal at the homeless shelter once a year doesn't do it, regardless of how great that makes us feel. Nor will a study or service trip to Guatemala do it. These activities can open our eyes, but my metaphors from athletics and performance are not accidental. Friendship with those among whom Jesus unfailingly walks requires at least the discipline that athletic or musical excellence requires. Jesus is not absent in charitable acts such as serving the Thanksgiving meal, but he is truly present in our ongoing daily friendships with the poor—and with all the give and take, ups and downs, and ins and outs of the relationships we have with classmates, co-workers, and the people at church.

The everyday mutual intertwining of lives in the most ordinary circumstances is guaranteed to bring us closer to Jesus. Such engagement is not easy—but it is a dependable way to "work out our salvation."[12] The new monastics[13] are getting this right—taking ourselves to the abandoned places of empire, as they put it, will put us in proximity to Jesus as surely as did Zacchaeus' climbing that tree.

In the Ancient Stories and Teachings of the Scripture

Finally, we know Jesus is present in the pages of the biblical text. I recently reclaimed the phrase "personal relationship with Jesus Christ"—language I long discarded as hopelessly, sentimentally pious—after I spent half a day every month for almost a year studying Luke's quest stories with some pastors. Over the course of those Friday afternoons, as we pored over the quests one by one, we got to know Jesus personally. We wondered why he said what he said and did what he did. As we read his words, we tried out different tones of voice. We imagined what he was thinking. We pondered the information Luke left out of the stories. Sometimes we discovered that Jesus frustrated us or puzzled us. Sometimes we were moved to tears, and often we laughed. But what we discovered above all is that Jesus is reliably present in the pages of the biblical text.

And as we pay attention to him there, we reliably experience him as being present in our midst. By the end of that study cycle, Jesus had become a vital part of our group; he had become not only our Savior but also our spiritual director, our friend, and our More-Than-Friend. That intimacy may happen most directly in working with texts that feature Jesus, but it also can happen in our engagement with the biblical canon more broadly.

I mentioned Paul's phrase about "working out our salvation." I like that term because the hard work of being a Christian is like going to the gym. Jesus is found reliably in the company of those who meet in his name, in the poor and hungry, and in the pages of the Bible. Going to the gym has little payoff unless we go regularly, whether or not we want to or feel like it. Showing up where we know Jesus is present is how we nurture our relationship with him. It is how we live in faith.

The Bad News is the *Best* News

Jesus never sugarcoated this Way to which he calls us. In the Sermon on the Mount he describes the way back to God, the path to salvation, as that narrow, twisty path that winds over the boulders and up the mountain.[14] You had better have your compass ready because there aren't many markers. It is not that broad, smooth asphalt boulevard that gets the tourists coming in on buses to the foot of the falls, with its convenient concession stands and ramps or stairs with sturdy handrails. This is a trail not too many people take. It winds on slippery, mist-wet rocks behind the falls and then finally emerges at the very top of the falls. It is breathtaking and dangerous.

> Jesus never sugarcoated this Way to which he calls us. In the Sermon on the Mount he describes the way back to God, the path to salvation, as that narrow, twisty path that winds over the boulders and up the mountain.

None of Luke's questers knew exactly what would come out of their encounter with Jesus. The paralytic wanted to be healed. He did not expect that Jesus would be as concerned about his sins as about his crippled legs. Nor was the woman who anointed Jesus' feet expecting that Jesus would describe her to his host as a model of hospitality, or tell her that her sins were forgiven. Simon the Pharisee, for that matter, was not expecting that his dinner invitation would turn into a lesson on the limits of his hospitableness and gratitude. Zacchaeus did not expect Jesus to come to his house. Nor did he expect to find his exuberant joy turning him into a generous fool.

> The only practical expectation with which we can approach this journey with Jesus is that we will be transformed—or in more traditional language—converted.

The only practical expectation with which we can approach this journey with Jesus, this relationship that becomes our most important relationship, is that we will be transformed—or in more traditional language—converted. Further along the way, we will not be exactly that person who first said yes to Jesus. In whatever way we encounter Jesus in life, part of the key to a saving relationship with him is to stick around and see what happens.

Transformation is not just an internal, individual process

that happens in some existential way. Transformation happens as we test insight and discern direction, day by day, in the same places where we go to find Jesus—where two or three are gathered in his name, in the forgotten places of empire, in the ancient stories and teachings of the Bible.

Nor should we be surprised if our twisting, turning salvation way leads us into hardship and suffering. Living in hope rather than despair is clearly no life for a couch potato.

• It is living for others rather than for ourselves.

• It is living *beyond* ourselves, living for something much larger than ourselves, for something that did not begin with our birth and does not end with our death.

• It is choosing not to build a monument to our own achievements but joining instead God's river of life. Paradoxically and inexplicably, losing ourselves in that river of life, that baptism, is also our truest life, our safest harbor, our cross, our great joy, and our salvation.

Questions for Discussion

1. *Salvation* is related to *sin*. It may help you to put both of these terms in your own words, even if that results in some unconventional metaphors. What do you need to be saved *from*? What do you want to be saved *for*?

2. Not everyone has or develops a sense of needing to be "saved." Such might be the case, for example, for many comfortable, middle-class North Americans who perceive themselves to be managing their lives quite well and with no need for any rescue plan or outside assistance. How should the good news of Jesus be communicated to people in this situation? Is the word *salvation* helpful in such a case, or would some other term be more appropriate and do a better job of connecting?

3. Likely the biggest problem with some common notions of salvation is that they are limited to that first-time, decisional moment of "accepting Jesus as Savior." Yet we go on being saved,

or in the terms of this article, we go on growing in our relationship with Jesus. What are some of your experiences of being saved or growing in Christ?

Notes

1. Many of the chapters in this book describe in more detail how God, the First and Primary "Quester" throughout the biblical story, has continually sought out the least, last, and lost of the world to offer hope and salvation. This chapter focuses more specifically on how people have responded to God's loving initiative in Jesus by exploring the salvation theme through the lens of seven "quest stories" found in the Gospel of Luke.

2. Luke 5:17-26.

3. Luke 7:1-10.

4. Luke 7:36-50.

5. Luke 17:11-19.

6. Luke 18:18-30.

7. Luke 19:1-10.

8. Luke 23:39-43. For more on Luke's quest stories, see Robert C. Tannehill, *The Narrative Unity of Luke-Acts: A Literary Interpretation*, vol. 1 (Philadelphia: Fortress Press, 1986), 111–27.

9. Matthew 18:20.

10. See Matthew 25:31-46. The "least of these" in this text may refer to the disciples rather than to the poor more generally. (Scholars have pointed out that elsewhere in Matthew, this phrase "the least of these" is always used by Jesus to designate the small disciple band he has assembled.) The key to the passage, however, is the knowing and not knowing. The sheep do not know they have been serving Jesus because they have "just" been serving the poor. The goats do not know that they have not been serving Jesus because they have not been serving the poor. Their question is telling: they imply that if they had seen Jesus poor, naked, etc., they would certainly have done something for *him*. They do not see the needs of the disciples (the least) because they do not see the needs of the poor.

11. Psalm 10:16-18.

12. Philippians 2:12.

13. "New monastics" is the name for a movement of Christians

who form communities of compassion, ministry, and transformation, often within impoverished and high stress neighborhoods. See Shane Claiborne, *Irresistible Revolution: Living As an Ordinary Radical*, (Grand Rapids, MI: Zondervan, 2006).

14. Matthew 7:13, 14.

Chapter 12

Jesus Our Peace

Mary Thiessen Nation with Matthew Krabill

———— Narrative: *The resurrected Jesus blesses his disciples* ————
with a greeting of "peace" and then shows them
his hands and side (John 20:19-29)

Dear Matthew,

I could write countless letters about the courageous peace I witnessed among my neighbors and friends in urban Los Angeles. Alternately, I could write a letter of confession, admitting that I sometimes ministered to the needs of others in an attempt to fill my deep need for inner peace. But as I reflected on the violence in our world today, I felt compelled to think about the despair, terror and suffering I encountered in L.A.—experiences in which the lack of peace defied human intervention. I asked myself if Jesus offered peace for such situations.

To be honest, putting Jesus and peace together in one phrase always creates some dissonance within me. To begin with, even though the angels announced the birth of Jesus with peals of "peace on earth," didn't Herod kill many innocent babies before Jesus could even walk? Even earlier, Mary's

> To be honest, putting Jesus and peace together in one phrase always creates some dissonance within me.

song[1] and Zechariah's prophecy[2] were packed with images of upheaval, not peace. True to these prophecies, Jesus' message of peace disturbed a lot of people. Perhaps the last line in Zechariah's prophetic poem—"to guide our feet into the way of peace"[3]—can carry some of the tensions I'm struggling with.

I should probably start again. You need to know a little more about me. Ten days after my college graduation in the early seventies, I joined an interdenominational Christian mission organization and moved into a violent neighborhood in Los Angeles. I lived there for the next eighteen years. I learned that peace is complex, sometimes paradoxical, often full of hard work, multi-faceted and full of a lot of mystery. Let me explain.

Not long after I moved to L.A. my housemates and I were threatened with dismemberment. I had naively called the police one night when I heard someone breaking into our garage. Alas, it turned out that the intruders were nine- and ten-year-olds. Their parents were understandably furious. The threats that continued relentlessly for three months were designed to drive us out of the neighborhood. When I couldn't stand the fear any longer, I lay on my bed and told God I was going back to my home in Canada unless he did something about my terror.

> Peace is complex, sometimes paradoxical, often full of hard work, multi-faceted and full of a lot of mystery.

I don't know how long I lay there but I remember hearing two messages: "They can't touch the real you," and "You can't create peace. It's a gift, a fruit of the Spirit."

I blurted out, "I'll take it."

The Holy Spirit responded. I received enough peace. I was not only able to stay, but through that experience I recognized that I couldn't impart peace to others. I could pursue and practice peace, but I couldn't create it within another person. I could and did watch and wait and expect and pray for it. And often others received the gift of peace just as I had. I've come to agree with Paul that "peace surpasses all understanding."[4] But I'm getting ahead of myself.

> The way of peace isn't placid or soft. It requires courage.

Did you catch the tensions in the previous story? Peace didn't

mean the absence of danger. You could even say that God's promised "way of peace" led me into danger. You see, although Jesus
says, "Peace I leave with you; my
peace I give to you. . . . Do not let
your hearts be troubled, and do
not let them be afraid,"[5] he goes
right on to prepare the disciples
for the world's hatred.[6]

> The incarnation, the life and teachings
> and miracles, the passion and cruci-
> fixion, the resurrection, the ascension,
> the sending of the Spirit, the present
> work and the promised future of
> Jesus must be held together.

Jesus explains himself still
further: "I have said this to you,
so that in me you may have peace.
In the world you face persecution. But take courage; I have conquered the world!"[7] The way of peace isn't placid or soft. It requires
courage.

David Bosch, the South African mission scholar and practi-
tioner who devoted his life to the gospel during the years of
apartheid, helped me to hold together some of the profound
dimensions in Christ's way of peace. Bosch, by the way, bled to
death after a car accident in a black township because the ambu-
lance driver, not realizing David was a white man, failed to hasten
to the scene of the accident. Get it? Anyway, David wrote that
we'd end up with a truncated, domesticated, and distorted gospel
if we didn't keep the full story of Jesus together. He taught me that
the incarnation, the life and teachings and miracles, the passion
and crucifixion, the resurrection, the ascension, the sending of the
Spirit, the present work and the promised future of Jesus must be
held together.

When I don't cut and paste or pick and choose, I recognize
how peace permeates and drives the story. And I can understand
why peace looks different in different situations. At times peace
includes wholeness, healing, forgiveness and blessing;[8] at times it
is expressed in feeding and clothing those who are poor;[9] and
sometimes it results in persecution and torture of the very worst
kind. I'm referring to the crucifixion of Jesus Christ.

I will never forget the night in the inner city of Los Angeles when twelve young women sat around a large piece of paper on which I had drawn a crude cross. I read from Isaiah 53 about the Suffering Servant who was despised and rejected, who was familiar with suffering and infirmities, who was considered unattractive. There was "nothing in his appearance that we should desire him" and he was as "one from whom others hide their faces."[10] I could see in the women's eyes that they knew what this felt like.

I continued reading, underlining that this Suffering Servant had borne our infirmities, had carried our diseases, was wounded for our transgressions, was punished in our place and was bruised so we could be healed. Next I read from 1 Peter 2:24, pointing out that the Suffering Servant was Jesus himself who "bore our sins in his body on the cross, so that, free from sins, we might live for righteousness; by his wounds you have been healed." I encouraged the women to let Jesus carry their suffering and sorrows, to let him bear their burdens, to let him heal the wounds of the sins they had committed and the sins that had been committed against them. I then encouraged them to write any of these pains and sins on the cross.

> That group of twelve young women wrote over three hundred things on that cross. And the mystery or miracle is, they didn't just write them there, they gave them to Jesus.

Almost as one they knelt by this cross and wrote intently for what felt like forever. They wrote of their experiences: "K.K.K. burned crosses in our front yard," "raped by stepfather," "molested by uncle," "not protected," "mother didn't believe me," "falsely accused by teachers," "watched suspiciously in stores," "not invited to the parties of white students," "brother murdered." They used words like "abandoned," "rejected," "mocked," "told I was ugly," "not welcome," "ignored." And they confessed their feelings: angry, bitter, afraid, insecure, depressed, useless, ugly, ashamed, guilty. . . .

That group of twelve young women wrote over three hundred things on that cross. And the mystery or miracle is, they didn't just write them there, some of them actually placed them there—they gave them to Jesus. Because they knew that Jesus understood their sufferings and longings, the Spirit convinced them that they could let go, could release these burdens and weights and injustices and sorrows to him. They sensed that the extreme suffering of Christ was strong enough to address the unbearable suffering they had experienced.

That memory captures my imagination, particularly because so many Christians are tempted to talk about following Jesus as though we're expected to experience one victory after another. The good news is that it was *after* the resurrection, while the disciples were hiding in shame and fear, that "Jesus came and stood among them and said, 'Peace be with you.' After he said this, he showed them his hands and his side."[11] He showed them peace—through his wounds. The risen Jesus is identified by his scars.

> Suffering, death, and resurrection victory—these are ever present companions on the way of peace.

I like the way Greg Jones said it in Northern Ireland: "We don't follow an uncrucified Christ." Suffering, death, and resurrection victory—these are ever present companions on the way of peace.[12] This combination becomes increasingly clear as you read through to the end of John's gospel and listen in on the lives of the early Christians. In fact, it was after Paul encountered the risen Jesus that he repeatedly wrote, "I preach Christ crucified."[13]

The way of peace can also, however, be very attractive. In the middle of violence, peace has magnetic power. I can't tell you how many people came to my home in Los Angeles looking for peace. One teenager came after part of her ear was bitten off in a fight; another came when she couldn't take the molestation any more. Some came after family members were murdered and others came during gang warfare.

One young woman whose reputation for violence was unequalled knocked on our door one evening. What could she want? She later told us, "When I came into your home . . . that was the first place I had been to where I wasn't watching my back." She felt safe. The peace disarmed her. She kept coming back. Several months later, on her graduation day from high school, she decided to follow the Prince of Peace.

I've begun to think that when Jesus challenged his followers to love one another, to be united as he and the Father are one,[14] it's as though he was implying, "They'll know that you are Christians by your *peace*." Yes, all neighborhoods, including violent neighborhoods, in fact, need communities of peace.

Here's another fun memory. One of the young women who wrote her junk on the cross became a most creative team member. At her wedding ten years later the photographer quipped, "What's this? It looks like the United Nations." With African-Americans, Hispanics, Caucasians, and even an Asian in the wedding party, the photographer didn't know how to set the lighting on his camera. There were simply too many skin tones. The photos didn't turn out well but the picture in my mind is strikingly beautiful. That's what the peace of Christ looks like in living color.[15]

The gospel of peace, the way of peace, the community of peace—all of these display God's reconciliation between humanity and himself and among disparate groups of people. This peace, this end of hostility, this dismantling of dividing walls, this communion in the covenant, this sharing of the same Spirit, is brought about through the body and flesh and blood of Christ.[16] Peace with God and peace with each other are inseparable. Reconciliation with God is inevitably entwined with interpersonal reconciliation.

> Peace with God and peace with each other are inseparable. Reconciliation with God is inevitably entwined with interpersonal reconciliation.

And once we're reconciled to God, we naturally join the other ambassadors of peace, the other ministers of reconciliation in the ongoing work of Jesus.[17] Because the story of Jesus who has reconciled us to God and to each other is ongoing, we are immediately conscious that there are still many strangers and aliens who need to be welcomed, that there are many walls that need to be broken down, that the family table has room for many more guests.[18] As disciples of Jesus we're reminded that we are the dwelling place of God, the building in which God's construction work continues.[19] And we're reminded that our tools, our instruments of reconciliation may well be blood-stained, shaped like a cross.

I wish I could tell you that we as missionaries always traveled on the way of peace, that we displayed the multiple dimensions of Christ's peace in a full way. Perhaps because we were living in what often felt like a war zone, we focused too narrowly on the micro issues in our neighborhoods, on whole-person peace through inviting Christ to address the emotional, social, physical, mental, and spiritual needs of individuals. Some of the macro issues, the structural and systemic and historic deterrents to peace, didn't get the kind of attention Christ's peace seeks to address.

> Jesus' words concerning loving our enemies were difficult to teach and practice when thinking about or meeting individuals who had raped, abused, molested, murdered, or oppressed the members of our community.

Three of my African-American friends from Los Angeles assisted my doctoral research. The peace of Jesus we discussed and examined did expand to include these broader dimensions of God's peace. And now when they call me about horrendous crimes in their neighborhoods or families, we let the peace of Jesus shed light on the multiple complex roots and systems and powers as well.[20] It's hard to keep all these things, the micro and macro, together isn't it? That's one more reason we need to minister in teams.

I also confess that Jesus' words concerning loving our enemies[21] were difficult to teach and practice when thinking about or meeting individuals who had raped, abused, molested, murdered, or oppressed the members of our community. I've recently been challenged again to entrust judgment and even vengeance to God.[22] I watched a fellow student in a contemporary Anabaptism course in Philadelphia struggle with the implications of Jesus' words concerning love of enemy. Because his parents had been brutally murdered, he purchased a gun and now justified his intention to protect his family through the use of force if necessary. As this minister from El Salvador heard the words of Jesus and listened to the testimonies of believers who refused to kill, even in war, he argued thoughtfully and humbly.

After the course this pastor wrote to my husband, Mark, who had taught the course:

> Thank you . . . you made me think and re-think some ideas planted very deep in my heart. It is obvious that my theology and ministry is changing after this class . . . you do not have a dichotomy between book and life or among academy, spiritual life, and ministry. That is great theology, basically the theology from New Testament.

Mark and I pray that this student will receive the gift of peace and will devote his life to peacemaking, to loving even his enemies, to entrusting judgment and justice to the higher courts. We pray that someday he will even get rid of his gun.

Yes, the peace of Jesus can transform the complex and multi-faceted roots of disorder, chaos, violence, injustice, suffering, sin, and evil within and around us. This peace is both free and costly. I want to pursue peace. I choose to accept the ministry of reconciliation. I do so with hope because the Spirit of Jesus groans on behalf of the current suffering of humankind and all of creation,[23] and because someday everything in heaven and on earth will be reconciled to God,[24] and because I know where this story will end—in the fulfillment of God's peaceful kingdom.[25] And in the middle of the horrors of the past and the terrors of the present, I keep watching expectantly for the fulfillment of the angels' announcement when Jesus was born: "Peace on earth."

I look forward, Matthew, to your response.

Shalom,
Mary

∂

Dear Mary,

I hear what you are saying. The world is a screwed up, violent, and messy place. People living on this planet experience tremendous pain and suffering. I resettled Liberian and Sierra Leonean refugees in Philadelphia and heard countless stories of unimaginable loss, fear, and devastation. I also lived with Palestinians in the West Bank and Gaza Strip and witnessed their daily humiliation, oppression, and violence. I currently live in the same city where you had lived, and I know the world you describe—a world where girls are raped, children abandoned, and siblings murdered. Your account describes in many ways the same Los Angeles in which I live in 2009.

So, Mary, I guess what I am saying is that the world as I see it is a very broken one—one that is very much in need of peace. And yet I find myself jaded—jaded because when I look at the world around me I see few signs of peace. And so I wonder how am I, or anyone else for that matter, to impart peace to others? What or who is the source of our peace? And what will happen if I choose to pursue the way of peace myself?

Fortunately I have learned a lot from my Liberian friends. John, a Liberian pastor and good friend, told me that in the midst of the Liberian civil war, when ethnic tensions divided neighbor from neighbor, when fear loomed and rebels frequently attacked his town, he felt convicted to preach a message of peace. In fact, he prayed for peace when neighbors huddled in fear night after night in his courtyard; he urged his neighbors to resist picking up arms against one another; and he was publicly proclaiming the message of peace when rebels surrounded his church one hot Sunday morning in July 1995. The rebels raped or killed half of his members, including his wife and two sons.

After hearing John tell his story the first time, I asked him, "How did you find the courage to live and preach that kind of message?" He replied, "Brother Matthew, listen to me. Our Savior was all about peace; that is the message Jesus preached when he lived among us. And when Jesus died on that cross and rose from the dead, he reconciled us with God and reconciled neighbor to neighbor."

Pastor John's story had a profound impact on me and got me thinking. It got me thinking about the cross and suffering, about the cross and peace, about the cross and reconciliation. And I realize now, Mary, that what John was telling me

Pastor John's story had a profound impact on me and got me thinking about the cross and suffering, about the cross and peace.

then is what you are saying to me *now*, that peace with God and peace with each other are indeed inseparable. Following the Prince of Peace is both free and costly. When people decide to follow the way of peace, it often leads them into danger and more often than not, great sacrifice. That Christ suffered is significant, because only a Christ that has experienced the same pain and suffering as the twelve women who placed their brokenness on the cross in your home is able to identify with the unbearable suffering of human experience.

But that is not all, because there is hope beyond suffering. There has to be if we believe in Jesus. What I mean is that the kind of peace that he preached, the kind of peace he died for, and the kind of peace announced, inaugurated, and embodied in his death on the cross and in his resurrection is none other than God's full-orbed response to the magnitude and scope of the world's pain and suffering. Human brokenness runs deep and wide—but God's response is equally as comprehensive.

Upon the crucified Jesus, humanity and the powers hurled their violent rebellion. Jesus absorbed the violence and forgave. In his forgiveness the cycle of violent retribution was stopped and reconciliation was made possible. This is the good news of the "gospel of peace"—that the reconciling work

Peace cannot be reduced to our own best efforts. Rather, peace is birthed, awakened, and sustained in and through us by Jesus our Savior.

of Jesus can transform the complex and multi-faceted roots of disorder, chaos, violence, injustice, suffering, sin, and evil, both within us and around us.

So yes, I too wait, Mary. I wait in the middle of the horrors of the past, the terrors of the present, and those yet to come for the angels' announcement, "Peace on earth"—the kind of peace only a Savior can bring.

Salaam,
Matthew

ço

Dear Matthew,

Sounds like our experiences have taught both of us that extreme suffering requires the extreme response that God provided in Jesus. And it sounds like both of us have our work cut out for us—learning how to live and teach that "peace with God through Jesus" and "peace with each other through Jesus" are inseparable. Will holding these two together fulfill Zechariah's prophecy that Jesus came "to guide our feet into the way of peace"? If this is true, Matthew, then peace cannot be reduced to our own best efforts. Rather, peace is birthed, awakened, and sustained in and through us by Jesus our Savior—as we journey together with him as our Guide.

> Human brokenness runs deep and wide—but God's response is equally as comprehensive. Upon the crucified Jesus, humanity and the powers hurled their violent rebellion. Jesus absorbed the violence and forgave. In his forgiveness the cycle of violent retribution was stopped and reconciliation was made possible.

On the way of peace,
Mary

Questions for Discussion:

1. Lots of people nowadays talk about peace. What is the difference between the kind of peace, for example, the Dalai Lama offers and that of Jesus?

2. Why are we tempted to separate peace with God and peace with others? Is this separation the root of our struggle to hold mission and peace, evangelism and social concern together? What happens to the "gospel of peace" when we treat them as separate themes or activities?

3. If you chose to list on a cross some of the sufferings with which you are acquainted, what would you write? You can think about yourself, others, your community or the larger world. Can you imagine how doing this could lead to peace with God and with others? Try it sometime.

4. Why is it important to walk in the "way of peace" within a community rather than attempting this path alone?

5. What aspects of Jesus' message of peace do you find most challenging?

6. Do you agree that peace is a gift? Can you give peace to someone else?

Notes
1. Luke 1:46-56.
2. Luke 1:67-79.
3. Luke 1:79. Bible text in this chapter is NRSV.
4. Philippians 4:7.
5. John 14:27.
6. John 15:18-21; see also Matthew 10:34 and Luke 12:51.
7. John 16:33.
8. Mark 5:34; Luke 7:50.
9. James 2:15-16.
10. Isaiah 53:2-3.
11. John 20:19-20.
12. L. Gregory Jones, "Embodying Forgiveness," in *Pathways* (Northern Ireland: ECONI), 2001.

13. 1 Corinthians 2:2; Galatians 6:14.
14. John 17:20-23.
15. Ephesians 2:11-22.
16. Ephesians 2:13-18.
17. 2 Corinthians 5:17-21.
18. Ephesians 2:19.
19. Ephesians 2:21-22.
20. Ephesians 6:12.
21. Matthew 5:43-48.
22. Romans 12:18-21.
23. Romans 8:18-27.
24. Colossians 1:15-20.
25. Revelation 21:1-4.

Chapter 13

Jesus and Mission

Wilbert R. Shenk with Jennifer Davis Sensenig

————— Narrative: *Jesus models God's mission and trains a team* —————
to continue the work (Luke 10:1-24)

Jack and Jenny Taylor are committed to following Jesus and sharing their faith with others. They bought a house in a new subdivision in Riverside, California, and moved in with their two small children. As they got acquainted with their neighbors, mostly Gen-Xers like themselves, it became clear they were about the only married couple in that suburb. The usual comment was, "Long-term commitment is too confining."

The neighbors were mainly upwardly mobile young professionals. Children were being born to these couples and raising children was on their minds. One neighbor recounted her journey out of the Christianity of her parents to Buddhism, then New Age, and now finally Judaism. "Each day I make up the spirituality that will work for me. What is your spirituality?" She was eager to hear about other people's experiences.

With their gift of hospitality, Jack and Jenny soon had groups of neighbors gathering at their home where conversation ranged over all sorts of topics, including discussions about the Christian faith.

The Taylors had two more children and were deeply invested in parenting. Jenny interacted with other mothers. Individuals would drop by for conversation with either Jenny or Jack. Raising children wasn't the only thing on their minds. They were wrestling with issues of meaning and purpose. They sensed the Taylors' lives were centered. With their gift of hospitality, Jack and Jenny soon had groups of neighbors gathering at their home where conversation ranged over all sorts of topics, including discussions about the Christian faith.

On Easter Sunday, the Taylors invited their neighbors to a city park for a picnic. Seventy people showed up for games and singing. They introduced several songs about the resurrection. "This fellowship is important to us," their friends said. The Taylors' grace-filled hospitality had drawn their neighbors into a circle where God's love was present.

As disciples of Jesus, the Taylors seek to be the presence of Jesus in their daily lives and relationships. This commitment is not something they wear on their sleeves and advertise. It is part and parcel of who they are.

Jesus' Self-Understanding

When Jesus was twelve years old Joseph and Mary took him on the annual Passover journey to Jerusalem. After the festival they began the trek back to Galilee. That evening the parents discovered that Jesus was absent. So they returned to Jerusalem to look for their son. Three days later they found him in the temple engaged in heavy theological discussion. Jesus' mother, visibly upset, scolded him for causing his parents such alarm. His reply to Mary might be paraphrased, "What else did you expect? I belong in my Father's house."[1] Jesus' answer shows he was completely absorbed in what the temple represented—God-centeredness. Nothing was more important than being in God's presence, seeking to know and do the will of God.

As the narrative of his life unfolds, Jesus' self-consciousness merges into God-consciousness. His all-consuming passion is to do "the will of the Father." Just before his arrest at the end of his earthly ministry and with crucifixion now inevitable, Jesus

> As the narrative of his life unfolds, Jesus' self-consciousness merges into God-consciousness. His all-consuming passion is to do "the will of the Father."

prays, "Not my will, but yours be done."[2] This was no attitude of weak resignation; Jesus embraces his mission. Jesus' self-consciousness was that God the Father and God the Holy Spirit had sent him into the world as God's Messiah.[3] This identity shapes his entire life and ministry.

Jesus Launches His Mission

The synoptic Gospels (Matthew, Mark, Luke) report that Jesus went to where John the Baptist was preaching and baptizing many people. John resisted when Jesus requested that John baptize him also.[4] Why would the Messiah require baptism? People might assume that ordinary sinful people obviously needed this ritual cleansing, but surely God's Messiah did not.

Jesus transformed the meaning of baptism. Receiving baptism meant identifying wholly with the kingdom of God and fulfilling God's work. It was far more than giving ritual assent. Baptism marked the first step in active participation in God's mission. When John baptized Jesus, the Holy Spirit put God's seal of approval on him.[5]

> Jesus transformed the meaning of baptism. Baptism marked the first step in active participation in God's mission.

One thing remained before Jesus launched his public ministry. Following his baptism, "At once the Holy Spirit sent him out into the desert."[6] For forty days Satan tested Jesus precisely at the point of his baptismal vow. The Devil dangled attractive alternatives before Jesus. But he rejected Satan's three overtures because they contradicted his covenant with God: (a) turn stones into bread, thereby currying favor with the people; (b) throw himself down from the temple dome, attracting the attention of the people; and (c) worship Satan in exchange for worldly power.[7] Having prevailed against Satan, "Jesus returned to Galilee in the power of the Spirit."[8]

Jesus Proclaims the Kingdom of God

Jesus' reputation as a compelling preacher spread quickly.[9] The central theme of Jesus' ministry was the new order or kingdom that God was establishing.[10] Jesus was passionate about the kingdom of God. His mission was to call people to follow him in serving God.

Matthew emphasizes that Jesus taught the people what it means to live the righteousness and justice of God in daily life. In his Sermon on the Mount, Jesus offered an alternative vision of life.[11] He called people to become his disciples in following God's way, rather than pursuing self-fulfillment. He assured the crowds that God longed to save them from the power of evil that was all around them. This was the good news that Jesus shared wherever he went. He used every means at his disposal to introduce people to God's compassion. At one moment Jesus was the master teacher; in the next he confronted evil powers that were holding people captive. He proclaimed the good news to the people but confronted the religious and political establishment that coddled the rich and powerful while riding roughshod over ordinary folk.

Jesus ministered to each person at the point of greatest personal stress. The encounter between the Samaritan woman and Jesus at Jacob's well begins with Jesus making himself vulnerable.[12] Needing water, he breaks all the rules by asking a woman with a scandalous reputation to help him. As the encounter unfolds, the woman sees herself and her circumstances in a new light. She had long been trapped by social ostracism. Jesus assures her that God is on her side. Transformed, this woman becomes an evangelist: "Many Samaritans from that town believed in him because of the woman's testimony."[13]

Luke traces the narrative of Jesus' ministry. He traveled

throughout Galilee liberating people from demonic oppression, healing the sick, and preaching and teaching in the synagogues. He attracted throngs of people. His teaching was strikingly different from that of other rabbis. Jesus' message had an authority that other teachers did not have.[14] He showed compassion to the people by inviting, "Come to me, all you who are weary and burdened, and I will give you rest."[15]

> Luke traces the narrative of Jesus' ministry. He traveled throughout Galilee liberating people from demonic oppression, healing the sick, and preaching and teaching in the synagogues.

He wanted the crowds to understand the contrast between this world that was controlled by the Devil and the kingdom of God.[16]

Rumors about Jesus' activities got back to John the Baptist in prison. He sent a delegation to check things out. John's key question: "Are you really the Messiah we have been promised?"[17] John had a stake in what was happening. His special role was to prepare for the coming of the long expected Messiah. Had John been mistaken? He wanted to be reassured that Jesus was genuine.

Jesus said, "Go back and report to John what you hear and see: The blind receive sight, the lame walk, those who have leprosy are cured, the deaf hear, the dead are raised, and the good news is preached to the poor."[18] Jesus was indeed following through on the messianic mission described by the Old Testament prophets and reiterated by John the Baptist's father Zechariah, cousin Mary, and the elderly Simeon in the temple.[19]

Jesus Calls and Trains Twelve Disciples

Jesus now began selecting individuals to be apprentices-in-mission.[20] The first was Simon Peter, with his business partners James and John Zebedee, who fished in the Sea of Galilee. Jesus does not tell Simon Peter to sell his business. Instead he deftly redefines the kind of fishing Simon Peter will do in the future— fishing for people. In a short time Jesus named twelve men to be his closest associates in mission. They were an odd lot—several fishermen, a tax collector, a revolutionary, one who eventually turned traitor, and others whose backgrounds are unknown.

Much of Jesus' teaching was in the form of parables that he used to tell people the good news of the kingdom of God. One thing was clear to the disciples. Jesus was passionate about winning men and women for the kingdom of God. He demonstrated the compassion of God through healing and delivering people. He was intent on overcoming the power of evil.

> Jesus does not tell Simon Peter to sell his business. Instead he deftly redefines the kind of fishing Simon Peter will do in the future—fishing for people.

Jesus constantly made use of the ordinary. The Gospels report various occasions when Jesus had table fellowship with people. In fact, one of the charges brought against him by the religious leaders was that he ate with sinners. The meal is a foremost symbol of hospitality. Jesus pictures God as the gracious host who invites all people to the messianic banquet. Table fellowship is essential to mission throughout the world.

> Jesus pictures God as the gracious host who invites all people to the messianic banquet. Table fellowship is essential to mission throughout the world.

Woven into Jesus' pattern of life and mission was the practice of prayer. Luke notes frequently the role of prayer in his life. Jesus teaches his apprentices-in-mission to pray. Both male and female characters in Jesus' parables reveal prayer as integral to mission.[21]

In addition to the twelve disciples, several women who had been healed or delivered from evil powers also joined Jesus' entourage that was moving through the "cities and villages" of Galilee. These women became witnesses of God's power that had touched them.[22]

Jesus Sends His Disciples on a Mission

One day Jesus announced to the twelve disciples that they were to participate in God's mission, too. "He gave them power and authority to drive out all demons and to cure diseases . . . to preach the kingdom of God, and to heal the sick."[23] They would travel light and depend on the hospitality of the people they met along the way. The disciples were not to impose themselves on anyone. "If people do not welcome you, shake the dust off your feet when you leave their town, as a testimony against them."[24] This would let people know that the disciples had not been welcomed there. After the disciples completed their missions, they returned and reported their experiences to Jesus.[25]

Later Jesus asked them what they overheard the people saying about him and his message. In an exchange that sounds familiar to us, the twelve reported all sorts of speculation as to Jesus' identity. Some were sure he was a resurrected John the Baptist, who had recently been beheaded by King Herod, or the prophet Elijah. Others thought he was another one of the ancient prophets who had reappeared. Jesus pressed the disciples, "Who do you say I am?" Peter asserted, "The Christ (Messiah) of God."[26]

Jesus Expands his Mission

In Luke's Gospel, the Galilean phase of Jesus' ministry ends at chapter 9:50. Jesus then began his journey to Judea and Jerusalem. He goes from the periphery, from the Galilean hinterland, toward the center of religious and political power where the mission of Jesus will reach its climax in his ultimate sacrifice and triumph.

> Luke wants his readers to understand that the messianic mission is ultimately to the nations, not only to the Jewish people. The seventy were commissioned to prepare the way for the Messiah's coming.

Luke shows Jesus engaged in ministry in Judea and Transjordan, followed by trial, death, and resurrection in Jerusalem.

Luke uses this movement to signal that the mission of Jesus was not confined to Galilee or even Israel. As a part of this new phase, Jesus commissioned a second group of disciples to serve as an advance party. "After this the Lord appointed seventy others and sent them two by two ahead of him to every town and place where he was about to go."[27] This signals Jesus' intention to evangelize the whole of the Jewish people—and more. Just as twelve represented the twelve tribes of Israel, *seventy* represented "the nations." Luke wants his readers to understand that the messianic mission is ultimately to the nations, not only to the Jewish people. The seventy were commissioned to prepare the way for the Messiah's coming.

Criticized by the Jewish religious leaders because he welcomed "tax collectors" and "sinners," Jesus told a parable about the lost sheep.[28] Imagine that you have a flock of one hundred sheep and one goes missing. What do you do? You leave the ninety-nine that are safe in the sheep pen and search until you find the lost one. Not only do you bring that one back to the safety of the pen, but you celebrate the fact that the lost animal has been found.

> Three times Jesus told the disciples that the outcome of his mission would be his death and resurrection. To the disciples this was unbelievable.

In contrast to the traditional interpretation that God will receive the sinner who repents, Jesus shifts the emphasis: God actively searches for the lost, i.e., the outcast tax collectors and sinners, and rejoices when they find salvation. The point was not lost on the crowd, who saw the religious leaders grumbling that Jesus showed compassion for ordinary people whom the religious leaders considered to be unrighteous.

Jesus knew that his expanding mission was stirring deep opposition. His message was a stinging critique of the religious and political order. The Roman occupation and the Jewish leaders all felt the threat Jesus posed to their power. Three times Jesus told the disciples that the outcome of his mission would be his death and resurrection.[29] To the disciples this was unbelievable.

Jesus' Mission Completed

After his ministry in Transjordan, Jesus began his final trip to Jerusalem. Near Jericho he healed a blind beggar and then went into the town, where he ate in the home of Zacchaeus, a despised tax collector, and in fact evangelized him.[30] From Jericho, Jesus and the disciples headed for Jerusalem. As they approached the city, Jesus rode on a colt, and the scene turned into the "triumphal entry into Jerusalem" with a "whole multitude of the disciples" that had witnessed "all the deeds of power" by Jesus joining in the procession. They exuberantly shouted, "Blessed is the king who comes in the name of the Lord! Peace in heaven, and glory in the highest heaven!"—a paraphrase of the earlier divine announcement by angels to shepherds at the time of Jesus' birth. This reveals that the crowd did not fully understand God's intention for peace *on earth*.[31]

By riding that colt into Jerusalem, Jesus was proclaiming that his mission was in fulfillment of the prophecy of Zechariah, who wrote that the promised Messiah would ride a colt thereby proclaiming his universal kingdom of peace.

By riding that colt into Jerusalem, Jesus was proclaiming that his mission was in fulfillment of the prophecy of Zechariah some five centuries earlier, who wrote that the promised Messiah would ride a colt thereby proclaiming his universal kingdom of peace.

> I will take away the chariots from Ephraim
> and the war horses from Jerusalem,
> and the battle bow will be broken.
> He will proclaim peace to the nations.
> His rule will extend from sea to sea
> and from the River to the ends of the earth.[32]

The singing throngs had no idea, of course, that this king of peace would be crucified! During the next several days Jesus was busy teaching in the temple. But he knew the showdown was fast approaching. Each night he retreated to the Mount of Olives where he prayed and prepared for the next day, "and all the people came early in the morning to hear him at the temple."[33] The people had high hopes. But within days these high hopes were dashed when Jesus was arrested, brought to trial and sentenced to death.

In spite of Jesus' attempts to prepare them for this outcome, none of the disciples could make sense of what was happening. They felt helpless and assumed that the messianic movement had failed. Their beloved Master had died an ignominious death, though he had at least been given a decent burial in the tomb of Joseph of Arimathea. When women from their group brought the news on Sunday morning that he was alive, they were incredulous.

Jesus' mission on earth was not yet finished. The Gospels report several post-resurrection appearances by Jesus.[34] Jesus used these occasions to give the disciples their final instructions. He reminded them of what he had told them along the way and that the prophets had predicted, "The Christ will suffer and rise from the dead on the third day." After that "repentance and forgiveness of sins will be preached in his name to all nations, beginning from Jerusalem." Their privileged position as "witnesses of these things" prepared them to lead this worldwide witness.[35]

Jesus now said, "As the Father has sent me, I am sending you."[36] But one more thing must happen before starting this movement to the nations. Echoing Jesus' own baptism, he tells the disciples that the Holy Spirit will empower them for this special task.

Until then there was no church. On the day of Pentecost, fifty days after the crucifixion of Jesus, the Holy Spirit came upon the disciples. At that time Peter preached a sermon in which he reviewed God's acts in history.

The church is a fruit of evangelization. Wherever and whenever evangelization ceases the church dies.

Pentecost links two developments: the formation of the church and the launching of the worldwide mission.[37] Apostolic proclamation of the gospel always comes first. The church is a fruit of evangelization. Wherever and whenever evangelization ceases the church dies.

Jesus the Messiah entrusted to his disciple community the mission that God the Father and God the Holy Spirit had given him when he was sent into the world. Mission is the heart of discipleship.

Witnesses of the Gospel in All Circumstances

The sixteenth-century Anabaptists understood the spirit and intention of Jesus. They rejected the idea that baptizing newborns made an entire society "Christian." An efficient religious system cannot guarantee a faithful church. They argued that discipleship must be based on an individual's heartfelt acceptance of the lordship of Jesus Christ and living as a witness of the gospel in all circumstances. It meant embracing the way of Jesus—love for all people and cultivating practices of compassion, justice, mercy, and peacemaking as a testimony to the transforming power of the gospel.

Jesus began his ministry announcing the kingdom. With his crucifixion only days away, he reminded the disciples that this good news "will be preached in the world as a testimony to all nations, and then the end will come."[38] After his resurrection Jesus told his followers that he was now entrusting to them the responsibility to share the good news of the kingdom with the whole world.

Mission permeates all of life—not just on Sundays, not just "special persons," but in all circumstances.

For the Anabaptists Jesus' final commission defined the church's permanent responsibility to the world. This called for concrete action. Baptism was for adults because it involved an unconditional commitment to discipleship expressed in witness to the gospel in all circumstances. Mission permeates all of life—not just on Sundays, not just "special persons," but in all circumstances. A contemporary application of this conviction affirms that, "Baptism is also an act of identifying with God's mission to the world." The person being baptized is asked, "Do you desire to be baptized upon this faith in Christ, and to be received into the church of Jesus Christ, identifying yourself with God's mission for the world through the church?"[39] This is the point around which all other life decisions revolve. Jesus the Messiah is our living model.

Questions for Discussion

1. What experiences have you had with persons committed to the mission of Jesus in all circumstances?

2. Jesus sent his followers to share his message of the kingdom and make this kingdom visible through signs of healing and deliverance. What do you do and say that point others to the kingdom?

3. Describe the connection between discipleship to Jesus and mission.

4. Immediately after Jesus embraced God's mission in baptism in the Jordan River, Satan challenged him. What challenges does the church face today in fulfilling its mission? Since Jesus did not arm his followers with physical weapons, how do we persevere in mission in the face of obstacles, challenges, and the powers of evil?

5. This chapter indicates God's mission is global and personal. "Jesus ministered to each person at the point of greatest personal stress." Examine one of the following scriptures in light of what you have learned in this chapter:

    1. The Paralytic and Four Friends (Luke 5:17-26)

    2. The Syro-Phoenecian Woman (Mark 7:24-30)

    3. Zacchaeus (Luke 19:1-10)

    4. The Rich Ruler—and Peter (Luke 18:18-30)

6. In what ways do you observe Jesus ministering to people in times of personal stress today?

Notes
  1. See Luke 2:41-50.
  2. Luke 22:42.
  3. Mark 1:10-11, and parallel passages.
  4. Matthew 3:13-17; Mark 1:9-11; Luke 3:21-22.
  5. Matthew 3:16.
  6. Mark 1:12.
  7. Matthew 4:1-11; Mark 1:12-13; Luke 4:1-13.

8. Luke 4:14.

9. Luke 4:15.

10. Mark 1:15; Matthew 4:17; Luke 4:18-19.

11. Matthew 5–7.

12. John 4:1-42.

13. John 4:39.

14. Luke 4:32.

15. Matthew 11:28.

16. Luke 6:17-49; see also Matthew 5-7.

17. See Matthew 11:3.

18. Matthew 11:4-5; see Luke 1:46-56, 67-79; 2:29-32.

19. Luke 1:46-55, 67-80; 2:25-32.

20. Luke 5:1-11.

21. Luke 3:21; 5:16; 6:12; 9:18, 28; 11:1-4; 18:1-6; Matthew 6:9-13.

22. Luke 24:10.

23. Luke 9:1b-2.

24. Luke 9:5.

25. Luke 9:10.

26. Luke 9:20.

27. Luke 10:1. Some manuscripts say that Jesus sent out seventy-two disciples.

28. Luke 15:3-7.

29. Luke 9:21-22, 43-45; 18:31-33.

30. Luke 9:1-10.

31. Luke 2:14; cf. Isaiah 57:19.

32. Zechariah 9:10.

33. Luke 21:38.

34. Luke 24:36-49; Mark 16:9-18; Matthew 28:16-20; John 20:19-23; Acts 1:6-8.

35. Luke 24:46-48.

36. John 20:21.

37. Acts 2.

38. Matthew 24:14.

39. *Mennonite Minister's Manual*, (1983) 21.

Chapter 14

Jesus and the Church

Robert J. Suderman with Andrew Suderman
and Irene, Bryan, Derek, Julie, Rebecca, and Karen
Suderman

— Narrative: *Jesus proclaims the kingdom and calls a community* —
of disciples to become fishers of people! (Matthew 4:12-22)

The church is a tough sell in the western world. Good words
are used to talk about Jesus—radical, revolutionary, countercultural, subversive, prophetic, alternative. Not so good words
are used to talk about the church—institutional, bureaucratic,
self-serving, conservative, slow, irrelevant, limiting, calcified,
resistant to change, out of date.

In Canada, where I live, a large majority (80 percent) of our
population identifies itself as Christian, but a declining minority
(16 percent) says it is connected to the church. In other words,
64 percent of Canadians prefer Christianity without the church.
This is serious. It could be described as a mutiny against the
church by Christians themselves.

Yet there is enormous interest
in spiritual matters in our society.
Evidence for the search and yearn-
ing for spirituality fills bookshelves
and the screens. Our western societies are not only secular, nor are
they atheistic. If anything, there is
a rejuvenated sense of the sacred and an increasing conviction that
there are powers beyond what is visible and knowable. There is a

> Sixty-four percent of Canadians
> prefer Christianity without the
> church. This is serious. It could be
> described as a mutiny against the
> church by Christians themselves.

sense of the transcendent nature of life and an understanding that there is more to life than the temporal, the visible, and the tangible. Science has not managed to demystify our human experience. We continue to be deeply spiritual people.

The Core Questions

Can Christianity address this deep spiritual longing without reference to the church? Is Christianity without the church still Christian? Is there a necessary connection between Jesus and the church? Is church an *essential* or *optional* part of the gospel? We want to explore these questions in this chapter.

A Step Closer

The New Testament was first written in the Greek language. The Greek word that is translated as "church" is *ekklesia*. Scholars have often pointed to the fact that Jesus doesn't use that word much. Indeed, there are only three times in the four gospels that the word *ekklesia* is used at all: Matthew 16:18 and twice in Matthew 18:17. This is remarkable when we think of the stature to which the church has risen since the time of Jesus.

> Is Christianity without the church still Christian? Is there a necessary connection between Jesus and the church? Is church an *essential* or *optional* part of the gospel?

The near absence of this word on Jesus' lips is striking given the fact that it is used 111 times in the rest of the New Testament. In Paul's letters alone it appears sixty-four times. Scholars have often pondered this significant shift of the use of *ekklesia* in the biblical text. There is another term that Jesus does use a lot, indeed it seems to be a favorite symbol. The word kingdom—*basilea* in Greek, appears 124 times in the Gospels. While Jesus favored this word, it is used less by other New Testament writers, especially Paul. This too has been noticed by New Testament scholars and has led some to observe that although Jesus proclaimed the kingdom, he got the church. They assume that there is a fundamental contradiction between Jesus' concept of the coming kingdom and Paul's commitment to forming the church.

The near absence of this word on Jesus' lips is striking given the fact that it is used 111 times in the rest of the New Testament.

Jesus' Definition of *Gospel*

We can test whether the church plays a significant role in Jesus' vision by asking how he understands what is good about the news that he proclaims. Fortunately, we have such a statement, and it is succinct and clear. These are the very first public words spoken by Jesus, according to Mark's Gospel, and we need to pay very close attention to them: "After John was arrested, Jesus came into Galilee, preaching the *gospel* of God, and saying, "The time is fulfilled, and the kingdom of God is at hand; repent, and believe in the *gospel*."[1]

In the Greek language, the word "gospel" is *evanggelion*. It is actually two words—*eu* (*ev*), which is the Greek way of making something normal into something very good and positive, and *anggelion* simply means a message. So Jesus is delivering a "positive message" from God. What he is saying is "good news," and the word is often translated that way.

This positive, inaugural message proclaimed by Jesus has two elements:

- The time (*kairos*) is fulfilled,
- The kingdom of God is at hand.

Nothing more. God's time is here (time is *kairos* in Greek). God's kingdom is at hand; it has arrived. This is it. According to Jesus, the gospel is that in God's timing, God's kingdom has become accessible. The rest of Mark's Gospel attempts to flesh out this good news.

Jesus' definition of gospel is only nine words in Greek. Because it is so brief, it is tempting to make it more complex than it is. We should not. This is the core of what the good news of God is. The time of God has been fulfilled; and God's kingdom is coming into our midst.

Jesus' definition of gospel is only nine words in Greek. Because it is so brief, it is tempting to make it more complex than it is. We should not.

Because the statement is so succinct, it also invites the reader to flesh it out more. The first century hearer would have made immediate connections to common understandings of God's time and kingdom. But they did not find it easy to move beyond their immediate impulses and assumptions. The rest of Mark's Gospel shows that although Jesus was saying some of the expected things, he meant some things that were quite different from what was commonly assumed. They needed to flesh out what this meant in their lives, and so do we.

Gospel is about Kingdom Presence

Jesus' gospel is that the kingdom of God is present among us. It presumes that there is a ruler, there is authority, and that people are being governed. This kingdom points to authority rather than geography. The kingdom arriving means that although God's authority is accessible and active everywhere, it is only recognized and accepted in some circles. Some people are willing to live according to God's will and authority for their lives. Others are not yet willing to do so. That's why we often say that while the kingdom is already here, it is not yet completely here. The presence of the kingdom is not limited to those who consciously reorient their lives to it. But God hopes that all will live kingdom lives.

What does the world look like when the kingdom of God approaches and becomes real in our communities? That topic is big enough to fill this entire chapter, book, and lifetime. But let's at least think about this in broad strokes. (Chapter 5 has already explored significant dimensions of the kingdom; here we are especially concerned with the relationship of the church to the kingdom.)

Jesus' parables, teaching, and actions try to paint pictures of what this looks like. Demons no longer rule the lives of people. Sick persons are healed. Lepers are liberated. Fisherfolk form kingdom communities. The rich share their wealth. The powerful are merciful and compassionate. The violent ones opt for peace. The revolutionary commits to nonviolent strategies. The hungry are fed. The naked are clothed. The prisoners are set free. Debts are forgiven. Land is distributed. Slaves are freed. Women are treated as equals. Samaritans become heroes. Children are held up as models. Leaders are re-defined as servants. People die for rather than kill each other. Forgiveness rather than revenge is practiced. Justice is the new norm. Oppression is eliminated. God is worshipped.

In other words, there is a new way to be and to live. Values and ethics are redefined. Strategies are transformed. Honesty and truth replace corruption and lying. Enemies are loved rather than hated. Money is shared rather than hoarded. The change is comprehensive. It impacts politics, economics, religion, culture, family and marriage, social structures, and military reliance.

When God's kingdom comes into a community and God's authority is accepted, life is not the same. And this transformation of life is good news. It is a positive message. It is a desired outcome, unless of course, you benefit from corruption and violence, hoarding and revenge. Then things may become uncomfortable for you. And you may think of this presence as an enemy. And you might wish to shut it down and drive it away. You may even think of killing all the babies under the age of two to make sure this idea doesn't catch on. This was King Herod's response to the arrival of a new king and a new kingdom. Or you may believe that it is best to crucify the one who promotes such thinking. This is what the religious and political authorities did with Jesus.

> When God's kingdom comes into a community and God's authority is accepted, life is not the same. And this transformation of life is good news.

But it's not enough to focus only on the social transformation that happens when the kingdom comes. The most important ingredient of the coming kingdom is that people can actually change their behaviors, habits, and self-understanding. They are given the power to do so. We don't fully understand this power in our lives, but we see it transforming us and others around us. People who are participants in the kingdom have a new identity for they believe in and are committed to Jesus Christ; they bear witness that the transformation is the gift of God in Christ.

> The most important ingredient of the coming kingdom is that people can actually change their behaviors, habits, and self-understanding. They are given the power to do so.

The New Testament says that believers in Jesus are participants in the power of the resurrected Christ, that is at work in our lives. The power of God that was mighty enough to raise Jesus from the dead is now available to change our lives too. It also says it is the power of the Holy Spirit, giving us the discernment necessary for transformation and the courage needed for implementation. It also talks about this as being born again (or born from above), and being saved by the grace of God. It is talked about as salvation, reconciliation, and liberation.

The point is that God's Holy Spirit makes it possible to live transformed lives that reflect the presence of God's kingdom among us. The presence of the kingdom is not an impossible ideal or a high-hanging fruit that we cannot reach. We are assured that the kingdom is among us and that it is possible to align our lives with it now and allow it to change our priorities and our purpose.

Kingdom is about Peoplehood

It is possible that God expresses authority through angels, lightning, earthquakes, and wind. It is also true that God exercises authority through people and systems without them being conscious that it is God at work. But God prefers that kingdom presence be intentionally lived out in the lives of people. Kingdom, rule, authority, and reign are all word pictures that point to the existence of a peoplehood—an identifiable group committed to living out the authority of God in their personal and corporate lives. Such a peoplehood is not simply a group of isolated individuals, each one searching for his or her self-fulfillment.

A kingdom people is a community with a common and corporate personality, a communal identity. It figures out what it means to be faithful to the common authority. It worships the one God whose authority ties us to each other. Although it is not yet what it is meant to be, it tries to live as a public community that can be watched because it practices what it preaches. If others wish to see love, justice, equality, forgiveness, compassion, mercy, and such in action, they can come and look. People are patient with one another and are willing to submit to each other when there is disagreement. If people want to line up their own lives with the presence of God's kingdom on earth, they will have a place to join, where the transformed life of the kingdom can be discerned and lived out with others.

Such people and such a community will be discipled (disciplined) in the ways of kingdom living, whose habits and instincts are informed by the values and preferences of the presence of the kingdom among them. It will be a

> God's preferred strategy is that the kingdom be visible in the lives of communities and people who trust that it is here and who intentionally live according to it.

community that is visible, touchable, knowable, and enterable. Such a community is a peoplehood, and it is God's preferred Holy Spirit home, where Jesus' ongoing presence is celebrated and the Spirit's power to transform individual lives and ultimately the entire world is made visible.

When Jesus announced this gospel, he added that the hearers have two responsibilities so that this announcement can be transformed into good news.[2] They have to believe it, and they need to repent. To believe is to trust that this news is true, and to repent means to turn our lives around in such a way that they are compatible with the presence of the kingdom of God that is now among us.

God's preferred strategy is that the kingdom be visible in the lives of communities and people who trust that it is here and who intentionally live according to it. This visible peoplehood transforms the presence of the kingdom into good news.

Gospel is about Peoplehood

The announcement of gospel as kingdom presence includes the premise of peoplehood. Good news must be lived out and demonstrated in order for it to be really good news for anyone. Good news must be possible, not just theoretical. It must be verifiable, not just speculation. Given that kingdom presence is a word picture that is communal, the living out and demonstration of this presence also needs a communal expression. It needs to be visible within a body of persons, not merely in an individual here and there. Kingdom presence is a communal, social, political, economic, and relational presence. It is not simply meant to be an individual, inner, or personal preference.

It is not surprising that Jesus' first action after his inaugural announcement of the gospel was to form a community that would live according to this proclaimed kingdom presence.

It is, therefore, not surprising that Jesus' first action after his inaugural announcement of the gospel was to form a community that would live according to this proclaimed kingdom presence. Mark points to this community-building initiative immediately after Jesus proclaimed that the kingdom is near, and he called his first disciples to follow him. Walking by the Sea of Galilee, Jesus saw Simon and Andrew, two fishermen, and he called to them and said: "Follow me and I will make you fish for people."[3]

Such a communal understanding was not new to Jesus. He was a Jew, and he knew very well the strategy for healing the world that was described in the Old Testament and that God had

initiated long before. It was a strategy that would form one peoplehood with common foundations but having diverse gifts. God's
intention was that Israel would be a peoplehood of covenant,
torah (law), and wisdom. It would be a royal, prophetic, and
priestly community. It would be a faithful community, sent into
the world to be a blessing of God. This peoplehood would be an
alternative to the communities of the many other gods and faiths
that surrounded them. As the watching world observed these
communities, they would see in them the will of God for the healing of the world. God's call to Israel was that this community be
a light to the nations.

Jesus was well aware of this ancient peoplehood strategy, and
he built upon it. Just as there were twelve tribes in the people of
Israel, so Jesus chose twelve disciples. Just as these people were
bound together by covenant, so Jesus binds his new communities
together by covenant, to himself and to each other. Just as the
Israelites were people of the Law of Moses, so Jesus indicates that
his communities are people committed to his authority, for he is the
fulfillment of the law. Just as the Israelites were asked to accept God
as their king, so Jesus announces that God continues to be the ruler
of the kingdom presence. There is,
however, a new element in Jesus'
understanding. It is that covenant,
law, prophetic presence, royalty,
priesthood, and wisdom now need
to be understood through his own
living out of these things.

From the beginning of Jesus' ministry,
the formation of a community was
integral to his proclamation of gospel,
and gospel was integral to his understanding of peoplehood.

From the beginning of Jesus' ministry, the formation of a community was integral to his proclamation of gospel, and gospel was
integral to his understanding of peoplehood. The two are inseparable. It is no longer good news when either one is neglected.

That was Jesus' intention, to form a peoplehood who would
embody the good news of the kingdom. For three years Jesus
taught and modeled the kingdom among his disciples. Nevertheless
the disciples did not entirely catch on. In many ways they failed the

test. The night of the Last Supper they argued quite combatively about who was the greatest among them. One of them went out into the night to implement his plan to betray Jesus. Later when soldiers came to arrest Jesus, Peter resorted to the violence of the sword in a futile attempt to protect Jesus. That very night as the trial of Jesus was unfolding, Peter three times denied knowing Jesus, and he even strengthened his denial with curses. The disciples fled. They abandoned Jesus. Three years of being with Jesus had not fully formed them into kingdom peoplehood!

However, within the next several weeks the disciples understood better. What happened? Jesus was crucified, and he was raised from the dead! Subsequently the Holy Spirit was poured out upon them. (See chapters 6, 8, 9, and 10.) The disciples, filled with the Holy Spirit at Pentecost, were astounded when they understood better what had transpired in Jesus crucified and risen. Reflecting many years later on the transformation wrought in his own life and others, Peter wrote, "[Jesus] bore our sins in his body on the tree, so that we might die to sins and live for righteousness; by his wounds you have been healed. For you were like sheep going astray, but now you have returned to the Shepherd and Overseer of your souls."[4] In those brief sentences Peter bears witness to his own experience of forgiveness, restoration, redemption and inclusion in kingdom peoplehood. This community is formed when people, like Peter, respond to the transforming Gospel of Jesus Christ as proclaimed in Jesus' life, teachings, crucifixion, and resurrection and in the ongoing ministry of the Holy Spirit in their lives.

Church is about Peoplehood

Jesus, Paul, and other New Testament writers understood the fruit of the gospel in terms of kingdom communities living under the authority of God's will in the power of the Holy Spirit. The church was conceived in Jesus' understanding of the arrival of God's kingdom; it was initiated by calling the disciples into a kingdom community; it was shaped by his teaching, death, and resurrection; and it was nurtured anew by the outpouring of the Holy Spirit on the disciples at Pentecost. These communities of disciples continued to struggle with the fuller implications of being this new church, as was evident when the church was formed at Pentecost when the Holy Spirit was poured out upon the disciples. Nevertheless from that day on, they understood that the good news needed to be livable and lived, and that committed communities were needed to be living signs of the gospel.

The New Testament pictures such communities in many ways—as living stones, a royal priesthood, a temple of the Holy Spirit, God's field, the bride of Christ, a city on a hill, salt, an open letter, and so on. Indeed, one scholar, Paul Minear, has indicated that the New Testament uses ninety-six word pictures to describe the depth, height, and breadth of what it means to be these kingdom communities. Many of these word pictures come from Jesus. And all of them point to the central and critical role of peoplehood as primary in the gospel of God.

> The New Testament pictures such communities in many ways—as living stones, a royal priesthood, a temple of the Holy Spirit, God's field, the bride of Christ, a city on a hill, salt, an open letter, and so on.

One of these ninety-six pictures, the one that has become a shorthand way of talking about all of them, is *ekklesia*, translated "church." This word picture is instructive. It is made up of two Greek words—*ek* and *klesis*. *Ek* simply means out of or apart from. *Klesis* means a calling or a vocation. When used to describe a community, the word *ekklesia* literally means a specially vocationed peoplehood, or a peoplehood with a special calling. This is an *ek* vocation—it is outside the norm. These are vocationed communities that serve as signs that the kingdom of God as taught and lived by Jesus of Nazareth is among us. This is the focus that makes the church uniquely Christian. Paul plays with these words: "Lead a life worthy of the calling to which you have been called. . . . You were called to the one hope of your calling."[5]

Being worthy of the calling, i.e., being worthy to be the *ekklesia*, is an awesome and exciting vocation. For example, Paul says: "*So that through the church* the wisdom of God in its rich variety might now be made known to the rulers and authorities in the heavenly places."[6]

At the heart of this vocation is a mandate to teach, to instruct rulers and authorities about God's wisdom and purpose. This is a critical responsibility and an amazing task.

This vocationed peoplehood will teach not only with words. The curriculum and textbook for teaching will be the life of the community formed by Christ and bearing witness to Christ. It is the vocation of providing alternative wisdom to the world, being a countercultural presence, inviting others to experience the qualities of life in kingdom communities, and worshipping the living God whose Spirit makes this all possible.

Does *church* mean an institutionalized, bureaucratic organization, irrelevant, slow to respond and limiting our potential? Obviously, this is not at all what Jesus had in mind. The church is meant to be an alternative community, subverting the values of our dominant society with kingdom of God priorities. It is to be radical, countercultural, and prophetic. It is to be a mobile and portable reservoir of kingdom living that can be present and contextualized everywhere. Because the agenda of the *ekklesia* is the agenda of God's kingdom, its interests are not narrow but broadly inclusive of all things that impact the welfare of society as well as creation.

> Does *church* mean an institutionalized, bureaucratic organization, irrelevant, slow to respond and limiting our potential? Obviously, this is not at all what Jesus had in mind.

As Jesus followers, we are instructed to cultivate the good news so that it is not forgotten, but is accessible and can be lived and experienced over and over. We are to discern evil and good, teach, baptize, and forgive. We are to break bread and drink the cup as again and again we receive Jesus' grace and forgiveness and remember and commit to the choices he made as our kingdom guide. He showed us how to organize in groups of two, fifty, and five thousand, heal the sick, overthrow corrupt tables, confront the powers, pray, and finance ministry. We are to celebrate the ongoing presence of Jesus among us.

Jesus wanted his movement to be continuous and viable. We are heirs of that intention and need to take it seriously, because the good news he announced is just as important today as it was then. If the church is not behaving as it should, then instead of inventing a churchless gospel, which in reality is no longer the gospel of Jesus, we should commit ourselves to changing the church so that it is worthy of its vocation. As the church of Christ, we want to make sure that the gospel can be experienced again and again in every context. And we want to make sure that this peoplehood is accessible to all people and to the nations, so that all can experience life under the authority of God.

Testimonials of Two Young Adults

In an age when in some regions of the West there is cynicism about the church, it is also true that across North America and around the world millions of young adults are finding a "home" in the church—a place of grace, forgiveness, healing and commitment to Christ and his kingdom people. Here are two testimonies of young adults and their experience with the church.

Andrew Suderman
I grew up in a home devoted to God and the church. When I was a child I remember asking my dad one Sunday morning, "Do I *have* to go to church?" "Only if you don't want to," he responded. Church participation was assumed.

When I was a youth, we lived in Colombia, South America. It seemed that the people of the Colombian Mennonite Church also assumed that participation in the church and its work were important. They have accomplished incredible things because every member is willing to be part of a body that witnesses to an alternate way of living in a country that has been ravaged and devastated by fifty years of civil war. People willingly participate as the church witnesses to a life of peace rather than war.

Back in Canada, I was disillusioned and skeptical because of what I perceived to be a stagnant, professionalized, bickering, and seemingly inactive church. This was difficult, especially because I was coming from a country where the church was so active, vibrant, hopeful, and purposeful. This led to a time in my life when I was very critical of the church in North America.

In college I began to realize that my perception of the North American church was not entirely accurate. There are members and churches that were active, striving to do God's will. There are those who live out and witness to an alternate way of living in their daily lives. Although the church is filled with imperfect people, I learned that even in their imperfection the church is also filled with people who care and want to be active in being God's missional people. I learned that instead of fighting against the church it is more helpful and fruitful to challenge the church by being part of it. Today I see people who strive to be faithful witnesses to God's mission in our world. My criticism of and love for the church are now also directed at me.

> I learned that instead of fighting against the church it is more helpful and fruitful to challenge the church by being part of it.

Vicki Butzer

I believe that Jesus intended the church to be a community of grace and forgiveness that generously welcomes all. That is how I have experienced the church.

I grew up in the neighborhood bar where my mother worked. By young adulthood my first marriage was broken and I was in despair. An older couple became the welcome of Jesus for me. As I came to Jesus, my life was transformed through a deep work of the Holy Spirit. On the Sunday morning when I became a covenant member of the church, I wept as I shared with the congregation the amazing grace of Jesus Christ for me.

With joy I shared: "Some among you might feel that I am not worthy to be part of this congregation. But I am worthy to be your sister, for I am a sinner redeemed through the grace of our Lord Jesus Christ."

Then I observed that it was not just me weeping. The entire congregation was weeping tears of joy at the wonder of it all.

Questions for Discussion

1. Are the two components identified by Jesus in Mark 1:14, i.e., "the time has been fulfilled" and "the kingdom of God has drawn near," central to your congregation's gospel understandings as demonstrated in the teaching, preaching, and strategic planning of the congregation? How are they evident in your congregation's practice?

2. This chapter suggests a connected sequence from Jesus to gospel to kingdom presence to kingdom people to church. In other words, the church is *essentially*, and not *marginally*, connected to the message that Jesus proclaimed. Is this connected sequence compelling to you? What difference does or should it make for your church?

3. The author states near the end of this chapter: "If the church is not behaving as it should, then instead of inventing a churchless gospel, which in reality is no longer the gospel of Jesus, we should commit ourselves to changing the church so that it is worthy of its vocation." Discuss the implications of this statement for your own faith and commitments to faith.

4. Jesus indicates in Mark 1:15 that the most important way of responding to the gospel is by *believing* that the Kingdom indeed has become present in our world and by *repenting*, aligning our lives with this presence. What are the obstacles that

make this difficult in our society? What are the elements that make it easy?

Notes

1. Mark 1:14-15 RSV (italics added).
2. Mark 1:15.
3. Mark 1:16-17 NRSV.
4. 1 Peter 2:24-25.
5. Ephesians 4:1-4 NRSV.
6. Ephesians 3:10 NRSV (italics added).

Chapter 15

Jesus Encountering the Religions

David W. Shenk with Linford Fisher
and Weston Shertzer, Jonathan Herr, Ryan Showalter,
and Jon Heinly

———— Narrative: *Jesus' encounter with the Samaritan woman*————
at Jacob's well (John 4:1-26)

The Sultan of Maguindanao in Mindanao, Philippines, hosted a dinner for five North American and Filipino representatives of the Mennonite Church, including me (David). The sultan described Muslim-Christian wars that had ravished his region. He told of Islam coming to Mindanao in centuries past; he was the descendant of the first Sultan.

Then the feasting paused, as the Christian guests absorbed his next statement. "You are peacemakers, and we welcome you. However, if you hope that Muslims become Christians, that is religious imperialism, and you should leave my community."

I responded, "Twice Muslim imams have wept as they pled, 'Become a Muslim!' They feared that my belief that Jesus is the Son of God will damn me. I experience these pleas as compassion, not religious imperialism. We are grateful that you have welcomed our people to serve among you. As they serve in the way of Jesus, sometimes others decide that they also want to walk in the way of Jesus. If we forbid them, wouldn't that be religious imperialism, to say that we and no others may believe in and serve Jesus?"

Surprisingly the Sultan responded, "Yes! To forbid others to follow Jesus is indeed imperialism."

The dialogue with the Sultan was about whether it is right to bear witness to the beliefs that form our life commitments. Christians confess, "Jesus is Lord!" For the Sultan, the Qur'an of Islam was his center. He believed that he was responsible to protect his community from temptations to leave Islam. That dinner conversation was really about truth claims in a world of many religions.

Surprisingly the Sultan responded, "Yes! To forbid others to follow Jesus is indeed imperialism."

Different 'Truths'

A key challenge is that there are different claims to "truth." The struggle about different truths within the home of the Sultan is our worldwide reality. My next door neighbor in small-town Pennsylvania is Muslim. A previous neighbor was Jewish. I've also had Buddhist neighbors and a patriot who has painted his birdhouses red, white, and blue. Linford and his wife, Jo, have lived in an international house with students professing a mosaic of religious diversity.

There are passionate advisers on what to do about conflicting claims to truth:

- *Agnostics* insist that we cannot know the truth.
- *Pluralists* proclaim there are many valid truths.
- *Universalists* believe that all truths lead to the same destiny; we climb the same mountain, but from different sides.
- *Relativists* are convinced that each society develops its own truth.
- American *individualists* honor the individual as the final authority in determining truth.
- *New Age* proponents see all phenomena as true expressions of the divine spirit. In Buddhism, they note, there is no

Creator God, whereas the Bible reveals the Creator God. This does not present a problem in New Age spirituality; both of these contradictory convictions are accepted as true.

So, what, we might well wonder, does Jesus contribute to this cacophony of counsel?

Jesus and the World of Many Religions

The world at the time of Jesus was enthusiastically religious, with people worshipping a multitude of gods. The Romans, who ruled Israel at the time of Jesus, worshipped gods such as the "genius" of the emperor; Mars, the god of war; Jupiter, the god of state—to name only a few. They never objected to the Jewish commitment to their God, Yahweh. However, they forthrightly objected to the Jewish insistence that Yahweh was the only true God. That drove the Romans crazy, for they expected citizens to honor all the gods. So, what can we learn from Jesus and his ministry, carried out in this religiously diverse environment?

The world at the time of Jesus was enthusiastically religious, with people worshipping a multitude of gods.

The account of Jesus and the Samaritan woman is an example of how Jesus related to religious people who were not of the Jewish faith. The history of the Samaritans was complex. Eight centuries before Jesus, the Israelite tribes living in the north of Israel with Samaria as their capital were taken from their land by the Assyrians. Only the poorest were allowed to remain. Non-Israelites were moved into this region. The Samaritan people derived from the mixed parentage of the remaining Jews and immigrant aliens. During the time of Jesus, the region of Samaria, occupied by these people of "mixed linage," was nestled between Judea in the south and Galilee in the north, both of which were predominantly Jewish.

The Samaritan religion was by Jewish standards "syncretistic," that is, a mixture of Jewish faith and polytheism. In the polytheistic religions of Canaan, natural phenomena were considered divine. The high hills, for example, represented pregnancy. So in the groves on the high hills the ancient Canaanites offered sacrifices and participated in religious rites to induce fertility among people and the land. Mount Gerizim in Samaria was viewed in a similar way by the Samaritans. They believed that this mount was the umbilical cord uniting heaven and earth, and they believed that Adam and Eve had been created on that mountain. Their mountain was the sacred center of the earth. In case the Jewish Yahweh was offended by their worship on Mount Gerizim, the Samaritans sometimes went to Jerusalem to worship in the Jewish way.

> The Samaritan religion was by Jewish standards "syncretistic," that is, a mixture of Jewish faith and polytheism.

The Jews were offended by all of this. When traveling between Judea and Galilee, Israelites took an extra couple days to detour around Samaria. Jesus, however, broke that taboo and traveled right through Samaria on one of his trips from Judea to Galilee. He met a Samaritan woman of dubious character at Jacob's well, while his disciples were in town to buy lunch.

In his multifaceted conversation with the woman, Jesus blessed her by asking for a drink, helped her to recognize and own her sin related to men and marriage, asserted that God invites worship in spirit and truth, sidelined the disputes about the most sacred place to worship—Gerizim or Jerusalem—and revealed that he was the Messiah. In essence Jesus declared that neither Jewish nor Samaritan religious practices save. It is God who saves and he himself, Jesus, is the Savior-Messiah whom God had promised through the prophets and the Scriptures.

> Jesus declared that neither Jewish nor Samaritan religious practices save. It is God who saves and he himself, Jesus, is the Savior-Messiah whom God had promised through the prophets and the Scriptures.

Salvation is from the Jews

The woman was astounded by the respectful way that Jesus related to her. Deep respect for the woman, however, did not imply that Jesus accepted her misguided beliefs or her lifestyle of attaching herself to different men. Jesus made this jolting statement, "You Samaritans worship what you do not know; we worship what we do know, for salvation is from the Jews!"[1]

When the woman asserted that when the Messiah comes "he will explain everything to us," Jesus exclaimed, "I who speak to you am he."[2] In jubilation she ran to the city proclaiming to the town that the Messiah was at the well and by evening much of the town had believed. They said to the woman, "We no longer believe just because of what you said; now we have heard for ourselves, and we know that this man really is the Savior of the world."[3]

This Samaritan town of "outsiders" had become "insiders." Although Jesus proclaimed that salvation was from the Jews, Israel found it more difficult to receive salvation than the Samaritans whom they rejected. Yet the bridge to salvation over which the Samaritans traveled from their religion to meet Jesus was the gift of salvation offered by the Jews. What does this mean?

Although Jesus proclaimed that salvation was from the Jews, Israel found it more difficult to receive salvation than the Samaritans whom they rejected.

If Jesus had positioned himself within Samaritan syncretistic nature-worshipping religion, the Samaritans would have viewed him as just another hero god. He rejected that option. "Salvation is from the Jews," he insisted. In other words the Samaritans with their Mount Gerizim cult had gotten it wrong. To get it right, they needed to receive the revelation of the Jewish scriptures and meet the Messiah that those scriptures revealed. (See chapter 2, "Jesus and the Bible").

Linford

I have concerns about that observation! The students at the international house have always been intrigued with the ethics of Jesus. They don't need Old Testament Jewish scriptures to appreciate Jesus.

David

I agree with you, Linford, that people can appreciate Jesus without the Jewish Scriptures. However, Jesus is more than a teacher of ethics. He is the Messiah. That is why I believe salvation in Jesus is best understood through God's revelation to the Jewish people wherein the vocation of the Messiah is revealed.

Through the ages God was preparing the world to receive Jesus the Savior. God called the Jewish people to be the carriers of the divine plan. About two thousand years before Jesus, God called Abraham and from Abraham's descendants he called forth Israel to be his covenant people through whom salvation would come to the whole earth. So when Jesus said, "Salvation is from the Jews," this was not just a statement about beliefs and worldviews. It was also recognition that through the covenant people, Israel, God was moving across the centuries to prepare for the coming of the Savior.

Linford

I consider that most remarkable when we consider how messy Israel's history was. Much is not edifying, and some just horrible.

David

I agree. Yet within the messiness, through these people of the covenant, God was preparing them and the world for the coming of the Savior. Unfortunately, however, when the Messiah finally did appear and begin his ministry, it was the Jewish religious establishment that gave him his greatest grief.

Truth Engaging Distortions of Truth

Every religion has narratives, myths, and belief systems that form its worldview. Nevertheless, salvation in Jesus is best understood in the context of God's revelation to the people of Israel and his call and covenant with them. The Old Testament is an essential bridge from the religions to Jesus, and it is a corrective to distorted beliefs.

For example, Buddhist philosophy has no awareness of a creator God and teaches that each person is his or her own savior; no person or god can save you. The goal of life is to get off the meaningless wheel of birth and rebirth so as to be absorbed into nirvana, that is, "emptiness." Jesus as Savior is nonsense within this Buddhist worldview.

Just as God's revelation to the Jews was a corrective to Samaritan beliefs, so also biblical revelation can become a corrective to the Buddhist worldview, preparing the way for the mission of Jesus to be understood. The Bible, for example, states clearly that God is the creator, that humans are created in God's image, and that God's gracious intention for all people is eternal life as persons. The Bible is also clear, however, that we have turned away from God and are in need of a Savior. When a Buddhist is introduced to biblical revelation, his or her worldview can be transformed, making it possible for Jesus as Savior to make sense.

Biblical revelation addresses all religions. Some religions worship nature gods, like the leopard for the Wakiroba people among whom I lived as a child. Biblical revelation frees from the terror of the leopard-god as well as all forms of nature worship, for it reveals that there is one transcendent creator God who is righteous, just, and loving.

Hinduism views the material world, including the phenomenon of bodily personhood, as an unfortunate illusion. Biblical revelation reveals that the material world, including the human body, is created good and real. This was affirmed most clearly when God in Jesus "became flesh and made his dwelling among us" in human, bodily form.[4]

Islam teaches that God sends his will down to us, but God does not come down to save us. The Bible on the other hand is the account of God coming down into our world through numerous acts of salvation and supremely in Jesus.

The gods people worship are often the projection of their own cultures. Warlike societies worship warlike gods; peaceful societies worship gods of peace. The Bible is clear—any god who is our creation is a false god. The prophet Jeremiah sarcastically likens the gods people create to a "scarecrow in a melon patch, their idols cannot speak; they must be carried because they cannot walk."[5]

> The gods people worship are often the projection of their own cultures. The Bible is clear—any god who is our creation is a false god.

Jesus believed the Old Testament worldview, although he also transcended it. He was forthright in his claim of authority to both clarify and fulfill the Old Testament.[6] It is, therefore, wise not only to believe in Jesus but to also commit to his worldview. For example, to believe in Jesus and also to worship nature gods is a contradiction that cannot be resolved.

The worship of false gods has immense moral implications, for the gods of nature or the gods people create are not noted for their morality. This is why the ancient Greek philosopher, Socrates, criticized the gods. He argued that one could not build a moral society when worshipping immoral gods, a critique that the Jewish scriptures also made.[7] The apostle Paul lamented the immorality of those who "exchanged the truth of God for a lie, and worshipped and served created things rather than the Creator."[8] Distorted religion justifies human sinfulness.

Like the Samaritan worldview, all religions are prone to distortion. Human sinfulness is mirrored in the religions. That was also true of the Jews. Amazing, isn't it? On the one hand Jesus said that salvation is of the Jews, yet he was often in conflict with the Jewish establishment, who seriously distorted the truth of God.

The biblical prophets proclaim that the only true God is the righteous, transcendent, personal Creator. Jesus is the clarification event in whom our Creator is fully revealed. He encounters us and calls for our repentance—that is, to make a U-turn away from all false gods and worship only the Creator. False gods do not call for repentance. However, God our creator, who is most fully revealed in Jesus, does call for repentance. That is why repentance is so central to biblical faith.

Signs of Truth

There are, of course, signs of truth within the religions, for God has not left himself without a witness.[9] The opening sentences of John's Gospel state, "The true light that gives light to everyone was coming into the world."[10] This suggests that there are glimmers of light within everyone, and Jesus brings to fullness those flickers of light. Paul observed, quoting from the teachings of Moses, "The word is near you; it is in your mouth and in your heart."[11] On one occasion Paul preached to the people of Athens and quoted from their philosophers, not from the Jewish scriptures, when he said, "In him we live and move and have our being."[12] Here and elsewhere Paul discerned truth within the writings of Greek philosophers, despite his deep and abiding commitment to the God of Israel revealed in Jesus.[13]

Wherever people receive the Gospel, they discern that God has been preparing them to hear and believe in Jesus. For example, even in their syncretistic worship, as we have seen, the Samaritans did believe that the Messiah and Savior would someday appear.

Likewise, although Muslims might not understand Jesus as Savior, all Muslims believe that Jesus is the Messiah. Nevertheless, as one reads the Qur'an it is clear that the full meaning of Messiah is obscured. However, that mysterious term has led many Muslims to faith in Jesus as they explore from the Bible the meaning of Jesus as Messiah. There are signs of truth in all religions, but the Samaritan woman got it right when she exclaimed, "When [the Messiah] comes, he will explain everything to us."[14] The signs of truth are only signs; the fulfillment of these signs is in Jesus the Messiah.

> Wherever people receive the Gospel, they discern that God has been preparing them to hear and believe in Jesus.

Reconciled to God!

An amazing sign of truth within the religions is the nearly universal awareness of a creator God. There are now some three thousand languages that have some portion of the Bible. With very few exceptions, the name for God in these Bible translations is a local pre-Christian name for a creator God. Buddhism is an exception, for Buddhism has no awareness of a creator God. However, in most translations the name for the Creator is the One that people had an awareness of before the Gospel message was proclaimed.

The understanding of God was of course different than that found in biblical revelation. In African traditional religion, for example, it was thought that God had gone away and would never return. Imagine the surprise when these people read in the Scriptures that the God they thought had abandoned them had never gone away at all. New believers in traditional societies dance with joy when they discover that in Jesus God has appeared among them in fullness and that they are reconciled to God. In these instances and others, biblical revelation radically transforms people's understandings of the God of whom they had had some previous knowledge, although, in the light of biblical revelation, that awareness was only partial or distorted.

I have engaged in conversations with people from diverse religions and cultures in some one hundred countries. I often ask new believers, "In what ways is Jesus good news?" Here are a few of their responses:

- South Korea (Buddhist)—In Buddhism there is no forgiveness; in Jesus I have received forgiveness of sin.
- West Kalimantan, Indonesia (nature worshipper)—Squawking birds terrified us, for they were the omens of the nature gods. Jesus has triumphed over the gods of nature, so we are not afraid of the birds anymore.
- Germany (atheist)—Jesus has freed me from guilt and depression.
- India (Hindu)—I was an outcaste; in Jesus I am included in the family of God.
- East Africa (traditionalist)—I have received salvation.
- Somalia (Muslim)—Because of Jesus I know God as my loving heavenly Father.
- Thailand (Buddhist)—Joy!
- United States (secularist)—In Jesus I have found abundant life and real purpose.
- Central Asia (Muslim)—Jesus has freed me from the burden of religious ritual.
- Burkina Faso (spirit worshipper)—The spirits were terrifying; Jesus has freed me from all the powers and now I am filled with the power of the Holy Spirit.
- Bulgaria (Muslim)—Jesus loves me!

A most astounding transformation is the revelation of God as loving heavenly Father. Jesus said, "I am the way and the truth and the life. No one comes to the Father except through me."[15] This does not mean that there is no awareness of God in the religions. However, in Jesus Christ we are forgiven, reconciled to God, and adopted into the family of God. We become daughters and sons of God; we know God as our Abba (Papa). Amazing!

Conclusion

Linford

For six years my wife, Jo, and I managed an international house for male students in Boston. We met hundreds of guys from around the world—Buddhists, Hindus, Muslims, atheists, agnostics, and every kind of Christian. We learned that presence and bearing witness for Christ had to be a two-way street, just as Jesus modeled in his meeting with the Samaritan woman. Until we really knew a student, he would not take our faith seriously. Developing friendship often opened the door for us to introduce students to Jesus.

Many students were interested in dialogue about faith. Most appreciated Jesus' ethics—"love your neighbor as yourself." However, the confession, "Jesus is the way and the truth and the life," was a perplexity for many of the students. Just as the Samaritan woman was intrigued with Jesus, so it was with these internationals.

Jesus used the metaphor of seed-planting and harvest to describe ministry among the Samaritans. Jo and I planted seeds. We do not always see immediate results of seed-planting; it is God who creates the harvest.[16]

Questions for Discussion

1. Describe your response to the way Jesus related to the Samaritan woman.

2. Unpack the meaning of Jesus' statement, "Salvation is from the Jews."

3. How do your friends who are not committed to the Christian faith respond to this statement: Jesus is the Way? How might you explain that statement in a way that they really hear the good news of the gospel?

4. Consider ways that modern culture communicates "a lie" about the meaning of life. Then consider signs of truth within modern culture.

5. How can the church more fruitfully bear witness to Jesus in our pluralistic world?

Notes
1. John 4:22.
2. John 4:25-26.
3. John 4:42.
4. John 1:14.
5. Jeremiah 10:5.
6. Matthew 5:17-48.
7. Jeremiah 10:1-5; Isaiah 44:6-11.
8. Romans 1:25.
9. Romans 1:18-20.
10. John 1:9 TNIV.
11. Romans 10:8.
12. Acts 17:28.
13. Epimenides, *Cretica*, c. 600 BC, from footnotes, *The New International Version Study Bible* (Grand Rapids, MI: Zondervan, 1985), 1680.
14. John 4:25 TNIV.
15. John 14:6.
16. John 4:35-38.

Chapter 16

Jesus and the Future

J. Nelson Kraybill with daughter Laura Kraybill

———— Narrative: God's kingdom will be fulfilled when Jesus ————
comes again (Revelation 21:9–22:21)

Archbishop Oscar Romero of El Salvador stood in front of a small congregation in the chapel of a hospital in the city of San Salvador in the spring of 1980. This shepherd of his people had enemies. For years he had called on his country's military dictators to use government powers to provide education and medicine and housing for the poor instead of assassinating their opponents and enriching a small circle of elites.

Romero painted a big picture for his little congregation: "The form of this world, distorted by sin, is passing away," he said. "We are taught that God is preparing a new dwelling and a new earth in which righteousness dwells, whose happiness will fill and surpass all the desires of peace arising in human hearts. Then death will be conquered." God will set creation free from bondage to decay, Romero insisted. "The kingdom is already mysteriously present on earth!"

At that moment a single bullet from an assassin came through the back entrance of the chapel, ending the life of a man whose faith gave him great hope for the future.

Referring to the communion bread and wine, Romero announced, "This body broken and this blood shed encourage us to give our body and blood up to suffering and pain as Christ did—not for self, but to bring justice to our people." At that moment a single bullet from an assassin came through the back entrance of the chapel, ending the life of a man whose faith gave him great hope for the future.

First-Century Jews Awaited Liberation

Two thousand years before Romero spoke out against the forces of greed and violence in Central America, people of Palestine suffered under the oppressive rule of the Roman Empire. Some Jews believed the kingdom of God—whatever that meant—soon would bring an end to human empire, sin, and suffering.

Old Testament prophets such as Amos long before had spoken of a "day of the Lord" when God would humble arrogant powers and bring justice. Isaiah got a glimpse of a *global* kingdom of God, a time when all peoples "shall beat their swords into plowshares, and their spears into pruning hooks; nation shall not lift up sword against nation, neither shall they learn war any more."[1]

Hopes for a universal, peaceful kingdom of God often seemed dim as the Old Testament era came to an end. Jerusalem was destroyed in 586 BC, and God's people went into exile in Babylon. Even though they were able to return to Palestine a generation later, other empires swamped the Jews in the following centuries—first the Persian empire, then the Greeks under Alexander the Great, and finally the Romans.

> Hopes for a universal, peaceful kingdom of God often seemed dim as the Old Testament era came to an end.

By the time Jesus was born, some Jews harbored hope that God would soon intervene in history with a messiah (one anointed by God) to throw off the yoke of empire and bring in the kingdom of God. While pregnant with the Christ child, Mary praised God with revolutionary language. God "has brought down the powerful from their thrones and lifted up the lowly," she said. God "has filled the hungry with good things and sent the rich away empty."[2]

When Jesus announced that the kingdom of God was near, he

quickly got an audience—and the lethal attention of people loyal to Rome. It was hard for Jesus' disciples to understand what kind of kingdom Jesus was proclaiming. Disciples James and John, thinking in political terms, put in a bid for senior positions in the new government! "Grant us to sit, one at your right hand and one at your left, in your glory," they said.[3]

> By the time Jesus was born, some Jews harbored hope that God would soon intervene in history with a messiah to throw off the yoke of empire and bring in the kingdom of God.

Jewish people tried in various ways to prepare for the kingdom and the awaited transition of history. Some in a group called the Essenes went into the desert next to the Dead Sea to study the Scriptures in permanent monasticism and await God's intervention. The Essenes literally planned the seating arrangement for their banquet with the Messiah. Others from another group called the Sicarii committed terrorist acts, thrusting daggers (*sicae*) into the backs of Romans or Jews who collaborated with the Romans.

A group that came to be known as Zealots eventually launched full-scale revolt against the Romans—a disaster that Jesus saw coming.[4] When the revolt flared in AD 66–70, a generation after Jesus' public ministry, it was a bloodbath. Tens of thousands of Jews died or were sold into slavery. The Romans destroyed much of Jerusalem, including the temple, which has never been rebuilt.

Jesus' Resurrection Means Hope for the Future

Except for periods of prayer and rest, Jesus did not withdraw into the desert like the Essenes. Nor did he support Sicarii-style violence, but rather told Peter to put away his sword when soldiers approached Jesus to arrest him. Instead of violent strategies, Jesus confronted the powers of sin and death with divine authority and transforming power. He forgave sinners, healed the sick, and freed people from demonic possession. He called his followers to give deep allegiance to God, not to Roman emperors or to the pursuit of wealth and security. He called them to radical obedience to God and love for others.

These actions were signs that the kingdom of God was bringing real change to the world. The powers of greed and prejudice were not amused. On a bleak Friday, Jesus died on a Roman cross, the victim of an oppressive empire. Jesus looked like a failed messiah. He had faced execution seemingly defenseless, even forgiving those who killed him. His closest followers abandoned him.

What witness to the crucifixion of Jesus could have imagined that this was the hinge on which all history would turn? Two days later the power of God that once transformed chaos into creation at the dawn of time now surged through the body of Christ. Jesus lived again!

> What witness to the crucifixion of Jesus could have imagined that this was the hinge on which all history would turn?

Because he lived, his followers knew that his vision of the future was the plan of the author of the universe.

If God raised Jesus from the dead, a new future was possible for all who turned to God. The world might still suffer from earthquakes and war and disease. But with the resurrection of Jesus, God had begun a process of transformation that someday would restore the farthest reaches of a broken world.

> No power can stand in the way of the future that God promises—not Roman emperors or modern dictators or the forces of greed and violence that warp our world today.

Paul, the great teacher of the early church, said that Christ was the first fruits of a new creation.[5] Jesus' resurrection was the beginning of a great harvest, like early fruits that the Israelites brought to the temple as an offering to God.

No Power Can Stand in God's Way

No power can stand in the way of the future that God promises—

not Roman emperors or modern dictators or the forces of greed and violence that warp our world today. People who believe in Jesus give their allegiance to a Lord who will "reign until he has put all his enemies under his feet" and ultimately destroy death itself.[6]

Laura

It's hard to wait for God to destroy death. When I was in England as a child, I knew a girl named Esther who was a cancer survivor. During the past two years, I have been director of a voluntary service house in South Bend, Indiana. One of the members of the household was Esther. She had a passion for social justice and sometimes would stand up in church and call people to pray for a part of the world where there was war or suffering. Then the cancer came back and Esther had to go home to England for treatment. Our household, the people at church, and friends in England prayed for healing. But a little over a year after her diagnosis, twenty-year-old Esther died.

It was hard to understand why God didn't save the life of a beautiful young woman like Esther. But in the last number of years I have come to see healing in a different light. While God didn't physically heal Esther, God brought or will bring healing in some other way. Perhaps Esther experienced the presence of God during her illness like never before, bringing spiritual healing. I know that Esther's testimony lives on, maybe bringing people who knew her closer to God. That is resurrection power—greater life after death.

Nelson

Your story about Esther is a small picture of suffering at many places on earth. Paul said already two thousand years ago that all of creation is groaning like a woman in labor.[7] We feel that agony when someone we love dies too young, or when war kills thousands, or when pollution and greed destroy whole species. Crying out to God for justice and healing in the world should be a regular part of our worship. We have the hope of looking to the future when God will make this world new again.

Disciples Ask about the Future

Forty days after his resurrection, Jesus took a band of disciples a short distance from Jerusalem to the Mount of Olives. His followers were thinking about the future, imagining that the kingdom of God would soon come to end the suffering of the Jewish people living under Roman rule. "Lord, are you at this time going to restore the kingdom to Israel?" they asked. Jesus steered his disciples away from speculation about the future, and instead gave them a charge, "You will receive power when the Holy Spirit has come upon you; and you will be my witnesses in Jerusalem, in all Judea and Samaria, and to the ends of the earth."[8] Do not become preoccupied with details of the future, he was telling them, but get on with sharing the good news about Jesus!

Having promised his followers empowerment for mission, Jesus was taken up into heaven. Two messengers appeared and announced that Jesus "will come in the same way as you saw him go into heaven." Ever since that day, followers of Jesus have waited for his return.

The (Second) Coming of Christ

Paul was the first to spell this hope out in writing, calling Jesus' expected return the *parousia* or "the coming." In political settings, this familiar Greek word referred to the arrival of an emperor or other ruler to a city. As the ruler approached, a delegation of leading citizens would go out to meet the approaching dignitary and escort the visitor back into their city. Then the ruler would hold court, conduct trials if necessary, and offer benefits such as new public baths or streets for the hosting city.

Paul uses this familiar image to describe the parousia or coming of Jesus.[9] Believers who have died when Christ returns will rise from the dead. "After that, we who are still alive, who are left, will be caught up in the clouds together with them to meet the Lord in the air. And so we will be with the Lord forever."[10]

Many modern Christians assume that believers will at that point be taken totally and forever out of this world to be in heaven with Jesus, but the Scriptures do not say that. Rather, like citizens of an ancient city going out to welcome a visiting king, we should expect to accompany our Lord back to the earth for him to complete the restoration of this suffering world.

Many modern Christians assume that believers will be taken totally and forever out of this world to be in heaven with Jesus, but the Scriptures do not say that.

In the meantime, Christians live changed lives in the present because of what God will do in the future. We follow Jesus in his ways of love, healing, and peace. God has given us power to live this way by the "first installment" of the Holy Spirit.[11] People who call Jesus Lord and live in his way are part of the kingdom of God that already is changing the world.

Laura

I wonder sometimes about what will happen in the future to people who do not know Christ. It's hard for me to believe that the Good Shepherd, who would search for one missing sheep, would eventually give up on anyone. Jesus himself said, "And I, when I am lifted up from the earth, will draw all people to myself."[12] How we live our lives matters just as much as what we believe. I'm intrigued in this story by what will happen when the Son of Man (Christ) comes in glory and separates people like a shepherd separates sheep from goats (see Matthew 25:31-40). In this passage it is Christlike actions that decide people's eternal destination, not their right ways of thinking. People who feed the hungry and clothe the naked inherit the kingdom.

Nelson

In the same chapter Jesus goes on to say that some people will face eternal punishment—presumably separation from God. That sounds harsh to western readers who prefer a God who is all sweetness and light. Certainly the God we know in Jesus of Nazareth is loving and compassionate. But we also see that Jesus could drive moneychangers out of the temple and blast hypocrites. It is part of God's mercy to hold accountable those who warp creation. The Christ who someday will judge is the same Lord who forgave soldiers who crucified him, so we can trust him to act justly. We mortals, with our limited understanding of God's design, do not need to—and are never asked to—determine the eternal destiny of anyone.

> Jesus goes on to say that some people will face eternal punishment—presumably separation from God. That sounds harsh to western readers who prefer a God who is all sweetness and light.

Laura

People who pay attention *only* to what they believe or only to what they do certainly are missing out on a huge part of heaven here on earth. Jesus invites us to both believe and do!

Heaven Comes to Earth

A first-century writer-prophet named John had a vision in which he saw a New Jerusalem coming down to earth out of heaven.[13] The city was a place of dazzling beauty, great wealth, and worship. At the center of the city was Jesus, the Lamb. This vision, like much of the book of Revelation, is theological truth in word pictures. The New Jerusalem is John's metaphor for the kingdom of God. Just as Jesus announced that the kingdom of God is "among you," John reported that the New Jerusalem is coming to earth.

Some Christians in the past two hundred years developed a view of the return of Christ that places the kingdom of God entirely in the future. This understanding is common on many Christian television programs and websites. Such a theology sometimes leads to the belief that the Sermon on the Mount and Jesus' teachings about love of enemy are only for the

> The New Testament teaches that the future has already started with Jesus' life, death, and resurrection, and followers of Jesus live into that future now.

future. That is a compromise that weakens the message of the gospel because it makes Christian faith all about beliefs and not about actions. The New Testament teaches that the future has already started with Jesus' life, death, and resurrection, and followers of Jesus live into that future now.

Nelson

When Esther died, she was wrapped in a quilt made from squares sent by people in Great Britain, the United States, Sweden, and Lithuania who had been praying for her. That did not take away the pain for family and friends who wanted Esther to be healed, but it represented something of the love of God and the caring community of the New Jerusalem.

Laura

I am sure that Esther is in heaven with her father—who died of a related form of cancer five years earlier. For Christians, death doesn't have the final word. Esther helped bring people to God, her life continues to bear fruit, and she is in heaven. I also have seen something of heaven come to earth. The voluntary service household I was part of in South Bend helped with children's ministry at an inner city Pentecostal congregation. We saw joy and hope in that church in the middle of an economically depressed area. Young men played drums, people sang with joy, and believers of another racial group embraced us. That was an expression of God's kingdom, a microcosm of what God eventually will do to bring all people together.

Salvation Belongs to God

The book of Revelation includes a vision of just such a celebration in heaven. Around Jesus the Lamb, John saw "a great multitude that no one could count, from every nation, tribe, people, and language, standing before the throne and before the Lamb. They were wearing white robes and were holding palm branches in their hands. They cried out in a loud voice, "Salvation belongs to our God who is seated on the throne, and to the Lamb."[14]

Earlier in his vision, John had seen a scroll in God's hand that was sealed with seven seals. Apparently the scroll contained God's plan or foreknowledge of the future. John weeps because nobody is worthy or authorized to open the scroll. The future is a complete mystery, since neither people on earth nor members of the heavenly court can know whether right or wrong will prevail in the end.

The Lamb is at the center of God's plan for the future. Through the Lamb that was slain, God will save the world and renew the earth.

But then the Lamb—Jesus—steps forward and begins to open the seals. Events leading up to the final transition to the kingdom of God start to unfold. There is suffering and violence. It is not always clear whether the chaos is simply the dramatic effects of sin on the world or punishment caused by God. But it is certain that the Lamb is at the center of God's plan for the future. Through the Lamb that was slain, God will save the world and renew the earth.

At the end of his vision, John sees the New Jerusalem coming down to earth. This is not just a future event but something that John saw beginning to happen already in his day. The New Jerusalem is the faith community to which all who know and follow Jesus belong. Wherever people believe in Jesus and begin to live in ways of the kingdom, something of the New Jerusalem comes to earth. The New Jerusalem in Revelation is another image for what Jesus meant when he taught his disciples to pray, "Thy kingdom come, thy will be done on earth as it is in heaven."

Laura

If the New Jerusalem is coming down from heaven, then that means that the earth is the house of God, and we are caretakers of it. You don't trash a house that God made, and you work to bring healing. In Pittsburgh I lived on the border between rich and poor neighborhoods. There Christians started the Union Project, a community center where people of all races and economic levels could meet. The project sponsored neighborhood parties, barbeques, a coffee shop that employed kids from low income families, and other events that brought people together. I'll never forget the diverse group of people who came together to celebrate Martin Luther King Jr. Day.

Nelson

The Union Project sounds like a sign of the future. Your mention of Martin Luther King reminds me of his statement that he had been to the mountaintop and had seen the Promised Land. King saw a future—God's future of reconciliation between all racial and ethnic groups—that many others could not see.

Our task in evangelism is to both live by ways of the coming kingdom now and invite others to know Jesus and become part of God's future. Both Romero and King were so confident that God's kingdom of hope and healing would win in the end that they were ready to give their lives for it. Can we do anything less?

Questions for Discussion

1. What Christian understandings of the future do you come across among acquaintances or in popular media? What kind of God do these views represent, and do they present good news?

2. Based on Acts 1:6-11, what might Jesus have to say about the popularity of Christian books about the future today? What

priorities did Jesus have when his disciples wanted to know about the future?

3. If the world around you became God's new creation, what suffering or brokenness do you expect God would heal? Can you describe ways God is using you now to bring healing?

Notes

1. Isaiah 2:4. Unless otherwise noted, Scripture text in this chapter is from the NRSV.

2. Luke 1:52-53.

3. Mark 10:37.

4. Luke 21:20-24.

5. 1 Corinthians 15:20.

6. 1 Corinthians 15:25-26.

7. Romans 8:22.

8. Acts 1:6-8.

9. 1 Thessalonians 4:13-18.

10. 1 Thessalonians 4:17.

11. 2 Corinthians 1:21-22.

12. John 12:32 TNIV.

13. Revelation 21–22.

14. Revelation 7:10.

Jesus Invites Us to His Table:
'Eat this bread, drink this cup'

Amy Barker
with James Puryear

The cross of Jesus is the foundation and pinnacle of our Christian faith. The New Testament Gospels narrate the story of Jesus' crucifixion and the Epistles work out its meaning. Yet so much remains a mystery. How shall we understand what transpired on the cross in Jesus, in God, for us? How shall we receive it as God's greatest gift of love? How can its historical reality be a reality in our lives, spiritually and in every other way?

> The cross of Jesus is the foundation and pinnacle of our Christian faith. The New Testament Gospels narrate the story of Jesus' crucifixion and the Epistles work out its meaning.

Jesus gave us the gift of the bread and cup at his table, the Lord's table.

> The Lord Jesus, on the night he was betrayed, took bread,
> And when he had given thanks, he broke it and said,
> "This is my body, given for you; do this in remembrance of me."
> In the same way, after supper he took the cup, saying,
> "This cup is the new covenant in my blood, which is poured out for you;
> Do this, whenever you drink it, in remembrance of me."
> For whenever you eat this bread and drink this cup,
> You proclaim the Lord's death until he comes.[1]

Jesus shared this Last Supper with his disciples the night before he was crucified. He commanded his disciples to continue to partake of the bread and cup and to remember and proclaim his death until he comes again. We come now to the table in obedience and in expectation. By the Spirit of God, we hope to know something of the mystery and power and love of God in Jesus Christ for us, especially on the cross.

Eat this Bread—the Body of Jesus

When we take and eat the bread, we remember the *body* of Christ, given for us. According to Scripture, Jesus took the bread, gave thanks for it, broke it, and said, "This is my body, given for you." Many Scriptures about the cross emphasize the body, the flesh of Jesus. There is great mystery here, yet what is clear is that in his very human body Jesus received and bore our sins.[2]

The passion narratives in the Gospels draw deeply from the Hebrew Scriptures to aid our understanding. The New Testament writers gave particular focus to the suffering servant songs of the prophet Isaiah, penned centuries before Jesus was born. The writers saw in these prophetic images a description of Jesus.

> Surely he took up our infirmities and carried our sorrows,
> Yet we considered him stricken by God, smitten by him,
> and afflicted.
> But he was pierced for our transgressions, he was crushed
> for our iniquities;
> The punishment that brought us peace was upon him,
> and by his wounds we are healed.
> We all, like sheep, have gone astray, each of us has turned
> to his own way;
> And the Lord has laid on him the iniquity of us all.[3]

This text from Isaiah 53 poignantly describes what the servant bore for us, in our place. More than any other Old Testament text, Isaiah 53 is used in the New Testament Epistles to explain the riches of God's gifts to us in Jesus' suffering and death. In the Gospels, however, Isaiah 53 is cited to reference Jesus' life and ministry *before* his crucifixion, not during or after it (e.g., Matthew 8:17).[4] From this we realize that the offering of Jesus as the suffering servant occurred not only on the cross but throughout his life. Jesus both died *and* lived as the suffering servant.

Whatever the mystery of his incarnation,[5] Jesus' determination to live in obedience and submission caused him to suffer, not only on the cross but throughout his lifetime. As the writer of Hebrews describes it: "During the days of Jesus' life on earth, he offered up prayers and petitions with loud cries and tears to the one who could save him from death, and he was heard because of his reverent submission. Although he was a son, he learned obedience from what he suffered and, once made perfect, he became the source of eternal salvation for all who obey him."[6]

> The offering of Jesus as the suffering servant occurred not only on the cross but throughout his life. Jesus both died *and* lived as the suffering servant.

We cannot comprehend the mystery, the condescension, and the love of God becoming flesh in Jesus. But Scripture suggests that the essence of Jesus' sacrifice was his *willing obedience*, wherein he yielded his divine rights, resisting all temptations to use his divine power, either to save himself[7] or to wield authority as king.[8]

> Sacrifice and offering You have not desired;
> but a body You have prepared for me;
> with burnt offerings and sin offerings You were not pleased.
> Then I said, "Here I am, . . . I have come to do your will, O God."[9]

The willing life-giving sacrifice of Jesus in his life and death—this we remember when we take the bread and eat. In his prayer the night before his crucifixion, Jesus offered himself willingly to the cross. "Father, if you are willing, take this cup from me; yet not my will but yours be done."[10] Jesus emptied himself of his divine rights as God, taking the form of a servant, being made in human likeness, and yielding in humble obedience to death on the cross.[11]

The broken bread signifies the love of God, who in Jesus condescended to become human and suffer and die. Not only did Jesus participate with us in our suffering as victims of sin, but he bore our sin as victimizers. Jews and Gentiles, the righteous and unrighteous alike, abandoned, mocked, taunted, humiliated, and even crucified Jesus. "There is none righteous, not even one."[12] When we come to the table, our confession of sin opens our hearts to gratitude for God's gifts of forgiveness, righteousness, and resurrection life, through Jesus Christ our Lord. "Amazing love," wrote Charles Wesley in the eighteenth century, "how can it be, that Thou, my God, shouldst die for me?"[13]

Bread is a sign of life. As we receive the gift of Jesus' death and life for us, we as the body of Christ bring to the world Jesus' abundant life that overcomes sin and death. But manifesting and sharing the gift of Jesus in this world may cause our suffering, just as Jesus told us to expect.[14] As the kernels in the bread are crushed and bonded together in the flour, we are to give of ourselves sacrificially for one another and so share in the sufferings of Christ.

We too are called to yield our lives, our wills, even our bodies, for the sake of the Gospel for others. As we eat the bread, we pray Jesus' prayer: "not my will, but yours, O Lord."

Drink This Cup—the Blood of Christ

When we drink the cup, we remember the blood of Christ shed for us. Shed blood connotes sacrifice. Yet to speak of sacrifice, we must first speak of love. The Old Testament abounds with

God's generous, longsuffering covenant love.[15] But God's people repeatedly rejected God's abundant love and faithful mercies, failing to return to God their love and obedience. For their failures they suffered discipline and judgment, yet never as they deserved. Rather, it was *God* who continually made the greater sacrifice in order to remain faithful to his covenant love for his people.[16] God's greater sacrifice on our behalf became manifest ultimately in the willing death of Jesus on the cross. The greater sacrifice of God *is* the blood of Christ—this is the cup we drink.

> God's people repeatedly rejected God's abundant love and faithful mercies. For their failures they suffered discipline and judgment. Yet it was *God* who continually made the greater sacrifice in order to remain faithful to his covenant love.

When Jesus offered the cup to his disciples, he said, "This is my blood of the covenant which is poured out for many for the forgiveness of sins."[17] God's covenant love and reconciling forgiveness, extended to each of us, is enacted and demonstrated when we share the cup. Communion powerfully portrays the reconciling love of Jesus between sisters and brothers in the Christian faith. Part of the communion liturgy invites participants to offer "the peace of Christ" to one another. People from every walk of life, diverse in race and culture and status, come together to be united as the family of God at the Lord's

> Salvation, atonement, victory, sacrifice, righteousness, justification, redemption, reconciliation, and eternal life are some of the rich terms in Scripture that portray the glorious gift of God's love for us on the cross.

table because "he himself is our peace."[18] At the Lord's table we may know the harmony and unity with God and with one another that all humanity longs for.

Such a bond of fellowship requires that we search our hearts to be sure that we are truly at peace with our sisters and brothers. In some churches, just before communion, a time of fellowship is offered to encourage people to ask forgiveness and seek reconciliation with one another, so that the peace of Christ in communion may be fully realized, and true.[19]

As we consider the meaning of the blood of Christ, we realize that this one term carries the full weight and glory of Jesus' crucifixion. *Salvation, atonement, victory, sacrifice, righteousness, justification, redemption, reconciliation,* and *eternal life* are some of the rich terms in Scripture that portray the glorious gift of God's love for us through the unimaginable means of Jesus' death on the cross. The blood of Christ is the signal symbol for the whole of the gift.

At the Last Supper, Jesus looked forward to the day when he would once again eat the bread and drink the cup with his disciples in the kingdom of God.[20] Likewise, when we partake of the bread and the cup, we eagerly anticipate the coming kingdom of God. Just as all creation groans under the travails of sin, so do we.[21] Yet "as often as we eat this bread and drink this cup, we proclaim the Lord's death until he comes."[22] We take communion both to remember Jesus' death and to proclaim his sure return. When Jesus comes again, he will restore all things in the perfect unity and peace and love of God. Until then, we join John the Baptist as we look to Jesus and proclaim, "Behold, the Lamb of God who takes away the sin of the world!"[23]

Come to the Table and Remember Me

We do not presume to come to your Table, our merciful Lord,
trusting in our own righteousness,
but rather in your loving kindness and great mercies.
We are not worthy to gather the crumbs under your Table,
but you are our God, whose mercy reaches to all people,
everywhere.
Grant us, gracious Lord,
so to eat this bread, the body of thy dear Son Jesus Christ,

and to drink this cup, the blood of our Lord and Savior Jesus
Christ,
that we may forever dwell in him, and he in us,
now and forever,
Amen.[24]

For we have been crucified with Christ,
and it is no longer we who live,
but Christ lives in us;
and the life which we now live in the flesh,
we live by faith in the Son of God,
who loved us,
and delivered himself up for us.[25]

Notes
   1. 1 Corinthians 11:23-26; Luke 22:19-20.
   2. Romans 8:3; 2 Corinthians 5:21; Galatians 3:13; 1 Peter 2:24.
   3. Isaiah 53:4-6.
   4. The primary Old Testament text referenced in the Gospels
during Jesus' crucifixion is Psalm 22, cited ten times in the passion
narratives.
   5. The incarnation refers to God *in the flesh* in Jesus.
   6. Hebrews 5:7-9.
   7. Matthew 4:3; cf. 27:40-43.
   8. Mark 9:31-35; Luke 22:24-30.
   9. Hebrews 10:5-10; cf. Psalm 40:6-8.
   10. Mark 14:32-42; Luke 22:39-45; cf. Psalm 40:6-8.
   11. Philippians 2:6-8.
   12. Romans 3:10.
   13. From the hymn, "And can it be that I should gain?" by
Charles Wesley, 1738.
   14. Matthew 5:10-12; Luke 6:22-23; John 15:20.
   15. Exodus 34:6-7; Deuteronomy 7:6-13; Psalms 103, 106 (v. 45),
136; Hosea 11:7-9.
   16. Genesis 6:5-7; cf. 8:21-22; Hosea 11:7-9.
   17. Matthew 26:28.

18. Ephesians 2:11-22, especially verse 14.
19. Matthew 5:23-25.
20. Luke 22:16-18.
21. Romans 8:19-23.
22. 1 Corinthians 11:26.
23. John 1:29.
24. Adapted from *Book of Common Prayer*, 1928.
25. Adapted from Galatians 2:20.

For Further Reading

Achtemeier, Paul J. *Inspiration and Authority: Nature and Function of Christian Scripture*. Peabody, MA: Hendrickson, 1999.

Arnold, Clinton E. *Powers of Darkness: Principalities and Powers in Paul's Letters*. Downers Grove, IL: InterVarsity Press, 1992.

Berry, R. J., ed. *The Care of Creation: Focusing Concern and Action*. Downers Grove, IL: InterVarsity Press, 2000.

Borg, Marcus J. and N. T. Wright. *The Meaning of Jesus: Two Visions*. San Francisco: HarperSanFrancisco, 1999.

Camp, Lee C. *Mere Discipleship: Radical Christianity in a Rebellious World*, 2nd Edition (includes study guide). Grand Rapids, MI: Brazos, 2008.

Claiborne, Shane. *Irresistible Revolution: Living As an Ordinary Radical*. Grand Rapids, MI: Zondervan, 2006.

Driver, John. *Understanding the Atonement for the Mission of the Church*. Scottdale, PA: Herald Press, 1986.

DeWitt, Calvin B. *Earth-Wise: A Biblical Response to Environmental Issues*. Grand Rapids, MI: Christian Reformed Church, Faith Alive Christian Resources, 2008.

Dula, Peter and Alain Epp. *Borders and Bridges, Mennonite Witness in a Religiously Diverse World*. Telford, PA: Cascadia, 2007.

Efird, James M. *Left Behind? What the Bible Really Says About the End Times*. Macon, GA: Smyth and Helwys, 2006.

Ekblad, Bob. *Reading the Bible with the Damned*. Louisville, KY: Westminster John Knox Press, 2005.

Gardner, Richard B. *Believers Church Bible Commentary: Matthew*. Scottdale, PA: Herald Press, 1991.

Gorman, Michael J. "Even Death on a Cross." In *Reading Paul*. Eugene, OR: Cascade Books, 2008, 78-90.

Green, Joel B. and Mark D. Baker. *Recovering the Scandal of the Cross: Atonement in the New Testament and Contemporary Contexts*. Downers Grove, IL: InterVarsity Press, 2000.

Green, Joel B. *Salvation: Understanding Biblical Themes*. Atlanta: Chalice Press, 2003.

Grimsrud, Ted. *Triumph of the Lamb*. Scottdale, PA: Herald Press, 1987.

Hays, Richard B. *Interpretation: First Corinthians*. Louisville, KY: John Knox Press, 1997.

Holmes, Stephen R. *The Wondrous Cross, Atonement and Penal Substitution in the Bible and History*. Colorado Springs, CO: Paternoster, 2007.

Johns, Loren L. and James R. Krabill, eds. *Even the Demons Submit: Continuing Jesus' Ministry of Deliverance*. Elkhart, IN: Institute for Mennonite Studies, 2007.

Johnson, Luke Timothy. *Living Jesus: Learning the Heart of the Gospel*. San Francisco: HarperSanFrancisco, 1999.

———. *The Real Jesus: The Misguided Quest for the Historical Jesus and the Truth of the Traditional Gospels*. San Francisco: HarperSanFrancisco, 1997.

Kreider, Alan. *Peace Church, Mission Church: Friends or Foes?* Elkhart, IN: Mennonite Mission Network, 2004.

Kraybill, Donald B. *The Upside Down Kingdom*, 3rd Edition. Scottdale, PA: Herald Press, 2003.

Krabill, James R. *Is It Insensitive to Share Your Faith?* Intercourse, PA: Good Books, 2005.

Kraybill, J. Nelson. *Apocalypse and Allegiance: Worship, Politics, and Devotion in the Book of Revelation*. Grand Rapids, MI: Brazos Press (forthcoming).

Leiter, David A. *Neglected Voices: Peace in the Old Testament*. Scottdale, PA: Herald Press, 2007.

Lewis, C. S. *Mere Christianity*. New York: HarperCollins, 2001.

McClendon, James Wm. Jr. *Systematic Theology; Vol. 2 Doctrine*. Nashville: Abingdon, 1994.

Nash, James A. *Loving Nature: Ecological Integrity and Christian Responsibility*. Nashville: Abingdon, 1991.

Nation, Mark Thiessen, "Who Has Believed What We Have Heard?" *Conrad Grebel Review*. Waterloo, ON: Conrad Grebel University College, (Spring 2009).

Ott, Bernard. *God's Shalom Project: An Engaging Look at the Bible's Sweeping Story*. Intercourse, PA: Good Books, 2004.

Peterson, Eugene H. *Reversed Thunder: The Revelation of John and the Praying Imagination*. San Francisco: Harper and Row, 1988.

Richardson, Don. *Eternity in Their Hearts*. Ventura, CA: Gospel Light, 1984.

Roth, John D. *Choosing Against War, A Christian View: A Love Stronger than Our Fears*. Intercourse, PA: Good Books, 2002.

Shelton, R. Larry. *Cross and Covenant: Interpreting the Atonement for 21st Century Mission*. Colorado Springs, CO: Paternoster, 2006.

Shenk, Calvin. *Who Do You Say That I Am?* Scottdale, PA: Herald Press, 1997.

Shenk, David W. and Ervin R. Stutzman, *Creating Communities of the Kingdom: New Testament Models of Church Planting*. Scottdale, PA: Herald Press, 1988.

Shenk, David W. *Global Gods: Exploring the Role of Religions in Modern Societies*. Scottdale, PA: Herald Press, 1999.

———. *God's Call to Mission*. Scottdale, PA: Herald Press, 1994.

———. *Surprises of the Christian Way*. Scottdale, PA: Herald Press, 2000.

Shenk, Wilbert R. *By Faith They Went Out, Mennonite Missions 1850-1999*. Elkhart, IN: Institute of Mennonite Studies, 2000.

———, ed. *The Transfiguration of Mission*. Scottdale, PA: Herald Press, 1993 (Reprinted by Wipf and Stock).

Showalter, Richard. *On the Way with Jesus, A Passion for Mission*. Scottdale, PA: Herald Press, 2008.

Swartley, Willard M. "Binding the Strong Man: Matthew 12:22-30." *The Mennonite*, Nov. 18, 2003: 16-17.

———. *Covenant of Peace: The Missing Peace in New Testament Theology and Ethics*. Grand Rapids, MI: Eerdmans, 2006, chs. 4, 5, 8, for victory over evil.

————. *Send Forth Your Light: A Vision for Peace, Mission, and Worship*. Scottdale, PA: Herald Press, 2007, chs. 4-5 for witness to government.

————, ed. *Essays on Spiritual Bondage and Deliverance*. Elkhart, IN: Institute of Mennonite Studies, 1988.

Van Dyke, Fred, et al. *Redeeming Creation: The Biblical Basis for Environmental Stewardship*. Downers Grove, IL: InterVarsity Press, 1996.

Volf, Miroslav. *After Our Likeness: The Church as the Image of the Trinity*. Grand Rapids, MI: Eerdmans, 1998.

Weaver, Alain Epp. *Under Vine and Fig Tree: Biblical Theologies of Land and the Palestinian-Israeli Conflict*. Telford, PA: Cascadia, 2007.

Widjaja, P. S. "Peace," *Dictionary of Mission Theology: Evangelical Foundations*, ed. John Corrie. Downers Grove, IL: InterVarsity Press, 2007.

Wink, Walter. *Engaging the Powers: Discernment and Resistance in a World of Domination*. Minneapolis: Fortress Press, 1992.

Wright, N. T. *Christians at the Cross: Finding Hope in the Passion, Death and Resurrection of Jesus*. Ijamsville, MD: Word Among Us Press, 2008.

————. "Evil and the Crucified God." In *Evil and the Justice of God*. Downers Grove, IL: InterVarsity Press, 2006, 75-100.

————. *Simply Christian*. Downers Grove, IL: InterVarsity, 2007.

————. *Surprised by Hope: Rethinking Heaven, the Resurrection and the Mission of the Church*. New York: HarperOne Publishers, 2008.

————. *The Resurrection of the Son of God*. Minneapolis: Augsburg Fortress Publishers, 2003.

Yoder Neufeld, Thomas. *Recovering Jesus: The Witness of the New Testament*. Grand Rapids, MI: Brazos Press, 2007.

Yoder, John Howard. *Preface to Theology: Christology and Theological Method*. Grand Rapids, MI: Brazos Press, 2002.

————. *Politics of Jesus*. Rev. ed. Grand Rapids, MI: Eerdmans, 1994, esp. chs. 8-9.

Contributors

Amy Barker resides in College Station, Texas, where she teaches piano, is a church pianist, and a substitute teacher at A&M Consolidated High School. She was campus pastor and assistant professor of youth ministry at Bethel College from 2003 to 2008. Amy's son, **James Puryear**, has attended Bethel College and Houston Baptist University, and now studies at the Art Institute of Houston in the digital filmmaking and video production program.

Lois Barrett, of Wichita, Kansas, is director of the Great Plains Extension for Associated Mennonite Biblical Seminary and associate professor of theology and Anabaptist studies. She writes on theology, church history, spirituality, and the missional church. Her publications include *The Way God Fights* (1986), *Missional Church* (1998), *Treasure in Clay Jars* (2004), and *Patterns of Missional Faithfulness* (2004). Lois also edited the Bible study *Mission-Focused Congregations* (2002). She is a consultant for Church Innovations Institute in St. Paul, Minnesota. **Susanna Barrett Mierau,** Lois's daughter, lives in Cambridge, Massachusetts, where she attends the Mennonite Congregation of Boston. She is a resident in neurology in the Harvard Partners program. A native of Wichita, she holds degrees from Massachusetts Institute of Technology, Oxford University, and an MD from Harvard Medical School. She enjoys traveling, sailing, and playing the French horn.

George R. Brunk III is professor of New Testament at Eastern Mennonite Seminary, where he has taught since 1974 and was dean from 1977 to 1999. He ministered in Italy under the Virginia Mennonite Board of Missions from 1964 to 1970 and was moderator of the Mennonite Church General Assembly from 1989 to 1991. Brunk is an ordained Mennonite minister. **Laura Lehman Amstutz** graduated from Bluffton University in 2003 and EMS in 2006. She is currently working for EMS as the Communication Coordinator.

Shane Claiborne is a sought-after speaker, prominent activist, a big fan of the circus, and a self-proclaimed "recovering sinner." He is also the co-founder of The Simple Way community in Philadelphia. His books *The Irresistible Revolution* (2006) and *Jesus for President: Politics for Ordinary Radicals* (2008) are reaching many young adults on issues related to Christian service and other important kingdom values.

Steve Dintaman and his wife, Betsy, are missionaries in Lithuania, where Steve is professor of theology at Lithuania Christian College International University. Steve formerly taught theology at Eastern Mennonite University. He is ordained to ministry by the Virginia Mennonite Conference. His young adult co-writers, **Gintare Giraityte** and **Daumantas Ivanauskas**, are both from Lithuania and are 2009 theology graduates from LCC.

John Driver has participated in community development, church-planting, and theological education in the Hispanic world for nearly sixty years. John and his wife Bonny have made their home in a half-dozen countries on three continents. John is the author of numerous books in Spanish and English on themes of the church, mission, peace, biblical theology, and New Testament and Anabaptist spirituality. John and Bonny are retired and live in Goshen, Indiana. **Daniel Driver**, John's writing companion and grandson, is studying pre-medicine and music at Goshen College. John and Daniel are members of the East Goshen Mennonite Church.

Stanley Green is executive director for Mennonite Mission Network, the mission agency of Mennonite Church USA. He has pastored congregations in South Africa, California, and Jamaica where he and his wife, Ursula were mission workers. **Sarah Thompson** is a scholar and activist from Elkhart, Indiana. She graduated from Spelman College in 2006 and is currently studying at Associated Mennonite Biblical Seminary. She volunteers as a translator and fitness instructor for a local women's shelter. She is the North American representative to AMIGOS, the youth and young adult executive committee of Mennonite World Conference.

Michele Hershberger, of Hesston, Kansas, is chair of the Bible and Ministry Division at Hesston College, where she teaches Bible and youth ministry classes. She enjoys preaching in a variety of venues and has written several books, including *God's Story, Our Story*, the catechism for Mennonite Church USA and Mennonite Church Canada. **Daniel Moya Urueña** is a Colombian who has lived for a number of years in Ecuador. He graduated from Hesston College in 2008 and is a student at Goshen College. Daniel plays a mean guitar. He and Michele got help in thinking about the resurrection from current and former Hesston College students **Erica Stoltzfus, Matt Boyts, Grant Sprunger, Zach Hurst,** and **Hope Weaver.**

James R. Krabill served for fourteen years in West Africa, primarily the Ivory Coast, as a Bible and church history teacher among African Initiated Churches. He and his wife, Jeanette, are the parents of three adult children, Matthew, Elisabeth Anne, and Mary Laura. James is the author and editor of numerous articles and several books, including, *The Hymnody of the Harrist Church* (1995), *Does Your Church "Smell" Like Mission?* (2001), *Anabaptists Meeting Muslims*, with David W. Shenk and Linford Stutzman (2005), *Is It Insensitive to Share Your Faith?* (2005), and *Music in the Life of the African Church*, with Roberta King, Jean Kidula, and Thomas Oduro (2008). James is senior executive for Global Ministries at Mennonite Mission Network.

Nelson Kraybill has been president of Associated Mennonite Biblical Seminary since 1997. Before that he was a high school teacher in Puerto Rico, a pastor in Vermont, and program director at the London (England) Mennonite Center. A frequent public speaker, he is author of *Worship Shapes Allegiance*, a study of the book of Revelation (forthcoming). He and his wife Ellen are parents of Laura and Andrea, and are members of Prairie Street Mennonite Church in Elkhart, Indiana. **Laura Kraybill** is a master's degree student in theater education at Emerson College. Previously she directed a Service Adventure unit—a young adult voluntary service program of Mennonite Mission Network—in South Bend, Indiana.

Mark Thiessen Nation has been a child protective services social worker, founding director of a Christian peace and justice organization, a pastor, and the director of the London (England) Mennonite Center. He is the author of many articles and the editor or co-editor of books including *The Wisdom of the Cross: Essays in Honor of John Howard Yoder* (1999); *Faithfulness & Fortitude: In Conversation with the Theological Ethics of Stanley Hauerwas* (2000); and *Reasoning Together: A Conversation on Homosexuality*, with Ted Grimsrud (2008). Mark is married and has two adult children. Since 2002, he has served as professor of theology at Eastern Mennonite Seminary. **Nelson Okanya** is an associate pastor at Capitol Christian Fellowship near Washington, D.C. Originally from Kenya, Nelson studied Christian ministries at Daystar University in Nairobi before coming to the United States in 1996. He graduated from EMS in 2002 and then served as an adjunct faculty at Eastern Mennonite University in 2005. Nelson enjoys reading, teaching, preaching, studying the Bible and theology, worship leading, pastoral care, and relating to people.

Mary Thiessen Nation is an adjunct professor at Eastern Mennonite Seminary and Palmer Seminary. She teaches trauma healing, conflict transformation, spiritual formation and mission and serves as a spiritual mentor and teacher for the wider church. Mary spent eighteen years in urban ministry in Los Angeles, and two terms with her husband, Mark, with the Mennonite Board of Missions in London. **Matthew Krabill** is a student at Fuller Theological Seminary. He graduated from Eastern Mennonite University in 2003 then worked for Lutheran Immigration and Refugee Service in Philadelphia, where he resettled Liberian, Sierra Leonean and Meskhetian Turk populations.

Tom Yoder Neufeld and **David Neufeld** are father/son collaborators in writing the chapter on "Jesus and the Bible." David graduated in June 2009 with a history degree from the University of Waterloo, after studying at Goshen College and with the Central American Study and Service program in Guatemala City. He is a member of First Mennonite Church, Kitchener, Ontario, and serves on the refugee committee, the sister church committee with a congregation in Colombia, and as a mentor and translator for recent arrivals to Canada. His father, Tom, teaches New Testament at Conrad Grebel University College. Among his publications are the *Ephesians Believers Church Bible Commentary* (2002) and *Recovering Jesus: The Witness of the New Testament* (2007). Tom enjoys numerous opportunities to preach and teach in church settings.

Mary H. Schertz is professor of New Testament at Associated Mennonite Biblical Seminary and director of the Institute of Mennonite Studies. She has written or edited many articles and is ordained for teaching ministry by the Indiana Michigan and Central District conferences. Mary is a member of Assembly Mennonite Church. **Ben, Sam** and **Luke Jacobs** are brothers. Luke is 16 and a sophomore in high school; Sam is 18 and a senior in high school; Ben is 21 and a senior in college.

David W. Shenk is Global Missions Consultant with Eastern Mennonite Missions. He has taught religions in several universities and seminaries and authored or edited more than a dozen books related to the gospel in a pluralist world. He and his wife, Grace, have served with EMM in Africa, in mission administration, and as academic dean and professor of theology at Lithuania Christian College International University. They have pastored or planted churches in the United States and East Africa. They are blessed with four children, Karen, Doris, Jonathan, and Timothy, and seven grandchildren. **Linford D. Fisher** is an assistant professor of history at Indiana University. Linford received his doctorate in American religious history from Harvard University in 2008. From 2002 to 2008 he and his wife, Jo, managed the International Fellowship House in Boston, where they lived in community with twenty students from a dozen countries. They now live in South Bend, Indiana, with their four children. Four other readers contributed to the chapter by Shenk and Fisher. They were **Weston Shertzer** and **Jonathan Herr**, university students; **Ryan Showalter**, director of EMM's Discipleship Ministries; and **Jon Heinly**, youth minister for Lancaster Mennonite Conference and Lancaster Mennonite High School.

Wilbert R. Shenk, of Elkhart, Indiana, directed Overseas Ministries of Mennonite Board of Missions from 1965 to 1990. He taught at Associated Mennonite Biblical Seminary from 1990 to 1995 and was professor at Fuller Theological Seminary from 1995 to 2005. He has written and edited numerous articles and books on mission history, missiology, and church renewal. **Jennifer Davis Sensenig**, is lead pastor of Community Mennonite Church, Harrisonburg, Virginia. She previously served at Cedar Falls (Iowa) Mennonite Church and Pasadena (California) Mennonite Church.

Robert J. Suderman is general secretary of Mennonite Church Canada. He has lived and worked in Costa Rica, Bolivia, and Colombia, and has related to the church in Cuba for more than two decades. He is the founding director of CLARA (The Latin American Anabaptist Resource Center) and the Mennonite

Biblical Seminary, both in Bogotá, Colombia. He is the author of several books in Spanish and English. He has taught in Mennonite high schools in Canada and been involved in educational efforts of the church. His chapter in this book on "Jesus and the Church" was a family project. **Andrew Suderman** is a graduate of Canadian Mennonite Bible College and is finishing a masters at Conrad Grebel University College. He is the director of a shelter for homeless men in Kitchener, Ontario, that is a project of the House of Friendship. Also involved in the chapter were Robert's spouse, **Irene**, his sons, **Bryan, Derek,** and **Andrew,** and his daughters-in-law, **Julie, Rebecca,** and **Karen.**

Willard Swartley is professor emeritus of New Testament at the Associated Mennonite Biblical Seminary, where he was dean for seven years. He has published numerous articles, and authored and edited many books, including *Slavery, Sabbath, War and Women* (1983), *Covenant of Peace* (2006), and *Send Forth Your Light: A Vision for Peace, Mission, and Worship* (2007). He is author of a forthcoming *Believers Church Bible Commentary* on the Gospel of John. His hobbies are gardening, fruit trees, and making special recipes. **Michael Fecher** is a student at Goshen College and a member at Benton Mennonite Church. He has completed the AMBS !Explore program—a theological experience for high-school youth that encourages vocations to church leadership.

April Yamasaki is lead pastor of Emmanuel Mennonite Church, Abbotsford, British Columbia. She has written several books and numerous articles with a special interest in Scripture as it relates to daily life. April's education includes a broad background in liberal arts as well as graduate school in Christian studies. Her husband, Gary, teaches New Testament at Columbia Bible College. **Peter Sensenig,** a graduate of Palmer Theological Seminary, is associate pastor at Oxford Circle Mennonite Church, Philadelphia, where he lives with his wife, Christy.